THE TASTES OF CRUISING

Your Passport to Cruising and Cruise Ship Recipes
Written and Compiled by Sonnie Imes

Copyright 1989 ©   ISBN # 0-934181-06-3

To Dick, Susan, Robin, Joyce, Kevin and Elaine.
Didn't we have fun!!!

DE LOACH VINEYARDS

SONOMA COUNTY RUSSIAN RIVER VALLEY CHARDONNAY

PRODUCED & BOTTLED BY DE LOACH VINEYARDS, INC.
SANTA ROSA, SONOMA COUNTY, CALIFORNIA
ALCOHOL 13.6% BY VOLUME

A Gold Medal winning Chardonnay. Complex rich flavors and aromas with a subtle warmth of oak and a lovely, lingering finish.

Food Pairing: Fish, seafood, fowl and creamy pasta dishes.

Table of Contents

INTRODUCTION	15
SS OCEANIC	27
PREMIER CRUISE LINES	
SS NORWAY	41
NORWEGIAN CRUISE LINE	
FAIR PRINCESS	61
PRINCESS CRUISES	
ISLAND PRINCESS	93
PRINCESS CRUISES	
CUNARD PRINCESS	113
CUNARD	
MISSISSIPPI QUEEN	141
DELTA QUEEN STEAMSHIP COMPANY	
BRITANNIA	173
KD GERMAN RHINE LINE	
CROWN ODYSSEY	189
ROYAL CRUISE LINE	
SS MONTEREY	213
ALOHA PACIFIC CRUISES	
SS COSTARIVIERA	231
COSTA CRUISES	
CARIBBEAN PRINCE	249
AMERICAN CANADIAN CARIBBEAN LINES, INC.	
MS CARIBE I	275
COMMODORE CRUISE LINE	
MV THE VICTORIA	295
CHANDRIS FANTASY CRUISES	

SS AMERIKANIS	315
CHANDRIS FANTASY CRUISES	
LADY A	331
BARGE FRANCE	
SONNIE'S FAVORITES	349
FOOD GLOSSARY	361
SHIP'S GLOSSARY	365
INDEX	371

INTRODUCTION

Until air travel became popular among well-heeled travelers in the 1920s and 1930s, steamships served the wealthy who wanted to see the world. They sailed from the United States to Europe, from France to Hong Kong, from Italy to Egypt. Accommodations were top-drawer and ship's fittings were opulent.

During prohibition in the U.S. - 1919 through 1932 - cruise ships became popular among ordinary Americans who wanted to drink in peace. From New York City and other major American ports, they could hop on a boat that would take them out to sea for a weekend of dancing, drinking and gambling.

And then, because of world-wide depression, the intervention of World War II, and eventual safe and relatively inexpensive air travel, cruise ship travel declined, almost to the point of extinction.

Until the boom of the eighties.

Traveling in style aboard a posh floating palace is back. Forty new cruise ships have been built in the last ten years. Because of the intense competition, rates are reasonable and destinations are varied and interesting. Cruise ship travel is the pleasure it always was - and now a bargain besides. If you want to go by boat, there is hardly a port in the world you can't get to in comfort and style.

It is estimated that only ten percent of Americans have ever taken a cruise ship vacation. This means that not too many of your neighbors will be able to tell you what it's like aboard a ship, what the costs are, what the etiquette is, where the ships travel to, what you should pack; what, in general, you can expect from any cruise, let alone a particular itinerary.

In the course of my cruise ship travels, I've formed opinions and a few pointers which have stood me in good stead. Much of the information I needed was unavailable to me when I began. Much of the ease of getting to and traveling aboard a cruise ship involves minor planning that will make your seven-day or two-week or month-long cruise a real vacation.

To begin, read this book, or browse through it, to get an idea of what cruise ship travel is like, where you might want to go and what kind of ship you might want to go on. Then call your travel agency and ask them for brochures that include prices on the cruise lines you're interested in.

Keep in mind that there are seasonal rates in most areas where cruise ships travel. These rates depend on the weather -- December through April in the Caribbean is prime time, for example; June through August is the high season in Alaskan waters. Remember that booking a cruise involves shopping around, taking advantage of advertising "deals" and "fly-to packages" -and knowing what you want.

Your interests may revolve around sightseeing - either historic or scenic - in exotic ports, or shopping for locally-made goods. You may want simply to lie on the deck in a chaise lounge for a week, or spend all available time snorkeling.

Some lines provide not only swimming pools aboard, but whirlpools, Jacuzzis, saunas, masseuses and masseurs, beauty salons and fitness facilities. Many cruises offer sessions in arts and crafts, lectures on such subjects as ice carving and vegetable carving, napkin folding and food presentation, gourmet food preparation and computer classes.

On some ships you can shoot skeet, drive golf balls off the fantail, play tennis, fly kites or play water polo. You can sign up for shuffleboard or Ping-Pong, indulge in bingo, horseracing, chess, backgammon or bridge, enter Trivial Pursuit contests, join a single's cocktail party or show up for the grandparents' "picture-proud" parties.

On other ships, you can see first-run movies, first-class comedians, singers and dancers, gamble in the casino from dusk to dawn, and disco into the wee hours.

Or you may choose a cruise that has a small TV in the lounge, a well-stocked library and proffers no on-board festivities or come-one, come-all games.

Do you want to dress for dinner or be casual? Many ships maintain two seatings for dinner, and you'll feel comfortable only if you put on your best. On other ships, you can show up having run a comb through your hair and put on your shoes.

Do you like twenty-four-hour room service? Do you need a sodium-free diet? Kosher or vegetarian? Some lines can offer these services, some can't. Inquire. Do you want a ship that has a casual cafe where you can get a hamburger at whim? On some lines, you cannot bring your own liquor aboard; on others, that's all you'll have. If you like your evening cocktail, find out what the drill is.

Do you prefer a large cabin, somewhere you can spend a lot of time in comfort? Or will you use your cabin as only a place to change your clothes so you can get on to the next event? Do you want a double bed or single? If you're prone to motion sickness, cabins at the center of the ship are the most stable as far as the roll and pitch of the ship. If you're sensitive to noise, ask for a cabin away from public rooms, stewards' stations and elevators. Some ships have cabin-controlled air conditioning. If it's important to you, ask the dimensions of the cabins, the closet space, the size of the bathrooms and if there is a tub/shower combination or shower only, the kinds (porthole or regular) and numbers of windows per cabin.

Two myths that need to be dispelled for the first-time cruiser are that cruise ship life is a slice of "The Love Boat" television series, and that the average cruiser is well past retirement age.

The Love Boat myth is that the cruise ship doctor, activities director and captain fall in love with a passenger on each cruise. In real life, all of these main characters, indeed the entire crew, are personable, friendly and outgoing - these are requisites for their jobs. But they don't have time to carry on shipboard romances. They are professionals at what they do, and they do it very well, with little time for dalliance.

As far as myth number two, forty-six percent of all cruisers are under forty-five years of age. Twenty-five to thirty-nine-year-olds are the most interested in cruises. Some cruises, however, may have a preponderance of older people, or some may have a lot of children and teenagers, some only middle-aged couples and singles. It depends entirely on the bookings of the moment, but don't fear that only well-heeled, retired executives who've made their fortune are the folks who will be your traveling companions. But you can press your travel agent to find out what your shipmates are going to be like for your particular voyage - insist, if you're really concerned. It is information the cruise line will have, and you may not want to travel with a large group of conventioneers, too many children, or maybe even a high percentage of folks who don't speak English.

What I have discovered in my shipboard travels is that life on a cruise boat is unlike life on land. Everyone has signed up for a good time, for fun, for a real let-go of worry and inhibition. I'm not saying that life on a ship is a dawn-to-dawn revel, that people are wild and brazenly uninhibited, but that an atmosphere of friendliness and camaraderie prevails. On the fifteen cruises I investigated for this book I found that the majority of people I met were ready to just "be" instead of trying to be someone. I laughed and had a good time, I met friendly folks full of goodwill and I came to know crews who were as gracious as they were hard-working and expert at their jobs.

Luxury line cruising may be your only chance in this lifetime to be waited on like royalty, to eat sumptuously for days on end, to be entertained constantly or to be constantly idle. It's worth it, at least once, to see what life on the high side can be like - especially now, because of the competition of cruise lines - at reasonable prices. When you take into consideration the expenses of land travel, accommodations and food, often cruise ship travel is less expensive.

Another plus to cruise ship travel is that there may be places you'd like to see but that you don't want to be in for an entire vacation. You want to view them in passing, visit them for an hour or two and then get on with your trip. Cruising is the way to do this. My Alaska cruise was a prime example, for me. I have always wanted to see Alaska, but I didn't want to travel there by air and stay. On my Cunard cruise of the coastal waterways of Alaska I had the option of seeing only the coast, of getting off at several ports to sightsee the historic and scenic high spots, or of traveling inland via bus, train or helicopter for more extensive sightseeing and visiting. Many cruises in the Caribbean, along Mexico's gold coast and in Hawaii offer this same kind of inland/waterland option.

You can also take a cruise to a certain port, stay for a while and get on another ship to continue your cruise. Or you can stay on either end of your cruise at a spot that offers what you want - relaxation, shopping or sightseeing.

The best part of a cruise is that you really don't have to get on the bus to see anything. You can stay aboard and revel in the quiet and luxury of doing nothing - in pleasant, catered-to-you surroundings.

Don't hesitate to join in, don't hesitate to opt for solitude. One of the pleasures of cruise ship traveling is that it is your own - whether you're traveling with eighty or 1,800 other folks. It is a made-for-you vacation, whatever made-for-you entails.

Following is a list of handy-checks and insider information. These are the things I learned in my cruise travels which may help your cruise experiences be as good as mine have been:

* Read up on cruise tours and pick one within your budget to a place you've always dreamed of visiting. Many lines offer theme cruises - special holiday packages, golf tours, baseball, tennis, football, basketball, fitness and beauty, skiing, country Western, jazz, great chefs and so forth. A few lines carry lecturers of renown - these are sometimes called educational cruises and are ideal for the perennial student.

* Obtain a passport and once traveling, never go anywhere without it. Many ships require that you carry a boarding pass whenever you leave the ship. Just be sure you have it when you cross the gangplank.

* Check on travel insurance before you go.

* Deal with a travel agent you know, or one who is reputable, or one who specializes in cruises. Most cruise lines operate not directly but through travel agents. They can be of immense help to you.

* Check with your area health office two weeks before departure to see if any updates have come in for vaccinations to the countries of your cruise destination.

* Read everything the cruise line sends you. Know your debarkation times, your airline leeway time in reaching your ship's port (in other words, know if you should fly the day before so you're not pushing the limit of when the ship sails. It will sail without you). Plan to board about three hours before sailing time.

* Find out, through this book, your own research, your cruise line or your travel agent what kind of clothing will be necessary and appropriate for your trip. This can be critical -- if you're in Alaska in the summertime where you know it gets to ninety degrees, do you also know it can plummet to twenty degrees? Be prepared.

* If you plan to fish, play golf or tennis, scuba dive or snorkel to any extent, bring your own gear. It costs less.

* If you decide in January that you're going to take a trip to the Bahamas and can get on the boat but can't find a swimming suit in Des Moines, ask if you can you buy one aboard.

* Unless you're on medication from your doctor, you don't need to take a pharmacopoeia with you. Aspirin or Pepto Bismol, Dramamine or even sunscreen and face cream, nail clippers and nail files, sunglasses and eyedrops, these sundries can be purchased on board most cruise ships. But don't go without your emergency digitalis, or whatever may constitute emergency to you (maybe an extra pair of prescription glasses).

* If a cruise ship has first and second seatings for dinner, sometimes you'll be asked to make a choice long before you leave for your cruise. In making your choice, consider these points: Early dining ensures you get a seat at any after-dinner shows. The cruise ship entertainment may be a Las Vegas-type review or a

more colloquial comedy routine. Early seating also means you have to be there on time after a day's excursion ashore where you may have tramped the wilds or shopped till you dropped. Later seating sometimes interferes with your getting a good seat at the show, but likewise, ensures you time to breathe between daylight activities and shower/shave and dress-up for dinner. Maybe even time for a nap to revive your enthusiasm.

* It's common practice on many large cruise ships to give cocktail parties in your cabin, or even in a small lounge. If you know you want to do this, you can notify the ship ahead of time, via your travel agent. If the idea pops up after you've met several swell folks aboard, you can still do it. You can order champagne, cocktails and hors d'oeuvres and throw a wing-ding of a party before dinner that you don't have to even lift a finger for except to call the maitre d' to make arrangements.

* Plan ahead via your travel agent for not only your dinner seatings, but any special diet you're on (sodium-free, kosher, etc.), and check with the maitre d' when you board to see if your requests are recorded.

* Shore excursions, which are a main part of many cruises, must be booked and paid for on the ship in advance. It can be difficult, if not impossible, to get in on the scuba diving class on St. Thomas or the helicopter ride over the glaciers in Alaska at the last minute. The cruise lines prepare you well in advance to make reservations. Port tours, in general, are good, but ask around - either fellow passengers or crew - for first-hand advice. Sometimes it's cheaper and more fun to take a taxi or a local bus, map in hand, and explore on your own in a port city.

* Be aware of the daily newsletters that are delivered to your cabin. Read them! Listen to the announcements over the intercoms. And it never hurts to go aboard knowing which excursions you're interested in (information you can get from this book).

* Find out if you can shop aboard for duty-free goods. In most cases, the dollar limit you can bring back with you is $400 worth of goods, one bottle of liquor and one carton of cigarettes.

* Commonsense advice: Never tamper with mechanisms or machinery on board a ship. Never throw cigarettes, lighted or otherwise, off the ship because they may blow back aboard and hurt someone or start a fire. Don't dispose of waste paper, refuse or any other objects in the bathtubs, washbasins, toilets or showers. In emergencies don't use elevators. Never smoke in bed. Don't waste water.

* Hang onto hand rails and wear flat shoes in stormy weather -- heels are treacherous on stairs and when the ship is rolling.

* Make a point to attend life boat drills.

* Carry traveler's checks as well as a small amount of cash and your credit cards. Check to see which credit cards are used aboard your ship and in the ports you'll be visiting.

* On some ships electrical appliances (razors, hair dryers, small coffee heaters) may not be used in the staterooms. Make sure you know the rules and the wattages.

* Pressing and laundry services are available aboard most ships, although for safety reasons some vessels cannot install dry cleaning equipment.

* When you leave a ship you can donate your books and magazines to the library.

* Photographers are snapping everywhere. They are hired by the ships and you are not obliged to buy their results. Usually the photos are posted the next day on a bulletin board so you can see if you want to order.

* Purser's offices are usually open twenty-four hours a day. Here is where you make currency exchange, deposit your valuables in a safety box, purchase postcards and stamps. A purser is also a complaint-taker.

* Religious services are usually a daily occurrence on the big ships.

* Ship-to-shore communications are usually available twenty-four hours a day but closed in ports. Telegrams, phone calls, Telex and FAX services are arranged through the ship's radio office. On-board calls can be made from your staterooms.

* On some ships, cabin radios are always on so that passengers can hear important announcements.

* Some cruise lines cater to kids, some refuse to take kids at all and some have age restrictions.

* Some ships have room service, some don't.

* Wines are usually extra at dinner, not part of your cruise fee. Most alcoholic beverages are extra charges, whether at table, in a bar or in your room.

* Most ships provide a free birthday cake if notified in advance of the birthday person's special occasion.

* Casino entry usually requires that passengers be eighteen years old. Most casinos offer slot machines, blackjack, roulette and sometimes craps. On many ships, instruction is available.

* Most ships furnish guidelines for tipping. And tips are usually due waiters, maitre d', stewards, luggage porters and for any special services, including drinks in the bars and lounges of the ship. A typical guideline: $2.50 per cabin steward per day; $2.50

per waiter per night; $1.50 per busboy per night; $1.50 per maitre d' per night; 50 cents per bag for porters. You pay baggage porters at the time of service, you tip the crew members at the end of the cruise.

* Courtesy, not complaints, will guarantee you a pleasant trip. And many new friends.

* The food on most cruise ships is so abundant you'll be almost overwhelmed. It's possible to stick to your diet. It's also fun to just eat your way through a cruise and diet later. Sometimes, the food is beautifully presented and tastes just okay. This will help you to not eat too much. There will always be a plethora of fresh fruits and vegetables. Skip the sauces and eat the fresh fish -- always a biggie on a ship, and good for you.

* Don't be intimidated by the "luxury" idea of cruise ships. If you opt for a cruise with a Captain's Cocktail Party, bring along your good black dress or your good blue suit and have a whale of a time meeting new people and visiting with the captain. The people who cruise are just like you - folks looking for adventure and a good time, for an idyllic respite from the real world.

ADDITIONAL TIPS

Phoning home - USADIRECT service, operator-assisted and direct dial are your usual options.

Exchange rates - the Wall Street Journal or the International Herald Tribune list daily rates throughout the world.

Temperature conversion - if a temperature is noted in degrees Celsius, multiply by 9, divide by 5 and add 32 degrees.

U.S. passport - keep it up to date at all times; it costs $42 to get one and it's good for ten years. If you are applying for the first time, go in person to a post office with proof of identity such as a valid driver's license, with proof of U.S. citizenship, such as a birth certificate and two passport-sized photos. Allow two to six weeks to get your passport. You can renew by mail. If you need a passport in a hurry, check your Yellow Pages for a passport expediting service. Leaving and re-entering the U.S. at Miami or San Juan, U.S. and Canadian citizens must carry documentary proof of citizenship, such as a passport, certified birth certificate, certified naturalization papers or a valid voter's registration card and a current driver's license. It is the passenger's responsibility to check with government agencies, embassies or consulates for requirements of leaving and re-entering the U.S.

In this book, I'll give you a sampling of cruise ships - and a generous sampling of the recipes they use aboard. I'll take you down the Mississippi for American Southern dishes with a little Cajun thrown in; we'll travel up the Rhine with good German food; we'll meander along the canals in France and taste-test a few restaurants. I'll guide you through the Caribbean, to Alaska's Glacier Bay, across the Atlantic, along the Mexican Riviera, and through the Hawaiian Islands with the endless tantalyzing foods the cruise chefs muster up.

Climb the gangplank, whether for vital information in order to line up your next cruise, for armchair travel at its most descriptive or for a collection of outstanding recipes.

Bon voyage . . . and bon appetit.

SS OCEANIC

PREMIER CRUISE LINES

SS OCEANIC

The best-priced package deal going is Premier Cruise Lines "Magic Vacation Combination." This is both a cruise and a trip to Walt Disney World. For exceptionally low rates you get a lot of sights and experiences. If you are a family-oriented vacationer, this cruise is ideal for you.

Of course, if you want to cruise only, this is a truncated version and may not satisfy your sea-going needs and dreams. Three-or four-day cruises combine with three or four days of the Magic Kingdom; Nassau is the port visited and another stop is a half day spent on a private island (where Gilligan's Island was filmed).

In typical Walt Disney style, the official cruise line of Walt Disney World gives you the treatment of the highest calibre - spic and span ships, smiling and eager crew, smoothly run activities. And, as at Disney's land-based resorts, a contagious friendliness spreads from the staff through the passengers. The goodwill, bonhomie and camaraderie are worth the trip.

Three ships serve this unusual vacation idea, the Star/Ship Royale, the Star/Ship Oceanic and the Star/Ship Atlantic.

The Atlantic, with a passenger capacity of 1,600, is the latest acquisition of Premier Cruise Lines, the official cruise line of Walt Disney World.

We cruised on the larger Oceanic, with a 1,500-passenger capacity. She was a Home Lines ship, built in 1965, when Premier purchased her in 1985 for $20 million. With $10 million worth of revamping, the Oceanic first sailed April 25, 1986.

The Oceanic's eight decks are worth exploring once you're settled into your stateroom - which, by the way, will be large enough to stem any fears of claustrophobia and pretty enough that you'll feel comfortable and special. Premier pays attention to detail, and the ship is spotless. Toilet items such as shampoo, conditioner

SS OCEANIC

and body lotion are furnished, just like in a first-class hostelry. For the moderate rates, this is a plus.

Check out the dining room, cafes, casino, swimming pools, purser's office, lounges and whirlpools while you're waiting for things to happen. It's a fun ship to explore.

EMBARKATION

Orlando Airport is midway between Walt Disney World/Epcot Center and Port Canaveral. An air/sea/land package is available, so be sure to question your travel agent about the program.

At Orlando, pick up your Hertz unlimited-mileage rental car which comes with the package and follow the easy directions to the Bee Line Expressway, forty-five minutes to Port Canaveral. (If you have opted for the Disney package pre-cruise, you would head to your hotel at this point.) Porters dockside will take your luggage aboard while your car is being secured in a parking lot and you are checking in (starting at 1 p.m.). At 4 p.m., you should be standing railside as your ship moves gracefully out into the Atlantic, bound for Nassau. It's a lovely sight, watching the land recede.

All your tickets and information will reach you well before your departure date, so don't worry about knowing what to do. You'll be well taken care of through Premier's Disney-style precise attention to detail - a comforting thought particularly if you've never been on a cruise before.

PORTS OF CALL

* On your second day at sea, about mid-day, you'll pull into the lovely harbor of Nassau, capitol of the Bahamas. Since the ship will be in port the rest of the afternoon and all night, you'll have

SS OCEANIC

ample opportunity to explore this small city of beauty, action, history and that all-important asset - shopping.

Christopher Columbus discovered the Bahamas in 1492; pirates used a few of its nearly 700 islands and 2,000 islets as hideaway for several decades of the eighteenth century; the British made the Bahamas an official colony in 1783; full independent Commonwealth status was achieved in 1973.

So, although the Bahamas is an independent nation, the head of state is still the Queen of England, and British tradition, architecture and culture are prevalent. Your first stop is Prince George's Wharf, which sounds rather British to me.

The handmade straw products are the best bargains, and the baskets, purses and every other conceivable article are beautiful and well-made. The stores offer everything from jewelry to liquor. Touring can be done on mopeds if you're brave and want to hit all the boutiques.

Nighttime Nassau is exciting and you'll love the music, the waterfront bars, the very posh casinos, the islands' native fire-dancer entertainment. If you prefer, you can book Nassau tours aboard ship before docking, and you'll be guided through the city and escorted through the casinos and night spots. You can return to the ship after an afternoon of shopping and sightseeing and come back to Nassau late in the evening for a show if you like.

* Salt Cay, one of the 700 Out Islands, is yours to explore from 9 a.m. to 4 p.m. on your third day of cruising. Five pristine beaches, peaceful lagoons, swaying palms . . . the whole nine yards of tropical paradise. Premier Lines tenders you ashore, offers you snorkeling, hiking, pirate treasure hunts, calypso music, exploring an old stone pirate tower (this island has EVERYthing), a barbecue and - get this - hammocks strung between the palms.

SS OCEANIC

I wonder if they have to beat the bushes to get all hands back on board?

If you're religious about your exercise, Salt Cay is equipped with an exercourse and a running track.

This island may look familiar. It was the location shoot for the opening scenes of "Gilligan's Island" for several years.

* The Magic Kingdom and Epcot Center at Walt Disney World are not exactly considered ports of call, but they are half of the package - and a major portion of the best deal in the industry.

The world's number-one resort is truly one of the most pleasant places in the world. With this package you can plan to see it for three days either before or after your cruise. The choice is a nice touch.

The package deal includes: Three- or four-night accommodations at an Orlando hotel (or an on-site Disney hotel for those booking six months in advance; available to others at an extra charge); a Hertz rental car for seven full days, unlimited mileage; three-day World passport to the Magic Kingdom and Epcot Center, tour of the NASA Kennedy Space Center; your three-night or four-night cruise aboard Premier Lines. All for the price of a four-night cruise.

Such a deal!!!

* It is also possible to extend your vacation by staying longer at your hotel in the Orlando area and keeping your Hertz rental car at a special day rate. All before or after your Cruise and Walt Disney World Week.

SS OCEANIC

This way, you'll get in on all the excitement in the Walt Disney World area. Visit nearby Sea World, Wet'n'Wild, Orlando's brand new Baseball and Boardwalk, and many other attractions.

SHIPBOARD

With a shipful of youngsters, life on board could be harrowing, but Premier, a la Disney, knows how to entertain children. Activities abound for the kids (ages seventeen and under) centering around automatic membership in the Junior Cruise Club. To accommodate the various age groups, Premier offers three fully supervised programs on board: Kid's Call (ages two to seven); Star Cruiser (ages eight to twelve); and Teen Cruiser (ages thirteen to seventeen).

Each club member receives a newsletter each day explaining the activities, ranging from art classes to swimming. All the activities are free and are directed by trained youth counselors. The teen center is a great idea, as is the ice cream shop where you can make your own sundaes, the games arcade, the kids' pool and the movie theater.

Babysitting is available after 10 p.m. when the children's programs shut down. Cookies are put in all cabins with kids, and special menus in the dining room accommodate young palates.

For adults, you name it. A casino, swimming pools, whirlpool baths, massage facilities, beauty salon and barbershop, gym, bars, duty-free shops, cafes.

Activities include backgammon or bridge, skeet shooting, bingo, dance classes, wine tastings, perfume seminars, talent shows and masquerades. You can sign up for snorkeling lessons so you'll be prepard to investigate that aqua blue lagoon at Salt Cay. The movies are first-rate and often first-run.

The Seasport Fitness Program is a honey, especially if you're eating as is expected of you on a cruise. If, as Premier Lines advertises this program, you're between five and ninety, you're eligible. The program includes an equipment demonstration on Nautilus, Universal and Aerobic Life Cycles. Cardiovascular charting is offered. A jogging path is set up on the Promenade Deck and a walk/jog/stretch is held while the tender is transporting folks to the Salt Cay ... a productive way to wait your turn.

A full morning workout includes Jumpercize, which is jumping rope, Dancercize and Stretchercize. You can take tap dancing and clogging lessons, play Ping-Pong or shuffleboard or learn to juggle. Techniques of jazz dancing are taught, including a few clues on how to move to a beat. Square dancing is available, as is a sports trivia contest for the armchair athlete/statistics buff.

While on the island of Salt Cay, the athletes can take the island walk, enter the "Olympic Competition," the tug-of-war, the potato sack races, the volleyball tourney and the limbo contest.

THE LOOK OF THINGS

Because the Premier ships are home-ported at Port Canaveral, Florida, the ships use "space" names for their public rooms. The Oceanic sports the Satellite Cafe, the Shooting Star Photo Gallery, the Milky Way Shops, the Space Station Teen Center, the Galaxy Disco.

Mirrors, glass and bold colors make for an oddly comfortable futuristic look.

Again, the spit and polish on this ship is something you'll notice, from the inside corners of your stateroom closets to the miles of corridors and expanses of teak floors.

SS OCEANIC

CLOTHING AND WEATHER

You're in the subtropics, so light clothing is best. Bring comfortable walking shoes for your port calls, dress-up shoes for the night life. Clothing, likewise. Although life aboard ship is casual, don't bring your cut-offs and your holey jeans - be appropriate and consider the sensitivities of your companions, strangers though they may be.

It does rain. Bring a light raincoat and an umbrella.

Don't forget your swimming gear, and if you're an exerciser, your sturdy tennies and comfortable attire.

BOOKING YOUR CRUISE

Premier Cruise Lines
101 George King Blvd.
P. O. Box 573
Cape Canaveral, FL 32920
Telephone 407-783-5061
Telex 2936541
or call your travel agent.

ENTERTAINMENT

Broadway-style reviews, again done with the typical Disney know-how and pizzazz, specialize in music to sing along with - the kind of entertainment that people join in with because the music is comfortably familiar. The costumes and dancing numbers are Vegas-spectacular - very professional.

Calypso bands play all over the ship; dance orchestras get your toes tapping and you out on the dance floor in no time; comedians are famous and funny; the disco DJ plays his tunes until the wee hours. It's good entertainment.

FOOD

Theme dinners on Premier ships mean that everything fits the theme - the food, the decor (walls move and panels turn from Caribbean to French to Italian - nice touch). The waiters and waitresses wear uniforms that fit the ethnic meal and the table settings reflect the country.

One night you'll get Texas Prime Rib and the next Piccata alla Marsala. Cuisses de Grenouilles Provencale is an example of French haute cuisine and Broiled Fillet of Grouper, typically Bahamian.

The two-seating evening meal is a ship's main attraction, but it's usually the Midnight Buffet that makes the flashbulbs pop and the folks ooh and aah. Premier is no exception. In fact, their ice carvings gracing the Midnight Buffet are so spectacular and so professional that you can go to an ice carving demonstration during the day to learn the secrets. Butter sculptures resembling Disney characters and Tinker Bell's Castle are breathtaking. The food displays are somewhat intimidating. Who wants to be the first to ruin those perfectly arranged and sometimes unidentifiable but beautiful edibles? Me!!!

Even if you can't eat anything, go in and take a look at the extravaganza. It's truly educational to see what creative people can do with food.

Breakfasts are hearty or slimming, depending on what you're capable of resisting (two seatings also), and there is a breakfast buffet for those who don't want to be obliged to appear at a set time.

SS OCEANIC

Luncheons can be elegant or just snacks at poolside. Late-night pizza parties are just about the last straw. But you can always diet later.

From 1 a.m. to 3 a.m., if you are still hungry, you can get soups and omelettes if you can find room.

RECIPES

Red Snapper Premier

1/2	stalk celery
1/2	carrot
1	2" section leek, white part only
1	6 to 8 oz. fillet of red snapper
	salt and pepper
1 1/2	Tbsp. lemon juice
1	tsp. Worcestershire sauce
2	dashes Tabasco sauce
1	c. flour
2	egg yolks, beaten with 1 Tbsp. water
2	Tbsp. corn oil
1/2	c. Pernod
1/2	lime, juiced
	salt and pepper to taste
	rice and beans, cooked and mixed together

Wash, peel and cut in 2" strips the celery, carrot and leek. Set aside. Season fillet with salt and pepper, lemon juice, Worcestershire and Tabasco. Marinate for 15 minutes. Remove fish from marinade and dredge in flour, then dip in beaten egg yolk mixture and dredge in flour again. In a large skillet, warm oil over medium heat. Add fish and cook 2 to 3 minutes per side or until golden in color. Remove to hot plate and keep warm. Add vegetable strips to oil in pan and saute. Add Pernod, lime juice, salt and pepper to taste. Cook on high heat 1 minute and pour over fish. Serve with rice and beans.

Serves 1

Coq au Vin

2	frying chickens
2	c. red wine
2	Tbsp. olive oil
2	carrots, diced
1	bunch celery, diced
1	onion, diced
2	Tbsp. tomato paste
1/2	c. cognac
	salt and pepper
1	clove garlic, minced
12	pearl onions, cooked
12	bacon strips, cooked
12	mushrooms
6	pieces dry toast
	rice, cooked

Cut each chicken into 8 pieces. Marinate for 2 hours in red wine, turning several times. In a large skillet heat olive oil. Remove chicken from wine, reserving wine, and place chicken in hot oil. Cook and turn pieces until brown. Add carrots, celery, and onion. Brown together with chicken. Add tomato paste and reserved red wine. Cover and simmer 1 1/4 hours, adding more wine if necessary. Remove chicken and keep warm. Add cognac to the pan and salt and pepper to taste. Add garlic and reduce on high heat 12 minutes or until sauce thickens slightly. Pass sauce through a sieve, mashing as much of the vegetables as possible through the sieve. Place chicken on platter and pour the sauce on top. Garnish with pearl onions, sauteed bacon strips and fresh mushrooms. Cut toast in triangles as garnish. Serve with rice.

Serves 6

Crepe Dame Blanche

1 1/2	qts. vanilla ice cream
2	c. whipped cream
1 1/2	Tbsp. Grand Marnier
1	Tbsp. Cointreau
12	crepes
2	c. hot fudge sauce
1	c. rum

Mix ice cream and whipped cream together. Add Grand Marnier and Cointreau and mix well. Fill each crepe with 1/2 cup of the mixture, roll up and place in freezer for 1 hour. When ready to serve, place on dessert plates and cover with hot fudge sauce. Flame with rum.

Serves 6

CRUISE BAREFOOT!

AWARD WINNING VARIETAL WINES AT POPULAR PRICES!

CABERNET SAUVIGNON	GOLD MEDAL WINNER! UNBEATABLE PRICE
NAPA GAMAY BLUSH	LA FAIR WINNER! TASTIER THAN WHITE ZINFANDEL
SAUVIGNON BLANC	GOLD MEDAL WINNER! SOFT AND FRUITY

Produced by Barefoot Cellars, Healdsburg, CA (707) 433-8828

SS NORWAY

NORWEGIAN CRUISE LINE

DOMAINE MICHEL

CABERNET SAUVIGNON
SONOMA COUNTY

PRODUCED AND BOTTLED BY DOMAINE MICHEL
HEALDSBURG, CALIFORNIA, U.S.A. ALCOHOL 12.8% BY VOLUME
CONTAINS SULFITES

Elegant structure, rich berry, vanilla, mint and a hint of spiciness. Delightful now or to be cellared for long-term aging.

Enjoy this Cabernet with grilled lamb, duck, beef or perhaps a chocolate truffle.

SS NORWAY

The SS Norway, sailing under the Norwegian Cruise Line, is one of the largest passenger ships sailing today. Formerly the SS France, launched in 1960, the Norway was purchased in 1979 for $18 million and rebuilt at a cost of $150 million. The SS Norway made its maiden voyage out of Miami on June 1, 1980.

With ten decks, three swimming pools, one dozen bars, two major dining rooms, one theater and other grandiose amenities, Norwegian Cruise Line's flagship may be one of the poshest palaces afloat. The rates reflect this. A grand deluxe suite (there are only two) is expensive. These are the money-is-no-object staterooms. They contain a living room, dining room, double bedroom with kingsize bed and vanity console, two full baths with showers, a television and a refrigerator.

Inside staterooms on the Biscayne Deck are moderate, whether peak season or "value" season. Cruisers traveling alone will travel cheaply if they don't mind sharing a four-bed stateroom with other singles.

The mid-level accommodations are adequate. Each stateroom has a shower and television.

You can eat nine times a day on the SS Norway.

EMBARKATION

Miami, Florida is the Norway's home port. The area airports are Miami and Fort Lauderdale. When purchasing your tickets for an SS Norway cruise, ask your travel agent about NCL's "Cloud 9" air/sea rates. These rates include roundtrip airfare to Miami/Fort Lauderdale, ground transfers, all transportation and airport security charges, plus a hotel, if applicable.

SS Norway's seven-day cruise leaves Miami on Saturdays at 4:30 p.m. Sunday and Monday are at-sea cruising days; Tuesday's port

SS NORWAY

of call is St. Maarten, 7:00 a.m. to 7:00 p.m.; Wednesday, St. John, 6:00 a.m. to 7:30 a.m. and St. Thomas, 9:30 a.m. to 5:30 p.m. (Ferry service is available from St. John to St. Thomas, a distance of a very few miles.)

Thursday is again spent at sea; Friday from noon to 7:00 p.m. NCL's private island, Great Stirrup Cay, Bahamas, hosts the passengers for a leisurely day of picnicking and swimming; Saturday the SS Norway pulls into her Miami berth at 8:00 a.m.

PORTS OF CALL

* St. Maarten/St. Martin is a thirty-seven-square-mile Caribbean island that is divided between the Netherland Antilles, which owns sixteen square miles, and French Guadaloupe, which owns twenty-one square miles. The duty-free island is a classic tropical paradise with a kind climate and hospitable people.

On the Dutch side, the capital of Philipsburg offers historical buildings, the Town Square outdoor market and Front Street's exclusive merchandise - clothing, perfumes, jewels, liquor, china and crystal from around the world - at duty-free prices. Two casinos, the Peacock and the Rouge et Noir, open when the Norway hits port. They offer slots, blackjack, craps and roulette.

On the French side, the capital city Marigot is, by comparison, quiet, quaint and very French-small-town with its cafes and boulangeries. In Grande Case, just east of Marigot, there are fine dining restaurants. And just beyond is the famous Orient Beach, nude sunbathers' haven, or as the guidebooks euphemistically call it, a "clothing optional" beach.

St. Maarten boasts three dozen magnificent beaches. Some are narrow strips below sandstone cliffs and some are wide curves of smooth white sand with palms encroaching and reefs offshore. Some come full of friendly sun-worshippers and others are so quiet and secluded you could pretend you alone know of their existence. Some offer calm waters and others wild, crashing breakers.

Transportation from Philipsburg to any of the beaches, to Marigot or to Paradise Peak (at 1,500 feet, the island's high spot), is plentiful. At the pier in Philipsburg where you are deposited from the ship, you can rent taxis, sightseeing buses, private autos, mopeds or motorcycles. The main road contours around the island and brings you back full circle to Philipsburg.

The majority of amusements naturally flourish on the water - scuba dive, snorkel, windsurf and parasail. You can rent jetskis and Sunfish, charter a fishing boat or sailboat or join a cruise boat for a scenic trip around the island.

For those who need a golf fix after three days at sea, Mullet Bay Resort's eighteen-hole championship links will satisfy the best duffer. There are also plenty of tennis courts on St. Maarten, and horseback-riding on the beach is so unusual and beautiful a pastime that you'll envision yourself and the Black Stallion in front of the movie cameras.

* St. John is the uncluttered, lightly populated natural sanctuary of the trip. The Virgin Islands National Park covers over two-thirds of the island and extends out into the sea to include nearly 6,000 watery acres. The Visitor's Bureau can set you on your path to discovery - maybe you'll spot the island flower, the yellow trumpet, or the island bird, the yellow-breast. An underwater scuba trail is famous, as is the beach at Trunk Bay.

Cruz Bay, the port town, is small but lines up exceptional clothing, jewelry and ceramics for its tourists in the small boutiques along the main street. In Cruz Bay you can also rent cars, taxis or - best bet - safari bus tours. The guides know their island.

SS NORWAY

The world-famous luxury resort, Gallons Point, built by the Rockefellers, is set in the lushness of St. John's tropical backyard. It offers a startling contrast to the island's untamed wilds.

* St. Thomas is billed as the most exciting of the U. S. Virgin Islands, and it may well be. It is difficult to do it all in your one day here, but if you plan it right, you can cover a lot of territory.

An island tour will clue you in to the enticements while highlighting the flora, fauna and history of this gem of the Caribbean. Then you'll be deposited back in the port city of Charlotte Amalie. Here you can shop duty-free. The best buys are diamonds, island-made straw goods and imported leather goods. You can then recoup your energy over a casual lunch at the Green House on the Waterfront or over a much fancier repast at L'Escargot in the center of town.

After lunch, take a walking tour of the intimate little port town with its Spanish-French-Danish-English influences and all the beautiful architecture those cultures left behind. Or you can hit the beaches. Magens Bay is one of the ten most beautiful beaches in the world according to National Geographic (and they've been everywhere), and the beach life is one of the pure joys of the Caribbean. You can snorkel, scuba dive, sail, windsurf, swim, laze in the sun . . . the good life.

Or you can tour Bluebeard's Castle and Blackbeard's Tower, the Mountain Top (highest point on the island) or Coral World (an underwater observatory).

* Great Stirrup Cay, Bahamas, is the private tropical paradise of Norwegian Cruise Line. On your last day, Friday, from noon until 7:00 p.m., you can explore the island on your own, snorkel in the quiet bay, picnic with the crew, swim, be a beach bum. It is, indeed, the way life should be. It is a somewhat bittersweet

afternoon, however, because this is your last barefoot idyll in the sub-tropics.

SHIPBOARD

Life on board the SS Norway can be anything you want it to be fast-paced, busy, informative, social; or quiet, relaxing, private. As I mentioned, you can eat nine times a day, or only now and then. You can dance all night and sleep all day. You can spend your hours in the library or in the casino. The world of the Norway is a world for all types and all whims.

Each day a newsletter is slipped under your door. "Cruise News" lists a dizzying number of daily events, from the 7:30 a.m. breakfast to the midnight buffet. A typical day will offer opportunities like this:

- morning exercise with the crew - a mile-long walk around the ship, outdoor fresh-air stretching class or aerobic dance class

- Catholic Mass, snorkeling lessons, presentation of what to do at ports of call, swimnastics class, palmistry reading, PGA golf pro seminar, shuffleboard, Ping-Pong and mini-golf programs and tourneys

- a talk on shopping tips in the islands, water volleyball, backgammon, basketball, library hours, touring of the Bridge of the Norway, arts and crafts, card games, beauty seminar, ice carving demonstration

- a wine tasting session, jackpot bingo, trapshooting, a question-and-answer session with headliner entertainers

- an Italian dinner, a fashion show, a roaring twenties review, a sing-along, a big-band dance, a disco dance, a midnight buffet

The service hours are listed in "Cruise News" for the gift shops, ice cream parlor, photo gallery, pools and healthspas, games room, casino, beauty salon, sauna and massage and the doctor's office. The bars are listed with their opening and closing hours. A few rules are pointed out: Where and when children are allowed (not in the casino, for example); where and when you can jog; what's on TV; how to order wine for dinner; how to find your steward and so on.

Other informative and interesting literature is available in your rooms about the ports of call. These magazines are well-done and they are valuable resources for your on-shore adventures. Also, the talks given by the cruise directors on tour information, how to shop and what to shop for in the ports, are worth attending. Forewarned is forearmed, and going ashore with an idea of the culture and what to look for gives you a definite advantage in the short time you have.

The snorkeling lessons on board will prepare you to get right down to the bottom of things in the bays of the Virgin Islands. This is, by the way, one of the favorite pastimes of Caribbean tourists. The waters are warm and the sights are worth the effort. Beside, you get a lovely backside tan.

THE LOOK OF THINGS

The staterooms are basic in decor - usually two twin beds with bunks above for the third or fourth person - but the public rooms live up to their advertised refinement, decorated as they are with the best in materials and more than $1 million worth of original art. In the Club Internationale in particular, ghosts of the past stir. The decor is pure 1930s. A feeling takes over that you are traveling aboard one of the grande dames of a gentler era.

The mall on the Internationl Deck evokes nostalgia also, with sidewalk cafes and fancy duty-free boutiques. The shops offer men's and women's clothing, gifts, jewelry, furs and toiletries. The clothing prices are generally below the cost stateside.

The library is well stocked with current best sellers.

The casino is always bustling and the card room is busy with backgammon, Monopoly, gin, pinochle and bridge. Sign-up sheets make for organized, full games.

MONEY ETIQUETTE

Tipping is a definite part of life aboard a luxury cruise ship. You generally tip on your last day out, taking care of the entire cruise all at once. The Norway suggests tipping your cabin steward, your waiter and busboy. At all the bars you sign for your drinks. A fifteen percent gratuity is included in the charge, but you are free to tip your bartender or cocktail waitress more if you care to.

Major credit cards are accepted in the beauty salon, health spa and for prearranged land tours, but personal checks and cash are accepted only in the duty-free shops on board.

CLOTHING AND WEATHER

The weather on a Caribbean cruise will hover in the seventies and eighties. It rains - remember, you're in the subtropics - so bring light raingear and a collapsible umbrella.

Cruise ship haute couture is a big item in major department stores, but clothes do not the man or woman make, and cruise ship attire should be first of all comfortable. A Caribbean cruise means sunsuits, swimsuits, straw hats, slacks, shorts, sandals, tennies and light shawls or jackets. You'll need nice but informal wear for evening dining in the two main dining rooms - a dressy dress, a jacket and tie. If you're so inclined, include a formal outfit

SS NORWAY

long dress/tuxedo - for the Captain's Cocktail Party and Farewell Dinner.

During the cruise, theme nights are common - Western, island, ancient Greek - and you may dress the part if you happen to have a cowboy hat, a hula skirt or a toga. But don't bother to bring theme outfits with you. There are too many possibilities and too few suitcases: 200 pounds of luggage per person is the NCL allowance.

BOOKING YOUR CRUISE

Norwegian Cruise Line
One Biscayne Tower
Miami, FL 33131
305-358-6670
or call your travel agent

ENTERTAINMENT

The SS Norway prides itself on its entertainment. It ranges from bingo to a Broadway production of "42nd Street." In between are movies, dancing to disco or big band, stand-up comedians, musical and comic legends such as Jack Jones, Norm Crosby, Phyllis Diller, Lou Rawls, Rita Moreno, Jim Nabors, the Fifth Dimension. This is an extravagant and highly touted plus to SS Norway cruises.

DEBARKATION

The Norway makes debarkation as painless as possible. Everything is clearly spelled out and the color-coding makes it easy to follow directions. This is a good time for people-watching or book reading. Don't become impatient - everybody can't get off at once but you will get off in good time.

SS NORWAY

STATISTICS

Facts and Figures about the SS Norway:

70,202 gross tons
1,035 feet long (over three football fields)
34.5-foot draft
26-knot top speed; 16-20 knot average cruising speed
2,400-passenger capability
24 life boats, capacity 3,218 seats
40 inflatable life rafts, capacity 800 seats
2 going-ashore boats, capacity 450 each
54,000 total horsepower in 2 steam engines

FOOD

What's your pleasure? Steak Diane or hot dogs, diet pop or Pouilly-Fuisse? The SS Norway is a floating cornucopia. Every Saturday morning they take on a few groceries for the coming week:

9,000 pounds beef
1,000 pounds veal
3,000 pounds seafood
6,000 pounds poultry
1,000 gallons milk
4,000 gallons juices
66,000 eggs
5,000 pounds flour
7,000 pounds potatoes
8,000 pounds fresh vegetables
10,000 pounds fresh fruits
30,000 pounds detergents

You can take a tour through the galley if you're interested in these kinds of fantastic figures. It's numbing, but interesting. They wash 12,000 pieces of china and 6,000 glasses every day. The bakery is manned twenty four hours a day and makes 100,000 rolls and 20,000 breads every week. One-hundred seventy-two chefs, cooks, bakers and cleaners provide 2,000-plus passengers their breakfasts, lunches, afternoon snacks, dinners and the midnight buffet - each day.

Dining is a pleasure, especially in the main rooms. Each evening a graphically beautiful menu announces the theme of the cuisine (you can obtain a menu in several languages besides English) and it is something to look forward to. You will start off the first evening with the Bon Voyage Dinner, progressing through the week with possibilities like International Night, Country and Western Night, Italian Night, the Captain's Gala and the Captain's Farewell Dinner. Chef's suggestions, from soup to nuts and from champagne to after-dinner drinks, line the left-hand side of the menu.

A typical example would read like this on Italian night: Marinated Hearts of Artichoke Verona; Rainbow Rotelli San Marco (special pasta with meat sauce and chopped tomatoes); Consomme Minestra; Boneless Breast of Chicken Parmigiana (breaded, topped with fresh tomato sauce and mozzarella cheese, served with linguine); Cassata alla Napolitana; Italian Coffee.

The best wines for the captain's suggested dinner will also be listed. On Italian night, for example, the following may be offered: (red) Chianti Classico, Ruffino; (white) Soave, Ruffino; (sparkling) Asti Spumante, Riccadonna. All alcoholic dinner drinks are extra, by the way, beyond the expenses included in your cruise rate.

From the right-hand side of the menu you will be offered four entrees, different salads, soups, appetizers and desserts, and always a dieter's main course. Cold hors d'oeuvres could be Smoked Norwegian Salmon, Papaya Nectar and Pate Maison

Waldorf; hot hors d'oeuvres may be Norwegian Fjord Mussels in Light California Chablis Sauce, or Stuffed Crab from the Gulf of Mexico. Soups are delectable, from the ordinary - Cream of Forest Mushrooms - to the unusual - Chilled Cream of Blueberries. Salads are crisped to within an inch of their green and leafy lives. You'll be offered one or two each evening. Lettuce with Cucumbers and Radishes, Celery and Shredded Carrots, Greek Salad with Feta Cheese or Hearts of Iceberg Lettuce with Chopped Eggs are just a sampling.

Two seatings are available, the first at 6:00 p.m. and the second at 8:30 p.m.

The entire fine-dining experience is just plain fun. The elegance of it - the hovering waiters and the excellent dishes, the glittery, high-life kind of feeling - is simultaneously soothing and stimulating. It is definitely a big part of the SS Norway's reputation. You couldn't dine better in the world's most prestigious and difficult-to-get-into restaurants. On the Norway you are treated to seven straight nights of being the boss, the influential, the catered-to, the fawned on rich and famous. It is irresistible.

RECIPES

Havana Oxtail Soup

1	oxtail, cut in chunks
1	carrot, chopped
1	stalk of celery, chopped
1	leek, chopped
1	onion, chopped
1	Tbsp. tomato paste
1	c. red wine
6	c. beef bouillon
1	bay leaf
1	Tbsp. butter
1	Tbsp. flour
	crushed black peppercorn, to taste
	chili powder, to taste
1	red pepper, sliced
1	green pepper, sliced
1	c. red kidney beans, cooked

In a Dutch oven, saute oxtail chunks until dark brown. Add carrot, celery, leek and onion. Reduce to simmer and cook for 1 hour. Add red wine, bouillon and bay leaf. Cook until oxtail is tender. Remove oxtail from the soup and cut it in small pieces. In second pan melt butter and add flour, peppercorns and chili powder. Bring to boil. Strain into soup. Add red and green peppers and kidney beans. Cook until peppers are soft. Add reserved oxtail.

Serves 4

Sauteed Dover Sole Fillets Genoise

4	pieces Dover sole, skin and bones removed (reserve for stock)
7	oz. butter
2	c. water
1	celery stalk, diced
2	onions, chopped
	salt and pepper to taste
	lemon juice
1/2	c. flour
2	oz. mushrooms, quartered
4	oz. white wine
2	oz.. cooked bay shrimp
1	oz. capers
	parsley

Make fish stock first by sauteing fish bones and skin in 1 ounce butter. Add water, celery and 1/2 of the onion. Simmer for 1/2 hour. Strain stock and reserve. Season the sole fillets with salt, pepper and lemon juice. Turn in flour and fry quickly in small amount of hot butter until golden brown. Remove from pan and keep warm. For the sauce, melt remaining butter and add remaining onions. Saute until translucent. Add mushrooms, saute until tender. Add white wine, strained stock and reduce. Add shrimps and capers, and heat. Pour sauce over warming sole. Garnish with parsley.

Serves 4

Sauteed Chicken Breast in Sorrel Sauce

8	chicken breasts, deboned
	salt and pepper to taste
1/2	c. flour
2	oz. butter
1	onion, chopped
4	oz. chicken stock
3	oz. heavy cream
2	lemons, for juice and grated peel
1	Tbsp. butter
1	oz. chopped fresh sorrel

Season chicken with salt and pepper. Turn in flour and saute in hot butter. Remove from pan and keep warm. Make sauce by sauteing onion in butter. Add stock, heavy cream, salt and pepper, if needed, and lemon juice. Simmer until slightly reduced. Place mixture in blender and add butter. Add sorrel and lemon peel at the last minute. Reheat sauce and pour over chicken breasts.

Serves 4

Carrot Cake

8	egg yolks
16	oz. confectioners' sugar
1	lb. carrots, peeled and grated
3	oz. flour
	zest from 1 lemon
1/2	tsp. cinnamon powder
1/2	oz. baking powder
8	oz. ground almonds
8	oz .ground hazelnuts
10	egg whites, whipped
4	Tbsp. melted butter

Whip egg yolks and half the sugar until stiff. Place carrots and remaining sugar into a bowl. Sift in flour, lemon zest, cinnamon powder, baking powder, ground almonds and ground hazelnuts. Fold egg whites into carrot mixture and add melted butter. Pour into a buttered cake pan or mold. Bake at 360° F for 45 minutes

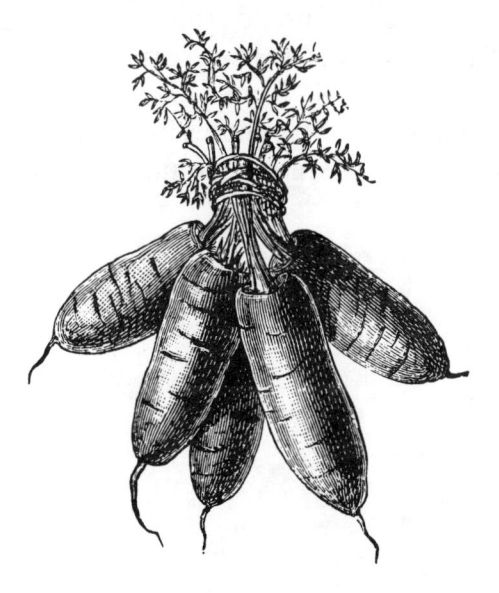

Serves 4

Vienna Apple Strudel

4	oz. flour
1	oz. oil
	salt
	water
12	apples, peeled and sliced
1/2	lemon, for juice, grated peel
1	tsp. cinnamon
2	oz. sugar
3	tsp. hazelnuts, chopped fine
1/2	c. melted butter
1	c. sweet bread crumbs
	powdered sugar
	vanilla ice cream

Add first 4 ingredients and mix to make a slightly soft consistency. For the filling, mix apples and lemon juice, lemon peel, cinnamon, sugar and hazelnuts. Roll out dough very thin. Sprinkle with some of the butter and sweet bread crumbs. Add apples and roll the dough up. Place on a cookie sheet. Brush with melted butter and bake for 20 minutes at 400° F, then lower heat to 350° F, brush with melted butter and bake 10 minutes longer or until crispy and brown. Sprinkle with powdered sugar and serve with vanilla ice cream.

Makes 1 strudel

SS NORWAY

Chilled Cream of Papaya Soup

2 papayas
4 scoops vanilla ice cream
1 c. sour cream
1 c. half-and-half
  juice of 1 lime
  mint leaves

In blender or food processor, blend 1 1/2 peeled papaya to a fine mousse-like consistency. Add ice cream, sour cream, half-and-half and lime juice. Mix until smooth. Dice remaining 1/2 papaya and use as garnish in the soup. Top with mint leaves.

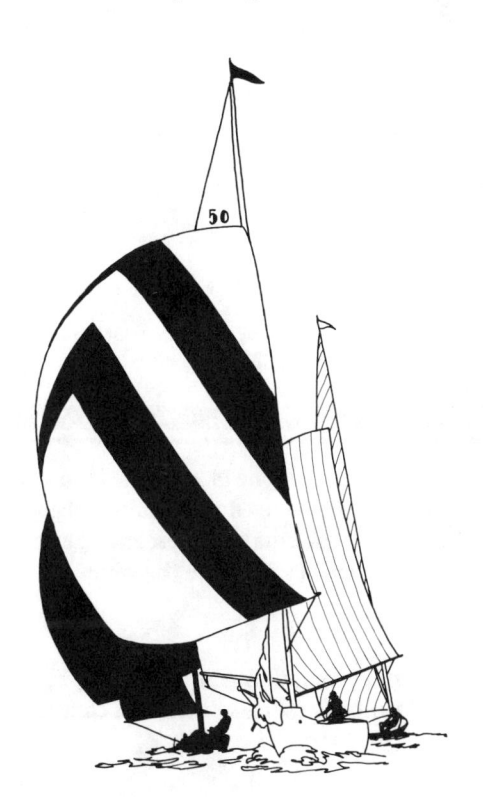

Serves 4

CLOS DU BOIS

MARLSTONE
Vineyard

Alexander Valley

62% Cabernet Sauvignon, 28% Merlot
7% Cabernet Franc, 3% Malbec

GROWN, MADE & BOTTLED BY CLOS DU BOIS WINERY
HEALDSBURG, CA USA • ALCOHOL 13.7% BY VOLUME • 750 ML

Like the great Bordeaux, Marlstone is a classic blend of four wine grapes. After fermentation, the wine is aged in 60 gallon French Oak barrels for three years, allowing the tannins to soften and the barrels to impart a vanillin flavor to the wine.

Marlstone is an exellent accompaniment to a hearty meal of roast beef, rack of lamb, or a fine selection of cheeses.

FAIR PRINCESS

PRINCESS CRUISES

FAIR PRINCESS

The Fair Princess, sailing under Princess Cruises, was built in the shipyards of Glasgow, Scotland, retrofitted in Trieste, Italy and remodeled in Norfolk, Virginia. It carries a truly international sophistication to it but is the least snobby of cruise ships.

Boasting eleven decks, 473 cabins, nineteen public rooms, three swimming pools, three elevators, a gymnasium and fully air-conditioned comfort, the Fair Princess is the luxury way to get to Baja California and just beyond. Many folks opt for the Fair Princess again and again - the repeat business is remarkable I discovered, and soon learned why. The crew here is exceptionally jovial and fun-loving, and many of them stick around for years. They're nuts and you'll love them. The majority of the seamen are Italian and Portuguese, and the cruise staff and people who work in the shops are mainly British or American. It seems that they are picked not only for expertise in their jobs, but for their gregarious personalities.

A Princess cruise is moderately priced, and considering the really friendly indulgence you receive, I'd call it a bargain trip.

EMBARKATION

San Pedro, near Los Angeles, California is the Fair Princess's home port for Mexican cruises. The seven-day cruise to Puerto Vallarta, Mazatlan, Cabo San Lucas and back departs on a Saturday afternoon and returns the following Saturday morning about 9 a.m. Three days are spent at sea.

PORTS OF CALL

* Puerto Vallarta - sounds exotic, doesn't it? Regulars to this world-famous spot call it "PV," which might come in handy if, like me, you find yourself twisting your mouth the wrong way around "pware-to vah-yar-tah."

FAIR PRINCESS

Tenders leave the ship at 11 a.m. for this lovely seaside village, but the Fair Princess sails again at 7 p.m., so it might be wise to take one of the three tours offered that will acquaint you with and inform you about the town.

The "Highlights Tour" lasts a little over three hours and is basically what it says - the scenic overview. Guides point out picturesque homes, the town square, Our Lady of Guadalupe Church. You will drive along the coastline past the famous Camino Real Hotel and on to the equally famous Mismaloya Beach. You will return to the plaza after being shown a few celebrity homes in "Gringo Gulch." Then grab a late lunch, shop, lie on the beach or explore.

If you're a sport of the golf/tennis/fishing persuasion, you can sign up to spend the day at your favorite pastime. Golf at Los Flamingos takes about six hours, including round-trip transportation and play. The eighteen-hole championship course is well-maintained and offers a good challenge. Green fees include cart or caddy.

Tennis reservations can be made on the ship. You'll find the clay courts of Playa de Oro in good shape.

Sportfishing may be the order of the day, for Puerto Vallarta is considered a sportfisherman's mecca. Six hours worth of fighting for your marlin could turn out to be a high point of your trip. Most of the cabin cruiser fishing boats offer a cash bar and serve a box lunch.

A three-hour bay cruise presents a relaxing day of sightseeing aboard a catamaran, plus time for snorkeling and swimming. This plan also leaves time for a bit of shopping and exploring on your own before the Fair Princess heads for Mazatlan.

* Mazatlan, with the exotic sound of the Aztecs in the name (it means "place of the deer" in the Nahuati language), is a port city on the mainland in the Mexican state of Sinaloa. It no longer maintains any such bucolic or woodsy connotations as the definition of the name implies, for it is a thriving and bustling city of more than 300,000 people, but a statue of a deer stands on the waterfront and a deer graces the city's coat of arms.

You'll have all day here, so make the most of it - there's more than enough to see and do. You have your choice of freelancing your own day or joining one of several tours. If you're on your own, take a "pulmonia," a three-wheeled cart. It's less expensive than taxis and more fun. Agree on a price to your destination before you take off and if nothing else, have the driver cruise along the Malecon. This is a seawall/walkway/avenue about five miles long that nearly circumnavigates the city.

The "City Tour" winds through a few classy residential districts and into the downtown section and can be booked for morning or afternoon. You'll see the eighteenth-century Temple of San Jose, the Indian Market, Olas Altas and the sidewalk cafe area. The mountain and beach views are spectacular as is hotel row. With this tour you'll get a chance to shop for Indian art and Mexican crafts before you return to the ship via Glorieta's Rocky Promontory where the cliff divers make their spectacular, splashy living.

The "Beach and Brunch Tour" lasts five hours and is a honey. You'll drive toward Vigia Mountain, a really lovely landscape, passing the hotels and fancy homes of Mazatlan, and wind up at Gaviotas Beach. Considered the most beautiful beach around, Gaviotas is also the home of one of the plushest resort hotels. This is where you'll spend the next few hours, sunning, swimming, slaking your thirst on unlimited free beer and complimentary champagne while enjoying an elegant lunch. Nice day.

If you really enjoy local color, opt for the "Shuttle, Shopping and Show Tour." It begins with a cab ride along the scenic seven miles of oceanfront homes to the Mazatlan Arts and Crafts Center. Here you have time to explore and shop and see the Folkloric Show of Mayan Indian dancers.

For the serious tourer, join the "Sierra Madre Tour," which buses you into the rugged Sierra Madre Mountains behind Mazatlan for a day of sightseeing. In the town of Concordia, you'll visit a church and a potter's home and have the opportunity to visit the local factories that make the ornate and classic colonial-style furniture. From there the bus wends its way through breathtaking mountain scenery to the ghost town of Copala, a gold-mining boomtown of old - really old. Copala was a Spanish settlement, a source of gold for Spanish kings. This place is much older than the ghostly boomtowns of the U.S. The streets are cobblestone, and restored homes and jailhouse add an authentic touch. Lunch is served in Copala at a historic hotel. Final stop is back in Mazatlan at the Arts and Crafts Center - one more chance to buy local goods - and then home to the ship. This trip takes more than six hours.

The "Sportfishing Tour" of Mazatlan waters is equal to Puerto Vallarta's. It lasts about seven hours, offering lunch, drinks and the opportunity to land your prize marlin, dolphin (the fish, not the mammal), sailfish, tuna or shark.

* Cabo San Lucas is on the tip of the Baja peninsula where the Pacific meets the waters of the Sea of Cortez (also called the Gulf of California). The time here is very short - three hours max - and although you may wish to simply relax on a romantic hideaway of a beach, first take the "Los Arcos Boat Tour." It lasts only half an hour and introduces you to what is labeled the most beautiful natural wonder in the country of Mexico - the rock arcades called Los Arcos. This is pristine seashore. Take your camera.

SHIPBOARD

Princess's "Daily Log" is a newsletter that informs you of the day's activities. (A nice touch in this daily newsletter is a reminder of how to dress for the evening meal, whether formal, semi-formal or casual. It leaves no doubt in your mind about what's de rigueur.) Lectures and talks, from cruise information to household hints, run often. If you're the information glutton, these lectures are good, valuable and fun. If you're a serious vacationer, however, you may prefer to lounge all day by the pool, with time out for a sauna, a manicure, a facial, new hair-do or a massage of one kind or another - Shiatsu, Swedish. For the cerebral, there's a library; for the health-conscious, there's daily exercise of the aerobic type, jogging paths, lectures and demonstrations, nutritional advice; for the athlete, there's volleyball, skeet shooting, Ping-Pong; for the social, there's dancing of all kinds, nearly constant eating opportunities, parties of a silly nature (pajama party, costume party, masquerade party), plus talent shows, sing-alongs, the liar's club and the what's my line game; for the gambler, there is the casino, with blackjack, and there are horse-racing contests and opportunities to set up card games where you can gamble to your heart's content. There are movies, radio of all persuasions (as in classical, pop, contemporary and easy listening), a daily newspaper that serves up more world news than anything but the "New York Times."

Visits to the ship's bridge, to the galley or to the engine room are worth the time, and simply exploring the ship, walking its decks and talking with its crew are simple pleasures that not too many people think about doing.

Each day a "SeaVid" is shown. This is a movie of the previous day's activities, whether it be your first day of just walking aboard, or the second day's Naughtie Nightie Contest or the third evening's lip-sync show. You can make arrangements to have your dinner table videoed and this can be added to the tape of main events, the whole of which you can purchase to take home with you. Obviously, some of this footage could be used against you by nefarious blackmailers, but on the other hand, your family at home will get a kick out of seeing you act in a manner they've never had the opportunity to witness.

A Catholic Mass is said each morning and on Sunday an interdenominational service is held. Friday evening a Jewish sabbath is celebrated. Explanatory talks are given about debarkation and about land tours for those interested. To check on what's to do and how to go about doing it, you can tune in to the ship's radio Channel 4, which explains it all.

One of the best ideas I've seen on a cruise ship is the Fair Princess's final day's White Elephant Auction. Anything you've purchased while in a buying frenzy can be unloaded before you are. If you really thought you wanted a mouse-shaped pinata and find you're too embarrassed to carry it home on the plane, auction the big rodent off. Conversely, someone else may also be suffering buyer's remorse and willing to sell off a great piece of Indian art you didn't even see while in port.

Youngsters and teens are as well thought of aboard Princess Cruises as are their parents. There's no hiding the kids while you have a good time. Rather, there are activities planned for the offspring that will appeal to them at whatever age - videos, movies, jukebox, board games, sports, tours on land and sea, Italian language lessons, ice cream sundae parties, scavenger hunts, parties, story time. The crew seems to sincerely like children, and the special activity counselors know their business and like it.

The Fair Princess is equipped with shoeshine service, laundry and dry cleaning service, a medical staff and satellite ability to "call home," even if you're not E.T. The duty-free shops had exceptional sales while we were aboard, including bonanza buys of formal attire the day of the captain's fancy cocktail party/dinner. A ship's bank cashes U.S. traveler's checks and exchanges money; no personal checks are accepted. Major credit cards are accepted, however, to pay for goods purchased aboard and to settle accounts at the end of the cruise.

SHIPBOARD ETIQUETTE

Each cruise line is basically the same, but one will be a tad more formal than another, or the tipping will be different.

Princess Cruises believes people should be left to tip as they see fit and does not suggest percentages. They do, however, offer guidelines if you need them: At the end of the cruise, tip the people you have dealt with directly, such as your steward (who really hops to on Princess Cruises, almost as if he's hovering at all times just outside your stateroom door) and your dining room steward and his assistants. Other service workers, such as bartenders, cocktail waitresses, wine stewards, barbers or hairdressers, blackjack dealers and so on, may be tipped at the time of service, even though you're signing for the bill. The cruise director gives a special lecture on tipping if you're interested.

On the ship, all charges for bar bills, wine, shore tours, shop purchases, sauna and massage services, photo orders, laundry, beauty and barber shop services and ship-to-shore radio calls will be applied to your personal account. A copy of your charges will be delivered to your stateroom at the end of the cruise.

General etiquette is no different on board ship than anywhere else. Simply be thoughtful and courteous. Smoking areas of large public rooms are designated on Fair Princess, and easily observable. Children should be reminded that running can be dangerous on shipboard, that rude or loud behavior is frowned on and that there are some things they are disallowed by law to do, such as enter the bars or casino.

It's such a relaxed atmosphere on this line that even on the most formal occasion there is no stiffness nor high and mighty behavior.

CLOTHING AND WEATHER

Although I haven't done this yet, if I ever do come with empty suitcases in order to buy what I need on board, I will do it on a Princess cruise because of the classy clothes in their shops and the reasonable prices. If this is too radical a move for you, pack your summer clothing, a few nice outfits, at least one very nice, suitable evening ensemble, your pool clothes, good walking shoes, a light jacket. The Mexican Riviera maintains an average temperature of seventy-five to eighty degrees, but if you venture into the mountains above Mazatlan, it may become chilly, so be prepared with a good sweater or windbreaker, possibly a hat. Depending on the time of year, Los Angeles, your home port, can be quite chilly also, down into the forty-degree range.

BOOKING YOUR CRUISE

Princess Cruises
2029 Century Park E
Los Angeles, CA 90067
Telephone 213-553-1770
Telex 215307
Reservations 213-553-7000
or call your travel agent.

CREW

Because the crew and staff are so enjoyable on the Fair Princess, the following will enable you to identify who's who. The Captain is the highest authority on a ship. He commands the three major departments: Deck, Engine and Hotel. The Deck Staff Captain oversees the cleanliness, safety and daily deck operations of the ship. Under him is the doctor.

The Chief Engineer keeps track of the Engine Department, which encompasses everything from propulsion to air conditioning. The Hotel Manager is in charge of dining, cabin, deck and front desk services. The Cruise Director and his or her staff is in this department. The Head Chef directs the butchers, the gardemanagers (who prepare antipasto, cold dishes, salads), the sauciers, the entremetiers (pasta, soup, vegetables), the poissoniers (breakfast, lunch and fish dishes), the rotisseurs (roasted and grilled dishes), the pantry cooks, bakers and the pizzeria guy.

FOOD

The galley of any cruise ship is a fascinating place. Even if you're not interested in cooking - or eating, if such a person exists - visit the galley. On the Fair Princess, food was brought in from all over the world. The Princess people pride themselves on their Alaskan salmon, French escargot, New Zealand spring lamb, Midwestern corn-fed beef, Virginia ham, Colombian coffee, French, Italian and American wines. (Sounds good just listing such items.)

The kitchen staff consists of about fifty cooks, chefs and sous chefs and serves an average 3,800 meals a day. A typical day aboard ship will see the following foodstuffs consumed by what appear to be starving and very thirsty passengers:

620 bottles of champagne
2,904 pounds of cheese
2,959 bottles of beer
1,600 bottles of wine
1,500 pounds of pasta
3,250 pounds of sugar

There is more, of course, but it begins to boggle the imagination. After the tour of the galley you'll want to just go and eat something. When you see how orderly and immaculate the galley is, you'll be impressed.

The menus for lunch and dinner are little works of art. The covers are reproductions of lovely watercolor paintings with a Mexican or tropical motif. They're framable enough to contain the artist's name, which they don't. Inside, the chef suggests a meal - for example, a typical luncheon suggestion is Homemade Fettuccine Primavera, Beer Steamed Knockwurst with Sauerkraut and Apple Slice with whipped cream.

If this doesn't appeal to you, a typical menu selection would include Tropical Fruit Cup with Grenadine, Deviled Eggs Zingara, Salad Nicoise, Sole Fillet Stuffed with Spinach and Cheese, Roast Spring Chicken with Dressing, Hot Sliced Roast Beef, Lemon Meringue Pie, Homemade Hazelnut Chip Ice Cream.

Remember, this is only lunch. . . .

Dinner is labeled with a theme, like Italian, Farewell, Welcome, French. The Welcome dinner suggested by the chef might be Assorted Seafood Cocktail, Homemade Cheese Ravioli, Medallion of Alaskan Salmon and Strawberries Romanoff, with wine selections from California's Jordan Winery, Sutter Home or Simi telling you what they accompany most companionably.

The regular menu on your first night out could read: Iced Fresh Fruit with Campari, Caesar Salad, Island Rock Lobster Thermidor or Fillet of Beef Wellington, Cauliflower, Assorted Italian Pastries and Homemade Pistachio Ice Cream.

Fit for kings, I tell you. It's tough not eating more than you should, but my latest theory is that one can always diet at home. Following are recipes that will make a dinner party such a success that your friends will think you've been to Le Cordon Bleu in Paris rather than dining your way from LA to Mexico and back.

RECIPES

Blush Fizz

1	6-oz. can frozen pink lemonade
6	oz. half-and-half
6	oz. vodka
1	whole egg
4	fresh strawberries

Fill a blender with ice and pour in frozen lemonade. Pour in half-and-half, vodka and add egg. (You can use the empty lemonade can to measure the vodka.) Blend thoroughly. Garnish with a fresh strawberry. This drink is great for brunch and may lift your spirits and those of your dinner guests also.

Serves 4

Electric Lemonade

1   oz. vodka
1   oz. gin
1   oz. tequila
1   oz. triple sec
1   oz. white rum
1 1/2   oz. sweet-and-sour mix
1 1/2   oz. 7-Up
        fresh lemon or lime slice

Fill a tall glass to the top with ice. Pour all the ingredients into the glass and stir. Garnish with a slice of lemon or lime. This is similar to a Long Island Iced Tea, except 7-Up is used rather than Coca Cola.

Serves 1

Kir

6   oz. dry white wine
3/4   oz. Campari
        twist of lemon peel

Fill a chilled wine glass with dry white wine. Pour in 3/4 ounce Campari; do not stir. Twist the lemon peel to release the skin's oil and drop it in.

Serves 1

Flaming Lampadina Cocktail

3	oz. heavy cream
1/3	oz. Tia Maria or Kahlua
1/3	oz. cognac
1/3	oz. Grand Marnier
3	oz. heavy cream

Steam cream until it begins to slightly thicken. Heat wine glass over a flame (use brandy heater or candle). Pour in all liquors. Hold a match over the glass and ignite the vapors. Be careful to hold glass away from your face and clothing. Pour out flame with steamed cream.

Serves 1

Marinated Mussels

2	c. dry white wine
1	small carrot, chopped
1	small onion, sliced
2	sprigs parsley
1/8	tsp. freshly ground pepper
5	lbs. fresh mussels, scrubbed and debearded
1/4	c. fresh lemon juice
1	Tbsp. fresh basil, chopped
1 1/2	tsp. capers, chopped
1/8	tsp. pepper
1/4	tsp. salt
1/3	c. olive oil

Combine wine, carrot, onion, parsley and pepper in stockpot and bring to boil. Add mussels, cover and cook until they open, about 5 minutes. Discard any unopened mussels. Let mussels cool in liquid, stirring occasionally. To make marinade, blend lemon juice, chopped basil, capers, salt and pepper. Whisk in oil 1 drop at a time. Remove mussels from shells and add to marinade. Refrigerate several hours or overnight. Bring to room temperature before serving.

Serves 12

Fried Zucchini

2	medium zucchini
2	large eggs
2	Tbsp. milk
	salt and freshly ground black pepper
1/2	c. all-purpose flour
2	c. bread crumbs
1	c. vegetable oil
4	lemon wedges

Wash zucchini, trim ends off and discard. Cut zucchini lengthwise into slices approximately 1/4" thick. Beat eggs and milk together in a shallow pan. Season with salt and pepper. Place flour in another shallow pan and season with salt and pepper. Do the same with the bread crumbs. Submerge zucchini slices in beaten egg, then dredge in flour, shaking off any excess. Dip slices once again in the beaten egg and then dredge in bread crumbs. Heat oil in a skillet and saute zucchini slices on both sides until golden brown. Remove and drain on paper towels. Serve on warm dish garnished with lemon wedges.

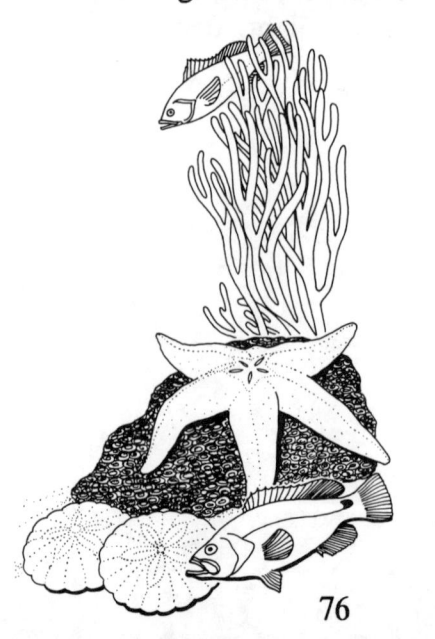

Serves 4

Calamari Salad

1 1/2	lbs. small squid
1/4	c. dry white wine
	salt to taste
1/4	tsp. freshly ground pepper
4	Tbsp. fresh lemon juice
1/3	c. olive oil
1/2	c. celery root, julienned
1/4	c. red bell pepper, finely julienned
4	Tbsp. fresh chives, minced

Clean calamari and cut body sacs crosswise into 1/2" rings. Heat a pot of water to boiling and add wine, salt and calamari. Simmer until tender (don't overcook), about 4 minutes. Drain and cool under cold running water. Combine salt, pepper and lemon juice, beat in olive oil and stir in celery root and red bell pepper. Toss calamari with dressing and marinate for 24 hours. Sprinkle chives on top.

Serves 6

Caesar Salad

1	clove garlic, halved
8	anchovy fillets, cut up
1/3	c. olive oil
1	tsp. Worcestershire sauce
1/2	tsp. salt
1/4	tsp. dry mustard
	freshly ground pepper
1	large bunch romaine lettuce, torn into bite-sized pieces
1	egg, coddled
1	lemon, halved
1	c. garlic-flavored croutons
1/3	c. Parmesan cheese, grated

Rub large wooden salad bowl with cut cloves of garlic. Allow a few small pieces of garlic to remain in bowl if desired. Mix anchovies, oil, Worcestershire, salt, mustard and pepper in bowl and toss with romaine until leaves glisten. Break coddled egg onto salad. Squeeze lemon over salad and toss. Sprinkle with croutons and cheese and toss.

Serves 6

Lobster Bisque

1	live lobster, 1 1/2 lbs.
5	Tbsp. butter
1/4	c. carrot, diced
1	small onion, chopped
1/2	bay leaf
	pinch of thyme
2	sprigs parsley
3	Tbsp. cognac
1/4	c. dry white wine
1/2	c. fish stock or chicken broth
1	Tbsp. sherry or Madeira
1/4	c. flour
3	c. milk
3	Tbsp. heavy cream, approximately
	red food coloring (optional)

Have the lobster split and cleaned at the market. Crack the claws and cut the body and tail into 4 or 5 pieces. Melt 2 tablespoons of the butter and saute the carrot and onion in it until the onion is transparent. Add the bay leaf, thyme, parsley and lobster. Saute until the lobster turns red, about 5 minutes, shaking the pan occasionally. Add 2 tablespoons cognac and ignite. Add the wine and the stock and simmer 20 minutes. Remove the lobster, cool and remove the meat from the shell. Dice the meat fine and add the sherry and set aside. Reserve the shell and broth. Melt the remaining butter in a saucepan, add flour and blend with a wire whisk. Meanwhile, bring the milk to a boil and add all at once to the butter-flour mixture, stirring vigorously with the whisK. Grind or crush the lobster shell and add to the sauce. Add the reserved broth with the vegetables and then simmer, covered, about 1 hour. Strain through a fine sieve.

Lobster Bisque (Cont.)

Bring the sauce to a boil and add enough cream to give the desired consistency. If desired, add a few drops of coloring to make the soup a delicate pink color. Add the reserved lobster meat, correct the seasonings and add the remaining cognac.

Serves 5

Chilled Zucchini Soup

1/2	c. olive oil
1	medium onion, chopped (about 1 cup)
8	medium zucchini, trimmed, scrubbed, cut into 1/4" slices
2	cloves garlic, minced
4	c. heavy cream
	pinch of fresh thyme
	salt and freshly ground pepper to taste

Heat oil in large, heavy skillet over medium heat until surface is rippling. Add onion and saute, stirring occasionally until softened, 5 to 10 minutes. Add zucchini and garlic, reducing heat to low. Simmer covered until zucchini is very tender but not browned, 20 to 25 minutes. Remove from heat. Stir in 2 cups of cream and the thyme. Let cool slightly. Place half the zucchini mixture in blender and blend until mixture is very smooth. Transfer to large bowl. Stir in 1/3 cup of cream. Repeat procedure with remaining zucchini mixture and remaining heavy cream. Force the mixture through a fine sieve. Add salt and pepper and refrigerate, covered, for several hours before serving.

Serves 6

Spaghetti Alla Puttanesca

1/4	c. olive oil
3	cloves garlic, finely chopped
1	large can plum tomatoes, drained, seeded and coarsely chopped
1	Tbsp. capers, rinsed and drained
15	black olives, pitted and thinly sliced
2	oz. anchovy fillets, rinsed, drained and chopped
1/2	(to 1) dried chili pepper, finely chopped
1	tsp. dried basil
1	tsp. dried oregano
1	lb. spaghetti
2	Tbsp. fresh parsley leaves, finely chopped

Heat oil in a large saucepan. Add garlic and saute until golden. Do not burn. Add remaining ingredients except spaghetti and parsley. Cook slowly for 15 minutes. While the sauce is simmering, cook the spaghetti in salted boiling water until al dente. Drain spaghetti and transfer to a warm serving bowl. Pour the sauce over the spaghetti and toss quickly. Sprinkle with chopped parsley.

Serves 4 to 6

Manicotti (Stuffed Crepes with Black Olives and Prosciutto)

2	lbs. whole-milk ricotta
1	large egg
1	c. Parmesan, freshly grated
1/4	c. walnuts, finely chopped
1/4	c. slivered almonds, blanched
1/4	c. black olives, chopped
1/2	c. fresh parsley leaves, finely chopped
1	Tbsp. dried basil or fresh basil, finely chopped
	salt and freshly ground black pepper
12	crespelle* or manicotti, cooked) See glossary
12	slices prosciutto, trimmed of fat and thinly sliced
2	c. Ragu Spaghetti Sauce
12	slices whole-milk mozzarella, thinly sliced

Preheat oven to 450° F. In a large mixing bowl combine the ricotta, egg, 1/2 of the Parmesan, walnuts, almonds, olives, parsley, basil, salt and pepper. Mix well. Lay the manicotti or crespelle, browned side up, on work surface. Place 1 slice of prosciutto on each crespelle or manicotti and top with a large scoop of ricotta mixture (about 1/4 cup). Fold 1/2 the crespelle over the cheese, fold in the sides and then fold over the other 1/2. The manicotti will be tubular shaped. Spread 1/2 the Ragu sauce over the bottom of a large baking pan. Arrange the manicotti, seam side up, in the pan. Cover with remaining sauce. Be careful not to drown the manicotti in the sauce. Cover the pan with aluminum foil and bake for 15 minutes. Remove the foil, cover each roll with a slice of mozzarella and sprinkle all with the remaining Parmesan. Return to the oven, uncovered, for 5 minutes, or until the cheese has melted.

Serves 6

Orange Roughy

3	orange roughy steaks, 1" thick (about 2 lbs. total weight)
1	tsp. salt
1/8	tsp. dried dill weed
1/2	small onion, thinly sliced
1/4	c. margarine or butter, melted
2	Tbsp. lemon juice

Grapefruit sauce:

1/2	c. unsweetened pink grapefruit juice
1/8	tsp. salt
	dash of dried dill weed
1	Tbsp. cold water
1	tsp. cornstarch
1	pink grapefruit, pared and sectioned
	dill weed or parsley for garnish

Heat oven to 450° F. Cut each orange roughy steak into halves. Place in ungreased rectangular baking dish, 11" x 7" x 1 1/2". Sprinkle with salt and dill weed and top with onion. Mix margarine and lemon juice and pour over fish. Bake uncovered until fish flakes easily with fork, 20 to 25 minutes. Prepare grapefruit sauce by heating grapefruit juice, salt and dill weed to boiling in 1 1/2-quart saucepan. Mix cold water and cornstarch and stir into grapefruit juice. Heat to boiling, stirring constantly. Boil and stir 1 minute. Carefully stir in grapefruit. Serve over fish. Garnish with dill weed or parsley if desired.

Serves 6

Duck a l'Orange

1	3 1/2 lb. duckling
1	pint demi-glace*
8	oranges
	juice of 1/2 lemon
2	lumps sugar
	a few drops of vinegar

Brown the duck and then pour off the fat. Cook the duck covered in a 400° F oven. Moisten with demi-glace. When cooked, skim off fat and strain the sauce. Add the juice of 2 of the oranges, the lemon juice, the sugar burnt to caramel and dissolved in a few drops of vinegar, and the rind of 3 oranges, julienned and blanched for 3 minutes in boiling water. Arrange the duck on a long dish and cover with sauce. Garnish with orange segments without seeds or skin. Serve the remaining sauce in a sauce boat.

Serves 4 to 5

*see glossary

Fillet of Beef in Dusseldorf Mustard Sauce

2	lbs. beef fillet (middle section)
	salt and pepper to taste
1	tsp. fresh marjoram, chopped
1	tsp. fresh thyme, chopped
1	tsp. fresh tarragon, chopped
2	tsp. fresh parsley, chopped
1/2	c. shallots, finely chopped
1	oz. butter
1	tsp. balsamic vinegar
1/3	pint white wine
1	tsp. sweet mustard
2	tsp. Meaux mustard
1	tsp. medium sharp mustard
3	oz. butter, room temperature
1	tsp. chives, finely chopped
3	Tbsp. whipping cream

Sprinkle beef with salt and pepper, rub with fresh herbs. Refrigerate for 3 hours. Brown fillet on all sides. Roast at 450° F for about 20 minutes or until pink in center. Allow meat to rest 10 minutes before slicing. Saute shallots in butter until transparent. Add vinegar and cook until vinegar is evaporated. Add wine and cook until it is reduced by half. Add mustards and cook until sauce thickens. Remove from heat. Whisk in small pieces of softened butter. Add chives and whipping cream. Place sauce on plate and place sliced fillet on top.

Serves 4

Lamb Roast with Pine Nut and Parmesan Crust

1/2	c. pine nuts, toasted
2	oz. Parmesan cheese, cut into 2" pieces
1	slice soft white bread with crust, torn into pieces
2	tsp. Dijon mustard
1	large clove garlic, minced
1/2	tsp. dried rosemary, crumbled
1/4	tsp. salt
	freshly ground pepper
1	egg white
1	3 1/2-lb. leg of lamb (sirloin end), boned and trimmed
	salt and pepper to taste

Position rack in center of oven and preheat to 450° F. Oil a roasting pan. Mix pine nuts, cheese, bread, mustard, garlic, rosemary, 1/4 tsp. salt and pepper to taste. Blend in egg white. Season underside of lamb with salt and pepper. Arrange seasoned side down in prepared pan. Using spatula, spread nut mixture over top of lamb, pressing gently to adhere. (Can be prepared 1 day in advance, covered tightly and refrigerated. Bring to room temperature before continuing.) Roast lamb 15 minutes. Reduce temperature to 375° F and continue cooking to desired doneness - 15 minutes more for rare (thermometer inserted in thickest part of lamb will register 125° F); cook longer for medium or well done. Let stand 10 to 15 minutes before carving in thin slices.

Serves 6

Pesto Genovese

2	c. fresh basil leaves, packed
2	cloves garlic, crushed
2	anchovy fillets
1/2	c. extra virgin olive oil
1/2	c. freshly grated Parmesan cheese
2	Tbsp. freshly grated Romano cheese
3	Tbsp. softened butter.

In blender combine all ingredients except cheeses and butter. When well mixed blend in cheeses and butter. Refrigerate for 24 hours.

Makes 1 1/2 cups

Macademia Nut Gelato

5	large egg yolks
2/3	c. sugar
2	c. milk
1	tsp. vanilla extract
1	tsp. macadamia nut essence

Beat egg yolks with a whisk in the top of a double boiler or a mixing bowl large enough to fit over a pan of boiling water. Add sugar and beat until the mixture becomes very light yellow. In a separate saucepan, bring the milk just to the boiling point, but do not let it boil. Place the bowl with the egg-sugar mixture over saucepan of boiling water but do not let mixture boil. Add the warm milk little by little to the eggs, whisking the milk completely into the eggs after each addition. Add vanilla and nut essence and continue cooking the mixture, stirring continuously with a wooden spoon until the mixture thickens. When it is done, it should be the consistency of thin pudding and should coat the spoon. Be very careful not to overcook it as the eggs will harden. Remove the bowl from the heat and set it in the refrigerator to cool. Stir occasionally to facilitate the cooling. Once cooled, transfer the mixture to a loaf pan. Place the pan in the freezer and stir the gelato every 30 minutes for 2 hours. The finished gelato will be thick, smooth and soft.

Serves 6

New England Cheesecake

6	lbs. cream cheese
1 1/2	lbs. sugar
6	eggs
1	tsp. vanilla extract
	rind of 2 lemons, grated
1	pint heavy cream
	butter
	cake crumbs or Graham cracker crumbs

With your fingers, blend together cream cheese and sugar. Stir in eggs with a spoon one at a time, blending well. Add vanilla extract, grated lemon rind and heavy cream to form a smooth batter. Mix as little as possible. Butter 2 10" cake pans, then line the bottoms with cake crumbs and pour the batter into the pans. Place pans in pan of hot water 1/4" deep. Bake in a hot oven 460° F for 10 to 15 minutes, then reduce heat to 350° F and bake for 1 hour and 45 minutes, or until the cakes are completely set. Serve with fresh strawberry sauce. (Recipe follows)

Fresh Strawberry Sauce

2	c. fresh strawberries
1	Tbsp. strawberry jam
1	Tbsp. fresh lemon juice
2	Tbsp. super fine sugar
2	Tbsp. framboise liqueur

Puree strawberries in food processor with strawbery jam and transfer to a fine-mesh sieve set over a bowl. Press puree through the sieve with the back of a large spoon to remove seeds. Discard

Fresh Strawberry Sauce (Cont.)

them. Stir lemon juice and sugar to taste into puree. Stir in framboise. Sauce can be refrigerated up to 3 days.

Makes 1 cup

White Chocolate Truffles

6	oz. white chocolate
2	Tbsp. whipping cream
2 1/2	Tbsp. butter, unsalted
2 1/2	Tbsp. butter, salted
1/4	tsp. kirsch, framboise, or any liqueur or champagne

Chop chocolate into coarse pieces and melt over hot water in a heavy saucepan with the cream and butter. Stir constantly until smooth and glossy, then remove from heat. Stir in flavoring, then pour mixture 1" deep into a container. Chill thoroughly. Use a melon baller to shape truffles, rinsing in hot water after shaping each truffle. If any truffles break, pinch them back into shape. Chill the chocolate if it softens too much while you work. If the truffles have softened during the shaping process chill them briefly. You can serve these truffles plain or rolled in toasted coconut or in toasted nuts. Be sure you use only white chocolate made with cocoa butter. Other white chocolate is disappointingly bland.

Makes 3 dozen 1" truffles

Chocolate Souffle

2	Tbsp. butter
2	Tbsp. flour
3/4	c. milk
	pinch of salt
2	oz. unsweetened chocolate
1/3	c. sugar
2	Tbsp. cold coffee
1/2	tsp. vanilla extract
3	egg yolks, lightly beaten
4	egg whites, stiffly beaten
	whipping cream

Preheat oven to 375° F. In a saucepan melt butter, add flour and stir with a wire whisk until blended. Meanwhile, bring milk to a boil and add all at once to the butter-flour mixture, stirring vigorously with the whisk. Add salt. Melt chocolate with sugar and coffee over hot water. Stir the melted chocolate mixture into the sauce and add vanilla. Beat in egg yolks one at a time. Cool. Beat egg whites until they stand in peaks. Fold into the mixture. Transfer to a 2-quart casserole and bake 35 to 45 minutes. Serve immediately.

Serves 6

Sacher Torte

1/3	c. butter, room temperature
6	Tbsp. granulated sugar
1/2	c. semisweet chocolate pieces, melted
4	egg yolks
1/2	c. plus 1 Tbsp. sifted flour
5	egg whites
2 1/2	Tbsp. apricot jam

Preheat oven to 325° F. Grease and lightly flour an 8" deep spring-form cake pan. Cream butter, add sugar gradually and cream until fluffy. Add chocolate and mix thoroughly. Add egg yolks one at a time and mix well after each addition. Stir in flour until no particles show. Beat egg whites until stiff but not dry. Gently fold them into the batter until no white shows. Turn the batter into the prepared pan and bake on the lower oven shelf until the cake shrinks from the sides of the pan and rebounds to the touch when pressed gently in the center, or about 1 hour and 15 minutes. Let the cake stand 10 minutes on a cooling rack before turning out of the pan (cake will shrink slightly on cooling). Turn the cake out on the rack, turn right side up and let cool. Stand the rack and cake on waxed paper and spread the top of the cake with jam. Pour any desired chocolate icing over the cake and spread it quickly to coat the top and sides.

Serves 6 to 8

ISLAND PRINCESS

PRINCESS CRUISES

ISLAND PRINCESS

The best ceviche this side of Akumal.

Marinate fresh mackerel or pez sierra in lime juice. Add tomato, onion, olive oil and spices. Include hot chiles, of course.

This is ceviche (say, seh-vee'-chay), from the Spanish verb, "to saturate."

Recipes vary region by region. The tangy ceviche of the Yucatan tastes distinctly different from the ceviche of Acapulco. In truth, the best ceviche is a matter of personal taste. From place to place. From mild to picante.

You can find our delicious ceviche served from the Riviera to our Caribbean. And in all our historic inland cities.

To get there, just ask your travel agent. Or call Mexicana at (800) 531-7921.

But the best ceviche, you really must discover yourself.

mexicana
We've got more cuisine going for you.

ISLAND PRINCESS

The Love Boat made Princess Cruises one of the most renowned cruise ship lines in the world. Because of the television show, which was about romance and fun on the high seas, the Love Boat also reinstated ocean voyages as the ultimate way to travel. Cruise ship vacationing is big business, and a cruise on the Island Princess to Mexico is a fitting introduction to the pleasures of travel by ship.

The parent company of the Princess Cruises is the prestigious P & O, the Peninsular & Oriental Steam Navigation Company. It went into business in 1837 carrying passengers from England to India and the Far East. This was the heyday of the British Empire. In order to satisfy the demands of the upper crust foreign servant bound for far-flung posts, a tradition of luxury and service was born. It continues today.

The British-registered Princess ships are crewed by British officers and seamen, and the dining staff is Italian, a good combination. The Island Princess staterooms are all first class, containing telephones, private bath facilities (the majority with tub/shower, a few with shower only), multi-channel music systems and individually-controlled air conditioning. The staterooms are soothingly decorated (as opposed to excitingly), and the public rooms are spacious and opulent. With one of the highest crew-to-passenger ratios, Island Princess guarantees that the service is personable and quick.

Princess cruise costs are in the moderate to pricey range.

EMBARKATION

Home ported in San Pedro, California, the Island Princess sails for Mazatlan on a Saturday evening at promptly 6:00 p.m. A bon voyage party is held on the Boat Deck and passengers can throw streamers and wave good-bye to the landlubbers just like in the movies. Each day in "Princess Patter," the activities newsletter deposited daily in your stateroom, the ship's navigator describes what his ship is doing, the route it will be cruising and what landmarks you'll be passing. The evening we sailed, his entry said, "Once clear of our moorings we will make our way down the San Pedro Channel, across Los Angeles harbour where we disembark our Pilot and thence into the open sea at about 6:45 p.m. During the evening we head south following the Los Angeles traffic separation lanes and then set southerly courses towards Cabo San Lucas. Sunset 6:10 p.m.; sunrise tomorrow 5:43 a.m."

PORTS OF CALL

* After two days of sailing, the Island Princess tied up in Mazatlan at 8:00 a.m. on Tuesday. Five tours are available before we set sail at 6:00 p.m., ranging from the simple to the sophisticated. All shore excursions are explained fully by the crew and you'll have plenty of opportunity to decide which suits you.

Tour A, the "Mazatlan City Tour," introduces you to the town and points out the highlights - Mazatlan's oceanfront drive, the world's second highest natural lighthouse, offshore islands, the old downtown market section - and deposits you at the Mazatlan Arts and Crafts Center for a browse-through of exhibits of Mexican and Indian arts and crafts. This is the largest crafts center in Mexico. You'll also be entertained by a folkloric dance troupe before driving across the city to the Shrimp Fishing Fleet Docks, one of the world's busiest fishing ports. This tour takes about three hours.

Tour B, dubbed the "Shopping, Beach and Lunch Tour," also takes you to the Arts and Crafts Center. Then you're pointed toward the Los Sabalos Hotel where you'll spend the rest of the day sunning, eating, swimming - a real lazy vacation day. Changing-rooms are provided at the hotel, which by the way, is one of Mazatlan's nicest beachfront hostelries. Whenever you're ready to return to the ship, a taxi is lined up for you.

Tour C, the "Best of Mazatlan," combines the morning sightseeing of Tour A with the afternoon relaxation of Tour B. You get the comprehensive look at the town and then the arts and crafts shopping and then the lunch, drinks and beach of Los Sabalos.

Tour D, the "Sierra Madre Tour," takes you into the coastal mountain range that separates the beaches from the interior. In the mountain community of Concordia you'll tour the colonial church, a factory where they make furniture that looks like the original Spanish colonial imports, and watch a potter at work in his cottage industry of throwing pots and fashioning dishes. The next stop is the former (and I mean former - we're talking the late 1500s here) gold mining town of Copala, now a touristy ghost town, but authentic-looking nevertheless. A good lunch is served here in the old hotel before you return to the city and the Arts and Crafts Center.

Tour E, "Sportfishing," is for the hardy trophy-hunter. The record marlin caught here weighed an astonishing 988 pounds, which sounds to me like it would have sunk the boat. The average marlin landed is a mere 140 pounds, the average sailfish about one hundred pounds. Most fishermen could live with that. The fishing boats are well-maintained and crewed by experienced sailors. Lunch is served on board and beer and soda are available.

If two days of being ship-bound have driven the golf nuts nuts, independent play at El Cid Golf and Country Club may save the duffer from the loony bin. All arrangements can be made, before leaving the ship, to play this eighteen-hole course or the nine-hole Club Campestre.

If you dislike the regimentation of a guided tour, you can plan your own look-see of this picturesque little city. Taxis await at the passenger terminal, as do the open "pulmonias," three-wheeled carts that make you feel like you're a part of the history of the place. Some of the greatest beaches in the world lie within a taxi

ISLAND PRINCESS

ride - Sabalo, Olas Altas (high waves), Playa Norte (a good swimming beach), or Las Gaviotas (the sea gulls) in the Golden Zone, near the best hotels, restaurants and shopping. You can also hire a boat and in just a few minutes be on Isla de Piedra, Stone Island, where the beaches are also worthy.

An interesting note: The Island Princess sponsors a Mazatlan orphanage and has raised a tidy sum over the years for its benefit. A nice touch. Whatever Mexican coins you have left over at the end of the day can be dropped into a container in the Purser's Office for this cause.

* Puerto Vallarta sounds sexy and jet-set. It is now, but until Richard Burton and Ava Gardner came here in the early '60s to film "Night of the Iguana," the place was a sleepy little hamlet. It was because of Burton's much-publicized love affair with Liz Taylor while on location in Puerto Vallarta that the seaside village earned its renown and soon became a spot of curiosity - and then, because of its extravagant natural beauty, an "in" spot of the traveling crowd.

Wrapped around the lovely Bahia de Banderas (bay of flags), Puerto Vallarta is the epitome of the lush, tropical, red tile-roofed village of your daydreams. The streets are cobblestone, the pink and purple paper-like flowers of the bougainvillea trail languidly over patios. The balmy days are unbelievably calming and peaceful.

You can walk the Malecon, the seawall, or hire a taxi to get you about. It is a friendly and prosperous little town, and many Americans have settled here. Their section of town is called "Gringo Gulch."

If you're on your own, some of the sights to see include the distinctive landmark cathedral, Our Lady of Guadalupe (patron saint of Mexico), crowned with a gold steeple that is a navigational landmark for sailors; Daiquiri Dick's (all taxi drivers will know these names); El Dorado, a restaurant under a palapa roof; the Joyeria del Mercado or La Fiesta, two of the main market areas; or Tlaquepaque, a market area just south of the Buenaventura Hotel.

Mismaloya Beach, where "Night of the Iguana" was filmed, can be reached by boat, taxi or bus. Here you can get the real feel of the best of Mexico's Gold Coast. There is a restaurant nearby, a changing area, white sandy beach and clear aqua blue water. If Mismaloya is crowded, negotiate with your driver to take you on, to Chino's Paradise. Chino's is a restaurant built into a cliff near a waterfall and natural pool. Rum punch in a pineapple is the drink here. This is the place for romance, or at least photos of the scenery.

For guided tours, make your reservations on the ship. Tour A, "Puerto Vallarta City," takes you from Marina Pier along the Malecon, past the cathedral and through Gringo Gulch. You'll have an opportunity to explore parks and shops and then drive past fancy hotels and even fancier private homes on your way to Mismaloya Beach. You'll end up at a famous restaurant called Chee Chee in the quiet Boca de Tomatlan for a drink before returning to the pier.

Tour B, "Fiesta Chee Chee," takes five hours and provides an opportunity to walk along the Malecon and through the main plaza near the cathedral. You will get a closer look at the stunning homes perched on cliffs, the exclusive Gold Coast residential area and Gringo Gulch. Then on to a view of Mismaloya before settling in at Chee Chee's for luncheon and cocktails. The fresh water pool here will soothe you for the afternoon unless you want to shop - which you can - or snorkel. Or you can rent a canoe to get you away from it all at a nearby private beach.

ISLAND PRINCESS

Tour C, "Banderas Bay Cruise," takes you aboard a fifty-foot catamaran for about three hours. You sail south a ways, past some of the more spectacular hotels, to a landmark of arched rocks where the pelicans feed. The boat anchors for a while so you can swim in to a secluded beach, snorkel or stay aboard and party with the crew.

There is time at the Puerto Vallarta stop to play a round of golf at the par-seventy-two, eighteen-hole championship course, Los Flamingos. Arrangements can be made on the Island Princess.

* Zihuatanejo is only half a day's stop, noon to about 6:00 p.m., but it's such a lovely, untouched place you'll be glad you took the time to go ashore. It's said to look like Acapulco did thirty years ago; it's also said to look like Bali or Tahiti. You're ferried ashore in a launch, as there is no pier large enough to handle the Island Princess. This is the place to relax on the beach and pretend you're far removed from civilization and its pressures. Easy to do in Zihuatanejo.

* Acapulco is big, modern, sophisticated, but as lovely a setting as the world offers. No doubt that's why it's become such a popular tourist spot. Here you can enjoy all the luxuries of the modern world amid the seductive climate and beauty of the tropics. Because of the diversity of the city, a tour is not a bad idea here, at least to get you oriented.

Tour A, "Acapulco City Tour," acquaints you with the commercial areas, the historic parts of this town which was a quaint fishing village not too long ago, the beaches and the Gran Via Tropical where many of the rich and famous live. A scenic highway takes you to a panoramic viewpoint and eventually you wind up at La Quebrada, where the most famous divers in the world take your breath away with their derring-do. This tour takes a little over three hours, introduces you to the area, offers a sample of shopping and is a good way to plunge into the glamour of Acapulco.

ISLAND PRINCESS

Tour B, "Acapulco Deluxe," takes seven hours and is therefore a little more leisurely. The Avenida Costera Miguel Aleman, lined with boutiques, restaurants, five-star hotels and the multi-million-dollar Cultural and Convention Center, is your first route of the day, with a stop at the Acapulco Princess Hotel, which is shaped like a pyramid. You'll watch the cliff divers here and then drive on to the elegance of the Pierre Marques Hotel on the lovely beach called Revolcadero where you'll be served a fancy lunch and then be invited to enjoy the hotel's pool, beach and lounges. Towels, changing rooms and showers are available.

Tour C, "Acapulco Bay Cruise with Lunch," is aboard a catamaran, which sails you past the luxury hotels, the cliff houses of some very wealthy folks and drops anchor at a secluded beach for a swim. An open bar aboard makes for a four-and-a-half-hour party.

Tour D, "Mexico City Tour," involves an airplane ride to the capitol and an interesting fourteen- to fifteen-hour day. Mexico City is one of the world's most beautiful and the Western Hemisphere's oldest city. It lives with an impressive past. You'll be shown the three eras of the city - the pre-Columbian, the colonial and the modern, all of which utilized this city as the capital of a large population. The largest religious structure on the continent is in Mexico City, the Metropolitan Cathedral. It is beautiful - a combination of French neo-classical and Spanish Renaissance. On this square, or plaza, called the Zocalo (constitution square), you'll also get a glimpse of the National Palace where a mural of the history of Mexico has been done by the world-renowned artist Diego Rivera. The Basilica of Guadalupe also sits here on this square that was once the ceremonial center of the Aztecs.

The tour takes you to the sacred grounds of the Teotihuacan Indians, an archaeological center of importance. Here you'll see the Pyramid of the Moon, the Pyramid of the Sun and the Temple of Quetzalcoatl. You'll eat lunch at a Teocalli restaurant and then return to the city via Chapultepec Park and the residential area called Las Lomas de Chapultepec. This is quite a trip and jam-packed with a lot of information and things to see.

* Once again, the golfers among you can play a round while in Acapulco, at the Pierre Marques or the Acapulco Princess hotels' courses.

SHIPBOARD

The Island Princess activities fill up the days, and if you prefer not to go ashore on tours, there is plenty to do on board. Movies, casinos, bars, nightclubs and showrooms afford sophisticated entertainment, but everyday fun activities never cease, either. The choices are too numerous to get them all in on one cruise.

As on most ships, Catholic Mass is said in the morning. An Episcopalian Communion Service is held on the Princess on Sunday, as well as a Friday night Jewish Seder. "Keep-Fit" classes begin early in the morning (right after the Early Risers Bloody Marys on the Sun Deck!), and Ping-Pong practice begins about 10:00 a.m. You can attend a gaming school to learn the tricks of playing blackjack, craps and roulette, or you can attend the cha-cha-cha school and learn the tricks of the dance floor.

Some of the highlighted entertainment includes Broadway reviews, a London pub night, cabaret singers and comedians, big band dancing and a fancy fiesta. A week-long involvement with a horse race event turned out to be a lot of fun. You get to pick your horse to train, choose your jockey's silks and so on, and then you might even win the derby come race day.

For one of the formal evenings, the Captain's Welcome Dinner, after the subtle suggestions of a fashion show, we spent a couple of hours late in the day being pampered with massage, sauna, manicure, pedicure, facial, make-up and hair-do primps. We felt like a million bucks for a surprisingly little bit of money.

Bridge and backgammon get-togethers attracted many people, and a few played Monopoly, chess and Scrabble. The gym was open all day for workout, and shuffleboard - the time-honored sport aboard luxury liners - was as popular as ever. I always feel duty-bound to play at least one game of shuffleboard whenever I'm on a ship.

The swimming pool and deck chair areas are the most popular, and rightly so, for the temperature hovers in the seventy-five- to eighty-degree range and is soothing in its balmy breeziness. Besides, there's something decadently satisfying about lounging on a luxury liner with a tall, fruity drink beside you, a best seller in hand and the company of other idle folk. If the opportunity happens only once in your lifetime, or every year, jump at the chance.

THE LOOK AND FEEL OF THINGS

The Princess ships are classy. Although your stateroom may see very little of you, it will be a comfortable and cheery place. A surprisingly large amount of closet and drawer space will accommodate your goods and the well-lit vanity may be better than what you have at home. No matter where your stateroom is on the ship you will enjoy comfort and convenience, some with picture-window views and a small refrigerator.

The service your steward is ready to give you will become addictive quickly. If you're really the reclusive type, you can depend on your steward for breakfast, lunch and dinner room service, snacks, drinks, laundered clothes, fresh ice - and all with sincere goodwill and friendliness.

The public rooms have a modern airiness to them and everything is immaculate. The line offers world-class accommodations.

BOOKING YOUR CRUISE

Princess Cruises
2029 Century Park E
Los Angeles, CA 90067
Telephone 213-553-1770
Telex 215307
Reservations 213-553-7000
or call your travel agent

ENTERTAINMENT

Princess Lines goes in for the review-type gala shows and they do a good job with them. Broadway music from celebrated long-runs like "Cats," "A Chorus Line," "Evita" and other oldie-but-goodie shows will warm your heart. The lighting, sound, costumes - everything is very professional and top-ranked.

The casinos play a big part on the Princess ships also, offering play most of the day and all night unless in port, where law generally forbids their opening. The dealers and croupiers are friendly and fun, unlike some of the ones you may have run into in the non-floating casinos stateside.

FOOD

The Italian cooking crew prides itself on its cuisine and service. There is a great deal of tableside preparation, which means your dinner is getting obvious special attention. These dishes include Fettucine Alfredo, Steak Tartare, Crepes Suzette, Cherries Jubilee - the kinds of things you'd be ordering at Four Seasons or in your favorite expensive restaurant. On the Island Princess it was a nightly occurrence - one good meal after another. It spoils you for many a day, believe me.

ISLAND PRINCESS

The Italian food is scrumptious - Italian chefs, remember - but they do all right with things like Beef Wellington, Broiled Lobster Tail and Roast Turkey if you want to pass up gourmet wonders like Tagliatelle Verdi, Gamberi Flambati, Scaloppine di Vitello and Zabaglione.

The diet society supposedly sins during cruises, but on Princess all dedicated thin-is-in folks can be taken care of with ease, for the chefs know how to order the best fresh fruits, crisp salad greens and many kinds of fish, chicken and lean meats. With twenty-four hour notice, the chefs will prepare just about anything your diet demands.

If, however, you're ready to sin, this is the place for chocolate, for pasta with cream sauces, for pastries, for five-course luncheons and bounteous midnight buffets. How does one resist caviar? Jumbo shrimp Newburg? Souffle au Grand Marnier with brandy sauce?

RECIPES

Calaloo Mussel Soup

2	onions, minced
1	small chile pepper, diced
1/2	c. Canadian bacon, diced
1	clove garlic, minced
2	Tbsp. chicken broth or dry vermouth
2	lbs. fresh spinach or 20 oz. chopped frozen spinach
12	pods okra, fresh or frozen
2	qts. water
2	Tbsp. fresh chives, minced
1	tsp. coarse salt
1/2	tsp. each ground pepper, cayenne, thyme, basil
12	mussels in shells

In a large stockpot saute onion, pepper, bacon and garlic in the broth or vermouth until the onions are translucent. Add all other ingredients except mussels and bring to a boil. Simmer over low heat for 30 minutes, stirring regularly. Add mussels and continue to simmer for about 1 hour, stirring occasionally.

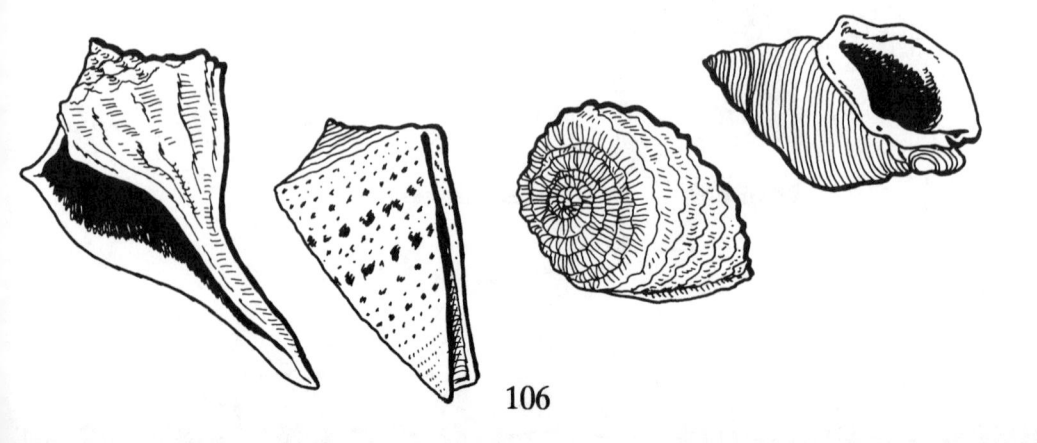

Serves 8

Duck and Orange Salad

2 1/2   c. duck meat, poached and diced
4   small navel oranges, peeled, de-membraned, sectioned
12   ripe olives, pitted and sliced
1   small red onion, thinly sliced
       salt and pepper to taste
       rosemary
       romaine and endive greens
       French dressing
       slivered almonds, blanched

Combine duck meat and orange slices with olives and onions. Sprinkle lightly with salt and pepper and a generous pinch of rosemary. Chill 1 hour. Toss romaine and endive with French dressing. Serve duck and orange combination on a bed of the tossed greens. Garnish with blanched slivered almonds. Serve cool but not chilled. (Greens must be crisp and cold but duck and orange mixture should be just cool.)

Serves 4

Shrimp Cocktail, American Sauce

Sauce
3/4	c. chili sauce
	juice of 1 lemon
1/8	c. horseradish or to taste
	celery, coarsely chopped
4-6	large cooked shrimp
	parsley for garnish
	lemon wedge

Place a small amount of sauce on the bottom of a shrimp cocktail glass. Add a mound of coarsely chopped celery. Cover the mound of celery with sauce. Place the shrimp into the sauce with the shrimp arched over the edge of the glass (the tails of the shrimp pointing outward). Do not remove the tail shell from the shrimp. Garnish with a sprig of parsley and serve with a wedge of lemon.

Serves 1

ISLAND PRINCESS

Dungeness Crab Newburg in Vol-au-Vent

2	Tbsp. butter
2	c. Dungeness crabmeat, cooked
1	Tbsp. flour
1	c. cream
1/3	c. dry sherry
2	egg yolks
1/4	c. cream
	salt to taste
	prepared vol-au-vent* pastry shells

Melt butter in a saucepan and add crab. Stir in flour and add cream. Cook the sauce, stirring carefully, until it is smooth and thick. Add the sherry and cook the sauce for 5 minutes longer. Mix yolks with 1/4 cup cream and combine with the crabmeat and sauce. Correct the seasoning with salt. Fill vol-au-vent shells and serve at once.

Serves 2

*Available in gourmet markets

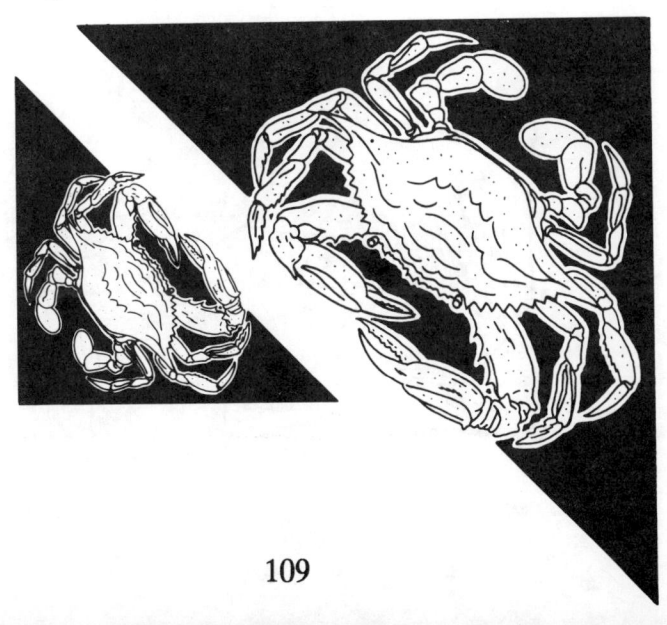

Cold Lemon Souffle

4	eggs
3	egg yolks
1/4	c. sugar
2	Tbsp. gelatin, softened in 1/2 c. lemon juice and dissolved over hot water.
	rind of 1 large lemon
1	c. heavy cream, whipped
	whipped cream for decoration

Beat eggs with egg yolks and sugar until the mixture is very thick. Use an electric mixer if possible. Gradually beat in gelatin mixture. Strain, then fold in the lemon rind and heavy cream. Oil a 6" band of wax paper and tie it around a 3/4 quart souffle dish to form a standing collar. Fill the dish with the souffle mixture (it should extend 2" above the rim of the dish) and chill until set. Carefully remove the paper collar and decorate the souffle with rosettes of whipped cream, pressed through a pastry bag fitted with a fluted tube.

Yields 1 souffle

Kugelhopf

1	cake yeast or 1 envelope active dry yeast
1/4	c. warm water
1/2	c. flour
1 1/2	c. flour
2	eggs
1/3	c. butter
1/2	tsp. salt
1	Tbsp. sugar
1	c. warm milk
1/4	lb. seedless California or Malaga raisins
	almonds, chopped and blanched (reserve some in half for decoration)

Dissolve yeast in 1/4 cup warm water. Add 1/2 cup flour and form the dough into a ball. Sift over this ball 1 1/2 cup flour and let the dough stand in a warm place until the ball of sponge rises up through the flour. Then work in eggs and butter, and knead to remove the water and to soften it. Add salt, sugar and warm milk, or enough to make a soft dough. Work the dough until it is elastic. Add raisins. Butter an 8" or 9" Kugelhopf mold (a fluted, round cake tin with a tube in the center), sprinkle the sides with chopped, blanched almonds and decorate the bottom with almond halves. Put the dough in the mold (the mold should be only about half full) and leave it in a warm place to rise. When the dough rises almost to the top of the mold, bake the cake in a hot oven (400° F) for about 40 to 45 minutes, until nicely browned and tests done.

Yields 1 cake

SILVERADO HILL CELLARS

NAPA VALLEY
CHARDONNAY

PRODUCED & ESTATE BOTTLED BY SILVERADO HILL CELLARS
NAPA, CALIFORNIA • ALCOHOL 13.0% BY VOL. • CONTAINS SULFITES

Character of Wine: Variety true fragrance derived from the grape, oaky montrachet bouquet from winemaking method.

Food pairing: Goes well with seafood and poultry.

CUNARD PRINCESS

CUNARD

If you are a ship of the line of Cunard parentage, you have a certain reputation to uphold. Cunard Princess, on her maiden voyage in March, 1977, sailed from La Spezia to New York City to be christened by none other than Princess Grace of Monaco, which is a nicely prestigious way to begin one's life if you're a ship.

Cunard Princess now plies the waters of the northern Pacific, transporting her passengers in leisurely, informal style from Vancouver, British Columbia to Ketchikan, Juneau, Skagway and Anchorage, Alaska - or the other way, starting in Whittier, near Anchorage. It is the Alaskan waters sightseeing voyage. The Princess glides past glaciers, sea life and wildlife, offering the wild grandeur of the north country amid the luxury and the attentive service that has made Cunard queen of the oceans for almost 150 years.

When Nova Scotia-born Sam Cunard launched his first steamship in 1840, he demanded that speed, comfort and safety be the watchwords of his captains. This attention to the right things made his the most respected steamships afloat, and since then more than a hundred ships have flown the Cunard flag.

Although Cunard's QE II and Sea Goddess are expensive, Cunard's other ships are in the mid-price range and worth every penny. The service and style are the same as on the prestigious Queen and Goddess, but the price is affordable. Cunard is still considered the illustrious way to travel.

EMBARKATION

All foreign passengers must pass through Canadian customs and immigration inspections before embarkation. This happens at whatever point you touch on Canadian soil, of course - at the U.S. border or at the airport. Because the Vancouver airport is small, many people fly into Seattle/Tacoma International, where Cunard provides motorcoach transfer to Vancouver. This offers a four-hour, worry-free close-up of the scenic Pacific Northwest and is a nice plus to an already worthwhile trip.

If you're southbound, you'll fly into Anchorage. Although this is American soil, always carry your passport with you; you will debark on Canadian territory in Vancouver.

THE TERRA FIRMA CONNECTION

Cunard in Alaska offers interesting inland trips that coordinate with the passing of the cruise ships. These are optional land trips that can occur before, after or in the middle of your coastal voyage. You receive the same special care as you do aboard ship - Cunard has a way of attending to detail in a friendly fashion. You might consider one of these side trips since you're way up there anyway, and when will you be there again?

"The Mt. McKinley" offers an overnight in Denali National Park (searching for wildlife, no less), a trip to Fairbanks, in the interior and some city excitement in Anchorage.

"The Eskimo" includes all of the above plus a flight across the Arctic Circle to visit the Eskimo town of Kotzebue and then on to Nome.

"The Fisherman" is the Mt. McKinley trip plus the Kenai Peninsula and an overnight in the town of Homer for a little halibut fishing.

"The Prudhoe Bay" trip features a stop at the northern end of the Alaskan pipeline on Alaska's North Slope, the Mt. McKinley tour, plus a trip to Coldfoot - a prospector's place - and a bus trip along the Dalton Highway through the tundra.

"The Midnight Sun Express" takes you through Alaska's wilds in comfort - to Denali National Park, up to Fairbanks and back to

Anchorage aboard a first-class train with an observation car, a dining car and a bar.

PORTS OF CALL

* Before I detail the Alaskan ports of call, I'd like to tell you a few things about Alaska in general. It is the only state in the land that has no nickname, but I suspect that a state which is bigger than many countries doesn't need a moniker to give itself prestige. The population hovers around 500,000 in a 587,000-square-mile area, which computes to about one square mile per resident. Its history, which can only be called wild, is also brief. Not much happened in Alaska, as far as the white man's involvement, until the late 1900s; it was - as it has so often been in this world - the discovery of gold that put Alaska on the map. The state is vast - one out of ten Alaskans owns a seaplane, utilizing one of the best ways to get around - and except for the coastal area, most of Alaska is untamed and as wild and lovely as it's been for millions of years. It may indeed be the last frontier, the last place where the deer and the antelope play with little interference from man.

Because Alaska is so far north, the summer sun literally never sets; because it is so huge, the types of climate range from moderate with plenty of rain to foggy, wet and windy, to dry (the Western Region is Arizona-hot in summer, Siberia-cold in winter), to the permafrost country in the north where a July high might be forty degrees and an average January noontime a chilling seventeen degrees below zero.

Alaska is a land of remarkable beauty and unprecedented sights. It's a place no traveler should miss, and especially no American traveler, for it gives one an idea what the lower 48 looked like and represented to nineteenth century pioneers.

Although Captain Cook, looking for the Northwest Passage, entered its harbor in 1778 and sailed up the main inlet (now called

Turnagain Arm, probably because he saw the endless forest and decided to turn around), Anchorage is only about seventy years old. As a construction camp for the building of the Alaska Railroad, the "anchorage" was merely a place for freighters to drop their goods for the railroad builders in 1914. It's now the biggest city in Alaska, at around 250,000, and although it's not what you'd call pretty, the setting is.

* Anchorage is a typical U.S. frontier town - progress and growth are the key words during this, its youthful period; it will take a few more decades for the preservationists and beautifiers to make any inroads. After the devastating earthquake of 1964, Anchorage city fathers just paved over the ruins and made a car park, and then began erecting new skyscrapers around the edges.

The Earthquake Park, however, in a residential area, is fascinating. One hundred thirty-two acres of once upper-class homes have been preserved as a reminder of the forces of nature - especially in this wild land of the north. Here you can see how nature is paving over in her own way, and in her irrevocable manner, camouflaging the havoc that she wrecked a quarter of a century ago. The twisted trees, the mounds of rubble, the new growth of greenery make for a sight worth taking time out to visit.

Mount McKinley, highest mountain in North America, can be viewed from Anchorage, most enjoyably from first-class restaurants such as the Anchorage Hilton's Top of the World, Josephine's in the Sheraton Anchorage, the Crow's Nest at the Hotel Captain Cook. The natives call the mountain Denali, the Great One, which may be more fitting. A relatively new national park called Denali is one of the largest in the national park system.

Shopping in Anchorage is worthwhile, especially if you're interested in furs and parkas, ivory and soapstone carvings, pottery, gold nugget and jade jewelry.

The Matanuska Valley, outside of Anchorage, raises cabbages as big as Volkswagens and turnips that weigh eight pounds. It's a combination of the fertile glacier soil, the warm, moist climate and the long summer days, of course, but it seems like never-never land. The flowers in Anchorage will astound you too - pansy faces as big as your hand, geraniums as tall as a twelve year-old.

One of the places to eat in Anchorage that is a must is Simon & Seafort's Saloon and Grill in downtown Anchorage. It overlooks Cook Inlet, serves huge portions, offers the best in food and service we have seen in a long time - and it's been chosen as one of the "Travel/Holiday Magazine" outstanding restaurants of the world.

Particularly exceptional items on their menu include the pasta, chicken, fresh fish (naturally), steaks, lamb, prime rib and salads. The Romaine with Egg Mustard Dressing and the Romaine with Bleu Cheese Dressing are both perfect. Look for recipes for both of these salads at the end of this chapter plus a couple of other especially good entrees.

If you're on the north-to-south trip as we were, you'll fly into Anchorage and be transported sixty-two miles by train to the port of Whittier, where the Cunard Princess docks. During this trip a guide points out all the sites - it's great fun and very relaxing.

PORTS OF CALL

* Skagway is not a pretty name, and it's not exactly a pretty town, but it is well-preserved, possibly the most authentic 1890s boom-town in all of America.

When gold was discovered in the Klondike, the tiny (and I mean tiny; two people lived in Skagway) hamlet became an overnight success. From 1897 to 1900 Skagway was the gateway to the

Yukon territory. In that brief period, $300 million in gold was unearthed, and then the "stampeders" moved on up to Nome, where the "pickins" were said to be richer.

At its peak, Skagway boasted 20,000 people. Today, about 800 hardy folks live there and keep it like it was, a Gay Nineties gold-mining town. The boardwalk survives and the old buildings are replaced plank by plank when need be. The saloons and general stores and hotels are in excellent condition, and the rye whiskey they serve will warm your toes. Jack London came here in 1898 (he was a prospector as well as a writer) and eventually wrote **Call of the Wild,** based on Skagway's huskie dogs and wild men.

Excursions in Skagway offer history and sights. "The Best of Skagway Gold Panning Tour" takes you up Taiya Inlet to the Chilkoot Trailhead, path of the miners on their way to White Pass and the gold. The White Pass trail is steep. It quickly becomes apparent why it was also called Dead Horse Trail. How could any animal traverse the treacherous trail at all, let alone while carrying his owner's worldly goods? In a tent city called Liarsville you'll get the real picture of how the miners lived - not too well - while they panned for gold. Over pie and coffee around a campfire, you'll hear tall tales and gold rush songs. A fun expedition.

The four-hour "Yukon/Carcross Excursion" will give you an even more expanded picture of what the gold seekers were willing to put up with to find their fortunes - although the true picture is that only about one out of 500 ever found anything yellow and valuable. This tour takes you sixty-five miles over White Pass, through valleys carved by glaciers and into Yukon Territory and the mining town of Carcross, which contains a very good general store. The scenery on this trip is, once again, out of this world, and the history you'll be absorbing from the guide is lively.

A guided tour of Skagway and its historic buildings and characters includes a stage show review, very professional and full of the bawdy atmosphere of the days of '98.

At Skagway you also have another opportunity to fly over glaciers - the "Haines/Chilkat Indian Dancers and Glacier Flightseeing Tour." On this flight you'll stop in a Chilkat Indian town, also the home of the first U.S. military post, Fort William H. Seward. This present-day art colony provides many examples of Indian art, including the master totem pole carvers. While you eat lunch in the Tlingit Tribal House, the entertainment is, naturally, Chilkat Indian dances. This tour ends with a brief history of Skagway as you drive back through town.

The "Glacier Queen Cruise" is a good way to see places along the coast that the cruise ship can't maneuver into. The excursion takes about two hours and gives you intimate glimpses of isolated bays and coves and then a ride up Burro Creek, where waterfalls tumble and a salmon hatchery provides an interesting subject for the guide. This trip is full of breathtaking scenery.

* Juneau is the capital city of Alaska - not Anchorage, not Fairbanks - and with its 20,000 population it is the smallest capital city in the United States. Juneau is charming, and coming into it from the sea, through Stephens Passage full of icebergs, you will be properly impressed by the lush green hills surrounded by mountains and the core of tall buildings downtown that constitute the state office complex.

The climate is mild, protected by the low mountains from the icefields beyond - glaciers named Mendenhall, Taku, Eagle and Herbert. It rains in Juneau two days out of three; it is a lush green seaport.

Excursion choices abound. "The Mendenhall Glacier Tour" will introduce you to what many people think Alaska is all about - ice and cold. Thirteen miles from Juneau, Mendenhall Glacier is twelve miles long and one-and-a-half miles wide, a creeping wall of ice that melts into Mendenhall Lake, which began forming in the 1930s. Mendenhall is receding at the rate of ninety feet a year, which is a pretty speedy meltdown for a glacier.

This tour also takes you through old Juneau, past homes hanging onto the precipitous hills, and then for a refreshment stop at the Red Dog Saloon, which is frontier drinking and eating at its most authentic, even removed as we are by a hundred years or so.

"Icefield Flightseeing" is an hour's worth of gazing down at the blue-white glaciers of the Juneau Icefield.

The "Taku Glacier Lodge Flightseeing and Salmon Bake" is billed as an "Alaskan Adventure." Aboard a float plane you soar beyond Mount Juneau and Mount Roberts for the eagle's-eye view of some of Alaska's most spectacular scenery (this is almost a redundant phrase when you're talking about Alaska), with the possibility of catching glimpses of caribou, mountain goats and black bears - maybe even an American eagle. You'll land on the Taku River next to Taku Glacier and visit a former hunting lodge where you'll be served salmon just out of the river, cooked over an open alderwood fire. After dining you'll have time to walk a nature trail or two to get the feel of the real wilds of Alaska.

Are you really a daring soul? Then go for the "Mendenhall River Raft Trip." It takes three and a half hours and costs about $75. A bus ride through Juneau ends at Mendenhall Glacier where you board eight-to-ten-person rafts - with an experienced boatman - to float down the Mendenhall River. At a convenient spot, your craft is beached in order for you to enjoy a snack of smoked salmon and reindeer sausage accompanied by apple cider. This is the trip where you wear warm clothes and bring extra socks.

If your wish is to walk on a glacier, opt for the "Mendenhall Glacier Landing Tour." A helicopter will set you down on top of the silent, frigid ice river - an experience you will talk about for days.

"The Gold Creek Salmon Bake" may be a highlight of your trip. This is the best salmon this side of heaven - and hundreds of thousands of visitors will back me up. In a mountain canyon just beyond town, Nancy Waterman and Bill Leighty serve salmon, salad and sourdough, alfresco. They've been doing it since 1972. They use a brown sugar paste with margarine and a little bit of lemon juice to baste the salmon - it's just a delightful and delicious experience. After dinner you can pan for gold in Gold Creek where the A.J. Gold Mine, now abandoned, was the largest gold mine in the world prior to 1944.

If you're interested in catching one of those famous salmon that everybody's always talking about, join the "Juneau Sportfishing Tour." From the Princess you'll take a twelve-mile drive along the Gastineau Channel with opportunities to view Mendenhall Glacier before you board your four-man, fully equipped, luxury fishing boat. Even if you don't catch the big one, you may spot a sea lion, a whale - we saw two just out of Skagway - an otter, a nesting eagle. It's better than most zoos and there are no crowds.

If you like the idea of being on your own, you can take in the salmon bake and then return to town and just look around, stop in at the Red Dog for a beer, and then shop and tour at your leisure. The Alaska State Museum is a gem. A movie worth seeing while you're there explains the history of Alaska, from its formation to its Russian days to the present vigorous Aleut and Eskimo cultures. The capitol buildings and grounds are interesting and beautiful as is St. Nicholas Orthodox Church with its Russian colony artifacts. Short walks and hikes in the hills offer spectacular scenery and close-ups of the prodigious summer greenery. Maps are available at the Information Center Kiosk.

A tip for the shoppers: the Russian Shop in the refurbished Senate Building downtown is a wonderful place. Here you can find what I'm sure Russians in Moscow never see - lacquered boxes, fine china from Leningrad, nesting dolls called Matreshka from Russian craftsman. An interesting place.

* "Thundering Wings of an Eagle" is just another name for Ketchikan. This is a village really, with fewer than 7,200 permanent residents. In one section of town there is a boardwalk called Creek Street, built on pilings over Ketchikan Creek. In typical Ketchikan style, Creek Street is revered and touted as "the most infamous red-light district in Alaska, the only place in the world where both the fish and fishermen went up the stream to spawn." Unusual and refreshing Chamber of Commerce advertising.

The town is small and you can obviously do your own exploring. Our ship's tour director suggested we go to Kay's Kitchen in Ketchikan. It's a little hole-in-the-wall spot with sandwiches, soups and pies, and everything was wonderful. We also went past a taxidermy place where they sell furs - I saw a white fox vest I'm still thinking about.

You might want to consider signing up for shore excursions. They offer a lot and may be the way to go for at least a portion of the approximately five hours you'll spend in Ketchikan.

The Totem Bight Tour takes you on a two-and-a-half-hour, thirty-mile trip to points of interest in and around Ketchikan: Creek Street; the commercial fishing harbor (Alaska's busiest waterfront, featuring many commercial fishing vessels, sports crafts, float planes and personal pleasure boats); a salmon cannery; a pulp mill (the largest of its kind in the world); and the Totem Bight State Park.

Here a park guide will lead you through the woods to ancient Alaskan Indian campsites crowded with towering totem poles. These beautifully and intricately carved works of art will awe and impress you. It is an eerie kind of place, full of power and ancient wisdom. If you've ever been to Stonehenge, you might catch hints of the same feelings that you had there. This is a must-see if you're interested at all in Alaska's cultural heritage.

For thrill-seekers, "the Misty Fjords Flightseeing Tour" is worth the money - around a hundred dollars. Aboard a float plane you'll cloud-cruise above and around the jagged granite cliffs and the waterfalls of Alaskan fjord country, then land on a high wilderness lake. The word "awesome" keeps popping up on this trip.

The "Historical Harbour Cruise," two hours, is excursion yachting at its best. Ketchikan's history is its waterfront, and this guided tour will give you the overview of a lively past, then transport you on up to the Totem Bight State Park and return you to the town, with tea and crumpets on the way.

The "Metlakatla Tour" takes you on a flight to a native reservation in Alaska. This thriving community of Metlakatla manages a commercial fishing industry in tandem with historical preservation of its heritage. It is, because of this combination, an interesting and vital village. One of the features of the tour is a native dance performed in the Tsimshian Longhouse, the tribal hall. This is a three-hour tour and it is expensive.

The "Ketchikan and Saxman Totem Park Tour" will appeal to the artisans among you, for the main portion of this coach excursion focuses on the Tlingit Indian village of Saxman, where the ancient art of totem carving is carried on daily. Watching this process and learning a little of the symbolism and interpretations of meaning involved with the totems will impress anyone interested in primitive arts. Other handcrafted items are made in the workshops of Saxman, including masks, beadwork and jewelry.

* Vancouver, your debarkation port, is one of the loveliest and most sophisticated cities in North America. It is clean, full of flowers, modern and energetic. A two-hour sightseeing tour begins at the pier and visits an area called Gastown, which was Vancouver's original name. "Gassy Jack" Deighton, saloon/hotel owner, is the town's spiritual patriarch, a fitting founding father figure for this West Coast city of over 400,000, incorporated a brief century ago during the heydays of Canada's western lumber boom.

The downtown area now is an architect's delight and there is obvious wealth here. Vancouver is the terminus of the Canadian Pacific Railroad and the Trans-Canadian Highway. It is also Canada's largest western seaport. Canada Place, the cruise ship terminal, is an outstanding building, which of course you'll see at close hand. Built to resemble a giant sailing ship, this building could be a masted frigate carved out of stone, protecting Vancouver's harbor. It's an impressive bit of architecture, inside and out.

Other points of interest in Vancouver are the Vancouver Art Gallery, Chinatown and the Chinese Cultural Center, Stanley Park and the fantastic and futuristic 170-acre Expo '86 - seventy pavilions and plazas that can be reached by monorail from downtown. The Van Dusen Botanical Gardens and Queen Elizabeth Gardens showcase Vancouver's love of flowers; the Centennial Museum, the Maritime Museum and the Museum of Anthropology showcase the town's history, both natural and cultural.

A stay-over in Vancouver after your cruise is something to consider. It is a very cosmopolitan city with a definite personality, part Canadian, part American and always refreshing. It's a city you feel safe in, also. You'll like it.

SHIPBOARD

Cunard's Alaskan cruise aboard the Princess is billed as relaxed, informal cruising at its finest. This translates into amenities and activities of every kind; it also means that you can wear your casual clothes, but be prepared with your dress-ups, as gentlemen are requested to wear jacket and tie in the dining room.

In each day's "Daily Programme," delivered to your room, you are not only advised of activities, but are told what kind of dinner will be served that evening - which will put to rest any dismay about, "Oh dear, what should I wear?" Formal means dinner jacket or suit and tie, cocktail dress; semi-formal/informal means suit or jacket and tie, regular or cocktail dress; optional means either formal or informal; casual/very informal indicates a theme night - Western, Caribbean and so on.

A few of the permanent activities and amenities (more than most small municipalities offer through city recreation programs) include golf driving, jogging, cinema, card room, basketball practice area, casino, swimming pool, library, paddle tennis, shuffleboard, table tennis, Jacuzzi, a gym with free weights, Nautilus equipment, cycling and rowing machines and a sauna.

Daily special activities run the gamut from arts and crafts to teen get-togethers, a financial lecture, the services of a handwriting expert, an ice carving demonstration. (This was a wonderful exercise. Crewmen went out in a life boat near a glacier and returned with a hunk of ice that must have weighed about 400 pounds. They then demonstrated the art of ice carving, turning the slab of frozen water into a regal Indian with headdress.)

Lectures about glaciers are informative and lively, worthwhile preparation for the voyage ahead, for the Princess slips alongside the Columbia Glacier, the most active glacier in North America, and Hubbard Glacier, a monolith six miles wide that brings you right down to size as you sail along beside it. I felt so small next to the biggest piece of nature I'd ever seen. I also felt so relaxed sitting on the deck watching the marvelous scenery. As we moved alongside the glaciers, every now and then we would hear what sounded like a cannon shot - it was ice breaking away from the glacier and falling into the bay, forming icebergs. The reason everything appears to be tinted blue along the coast is the refracting of light off the endless ice and snow.

The well-versed lecturer, John Brand, a glaciation expert for twenty-three years, talked about the problems caused by receding glaciers when they raise the level of the world's oceans - the prominent Greenhouse Effect theory. It's a well-done talk.

There was really so much of note to do on this cruise, so many things that I wanted to fit in, I barely had time to catch my breath. What with the ports of call, the staggeringly overpowering scenery and the activities that called to me - and which I participated in - I was sleeping like a log every night. The cool, invigorating air surely contributed also. It was sunny but cool, very comfortable traveling weather.

Our cabin was great - roomy and comfortable although we didn't spend much time there, mostly a lot of changing of clothes and then falling into bed to sleep the sleep of the happily weary.

The Talent Show on the Princess, an activity that many cruises offer, was particularly hilarious. Our dinner table companions decided to go as a group and we prepared well - buying garbage bags and string in Juneau, and dancing onto the stage as the California raisins. We had a ball. This phenomenon of making friends aboard ship happens often, sometimes with your dinner mates, sometimes with the folks next to you on the deck chairs, or maybe at the evening's entertainment. It's one of the pluses of cruising, something that doesn't happen during land traveling.

CUNARD PRINCESS

The captain of the Princess was a friendly Britisher, a delightful man. We had as much fun at his dinner table each evening because of him as we did in any of our activities. The jokes were flying and the private dinner party atmosphere was like being at a friend's home, dinner for eight. His nicely wry wit continued without stop, and his thoughtfulness was touching. The pleasure of the captain's company is not always available on cruise ships, but if you have the opportunity to sit at the captain's table on board the Princess, and Captain Ronald Warwick is in charge, get to know him. He is charming and sincere and made our trip very special.

His crew was easygoing and gregarious also. Close to forty nationalities are represented among the crew of the Princess, which totals close to 350 talented and hard-working souls. Although they're all busy and work diligently to keep the passengers happy, this particular crew was especially fun to be around and always willing to stop for a chat. We left feeling that we had made friends. It was a good feeling, a kind of secure knowledge that we were not just tourists. This is one of Cunard's extra touches that may just be the most important touch needed. (This particular cruise was comprised of mostly retired people, very few singles.)

CLOTHING AND WEATHER

Casual and comfortable are the packing order here. Also warm. Daytime temperatures along the Alaskan coast can range from thirty degrees to ninety degrees, and evenings can fall ten to twenty degrees cooler. The way to plan is to go for the layered look - items of clothing that can be added or removed according to what happens with the sun and the wind when you're off discovering gold in the Klondike. It wouldn't hurt to take a medium-sized daypack to carry your extra socks, your sweaters and wind breakers, mittens and gloves. Being too hot can be taken care of by removing some of your clothes. Being too cold and not having a jacket to put on can make for a miserable afternoon. Bring an umbrella, good, solid, preferably waterproof walking shoes and a raincoat.

BOOKING YOUR CRUISE

Cunard
555 Fifth Ave.
New York, NY 10017
Telephone 212-880-7500
or call your travel agent.

ENTERTAINMENT

The nightlife is good and varied - comedians, magicians, a French revue, an American Broadway show song revue, an international dance troupe. Cocktail parties are plentiful and the casino provides a chance to make a buck or two. Or lose, depending on your luck, of course. The Topsail Piano Lounge is a nice, cozy place to listen to good keyboard and the movies range from current to classic.

FOOD

Beginning from the top o' the morning, the dining arrangements follow first and second seating. When you indicate your preference, it means that all three meals will be the same for you - first or second seating. Breakfast first and second seatings are 7:30 and 8:45 a.m.; lunch at noon and 1:30 p.m.; dinner at 6:30 and 8:30 p.m.

If you are the unscheduled type, eating alternatives abound. Early Riser's coffee/tea/Danish is served in the Outrigger Cafe from 6:30 to 11:30 a.m. Continental cabin breakfast is served from 8 to 10 a.m. What is called a Light Breakfast is served in the Outrigger Cafe from 7 to 10 a.m. Mid-morning bouillon is served in the Lido Pool Bar from 11 to 11:30 a.m. Light Luncheon can be obtained at the Outrigger from ll:30 a.m to 2:30 p.m. After-

CUNARD PRINCESS

noon Tea is served in the Showboat Lounge at 4:00 p.m. Midnight Buffets are served in the Meridian Dining Room between 11:30 p.m. and 12:30 a.m.

The food is as you would expect - wonderful. The morning menu is clever. It lists Juice, Yogurt, Eggs, Meat and so on and then tells you what flavors are available or how you can order things cooked. Very simple. And very thorough.

Special dinner parties include the Welcome-Aboard dinner, the Captain's dinner, the Gala and the Farewell. This is definitely the trip to order seafood. It's so fresh and so delicious - Alaskan king crab legs, scaloppines of seabass, Alaskan halibut brochette, broiled Alaskan salmon steak, Alaskan white fish, Alaskan rockfish. You've possibly never tasted such fresh fish so well prepared.

One of the crew caught a twenty-five-pound halibut and it was cooked specially for the Captain's table - it was succulent, out of this world.

The choices for each meal are plentiful and go beyond seafood - always a steak of some kind or prime rib. Chicken, quail, pork loin, veal, cornish game hen, turkey, lamb are offered during the trip, too, along with the accoutrements: maybe fresh garden peas, Kalkemy potatoes, dilled yellow squash or baked Brussel sprouts. Appetizers are particularly fun - items like Alaskan smoked salmon rolls with crabmeat stuffing, Kentucky country pate, Coquille of seafood, baby scallops ragout.

Three or four soup choices come with each dinner - a creamed corn soup was outstanding, made with fresh corn and flavored with whiskey. The most unusual, one I'd never heard of, was a chilled olive soup made with black olives from Spain, garlic, eggs, light cream and sour cream.

Desserts on board ship are often a production, and Cunard won't let you down in this department. Besides being beautiful they are delicious - Baked Alaska (could you have guessed?); praline nougat torte, chocolate eclair, close to twenty flavors of ice cream each evening... and on and on.

The dining room on the Princess is on one of the top decks, and rather than the traditional portholes it is designed with huge picture windows. Being in the land of the midnight sun, we enjoyed spectacular dinner-time views, the sun lingering along with us as we sipped our cordials.

RECIPES

Jaeger Tea

1	liter red wine
1/2	liter Russian Caravan tea (a tea blend)
1/4	liter dark rum
1/4	liter pear schnapps
	sugar to taste

Place all ingredients in a large pot and bring to boiling. Keep tea at this temperature for about 10 minutes. Do not allow tea to boil. Strain and serve in tea mugs.

Serves 4 to 6

Alaskan Gluhwein (hot spiced wine)

1	bottle red burgandy wine
3	oz. Yukon Jack
1/2	c. sugar
1	cinnamon stick, whole
18	whole cloves
	peel of 1 orange
	orange slices for garnish

Mix together all ingredients in a pot and bring to a boiling point. Keep mixture at this temperature for 10 minutes. Do not allow it to boil. Strain and serve in wine glasses. Garnish with orange slices.

Serves 4 to 6

Northern Lights

4	oz. Smirnoff vodka
2	oz. Galliano
2	oz. cherry brandy
12	oz. orange juice
4	oz. sweet-and-sour mix
2	oz. grenadine syrup
	oranges and cherries for garnish

Combine all ingredients. Shake and serve over ice in highball glasses. Garnish each with an orange slice and a cherry.

Serves 4

Lancashire Hot Pot

4	oz. onions, finely shredded
12	oz. potatoes, sliced 1/8" thick
2	lbs. lamb leg, cut in 1/2" cubes
	salt and pepper to taste
1	bunch parsley, finely chopped
1	pint stock
	meat drippings or shortening

Grease a baking dish. Place a layer of onions and potatoes in the bottom. Season lamb with salt and pepper. Place in baking dish with remaining onions and the parsley. Cover with remaining potatoes, arranging the slices neatly overlapping. Half fill with stock and bring to boil on top of stove. Paint the top with heated drippings or shortening. Place in 350° F oven to bake for 1 1/2 to 2 hours. Press down with a spatula at intervals. Remove surplus fat from surface before serving.

Serves 4

Korean Barbecued Beef (Pulgogi)

1 1/3	lbs. top round beef
3	Tbsp. sugar
2	Tbsp. rice wine
6	Tbsp. soy sauce
1	clove garlic, chopped
5	green onions, chopped
1	Tbsp. sesame salt
2	Tbsp. sesame oil
	black pepper to taste
	lettuce

Slice the beef thinly against the grain and cut into bite-sized pieces. Marninate with sugar and rice wine for 1/2 hour. Mix in soy sauce, chopped garlic, green onions, sesame salt, sesame oil and black pepper. Broil the beef on a grill or in a hot frying pan. Serve on a bed of lettuce.

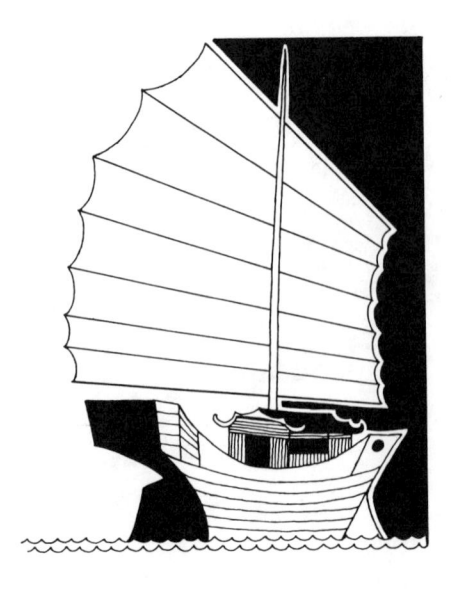

Serves 4

CUNARD PRINCESS

Steak au Poivre

2	oz. butter
1	clove garlic, crushed
1	shallot, chopped
2	tsp. Dijon mustard
4	filet mignons
	Worcestershire sauce
2	Tbsp. green peppercorns, crushed
	brandy
1/2	pt. demi-glace*
1/2	glass red wine
1/2	pt. heavy cream
	salt to taste

Melt the butter in a thick-bottomed copper frying pan. Add garlic and shallot and cook gently. Spread mustard thinly on both sides of fillets and sprinkle with Worcestershire sauce. Liberally coat both sides of fillets with crushed peppercorns. Add the meat to pan and sear on both sides, then cook until done to your liking. Flame the fillets with brandy, add demi-glace and wine. Reduce by half and add heavy cream. Heat through, adjust seasonings and serve immediately.

Serves 4

* see glossary

Zuppa Inglese

1	chocolate sponge cake
2	pts. pastry cream
	vanilla
4	oz. chocolate, melted
	dark rum
	Creme de Cacao
	Marsala
1	qt. whipped topping
	candied cherries
	candied Angelica

Split sponge cake horizontally into 3 equal portions. Divide pastry cream into 2 parts. Add a few drops vanilla to taste to the first part. To the second part, add melted chocolate, rum and Creme de Cacao according to taste. Sprinkle each layer of cake with Marsala and spread 2 of the layers with a different flavored pastry cream. Top with the third layer. Cover the whole cake with whipped topping. Decorate with candied cherries and Angelica.

Serves 8

Salzburger Nockerin (Austrian/Bavarian dessert)

	cranberry jam
6	whole eggs, separated
1	tsp. vanilla-flavored sugar
2	oz. regular white sugar
1	oz. flour

Grease circular cake pan and spread jam evenly on the bottom. Whip egg whites until peaks form. Carefully fold in sugars, 2 egg yolks (reserve remaining yolks for another purpose) and add flour. Pour into cake pan and bake 15 to 20 minutes at 180 to 200° F. Important: Do not open oven during baking. Serve hot.

Serves 2 to 3

SIMON AND SEAFORT'S RECIPES

Romaine with Egg Mustard Dressing

3	eggs, hard-boiled
1 1/2	tsp. yellow mustard
3	Tbsp. cider vinegar
3	Tbsp. sugar
16	oz. romaine greens
1/3	c. warm bacon drippings
4	slices bacon, cooked and chopped
2	green onions, chopped

Egg Mustard Dressing (Cont.)

Separate hard-boiled eggs into whites and yolks. Chop whites. Mix yolks with mustard, vinegar and sugar until smooth. Put the romaine in a salad bowl and toss with egg dressing, then lightly mix in the warm bacon drippings. Sprinkle top of salad with egg whites, bacon pieces and green onions.

Serves 4

Romaine with Bleu Cheese Dressing

1/8	tsp. white pepper
3/4	tsp. salt
1/4	tsp. onion salt
1/4	c. salad oil
1/4	c. water
1	Tbsp. wine vinegar
1	c. mayonnaise
1	c. sour cream
2	oz. bleu cheese
	romaine greens
	hard-boiled egg, chopped
	slivered almonds
	crumbled bleu cheese for garnish

Mix all the spices with the salad oil and water. Blend in the vinegar, mayonnaise and sour cream. Mash the bleu cheese and stir into the dressing. Serve on romaine greens. Garnish with chopped hard-boiled egg, toasted slivered almonds and fresh crumbled bleu cheese

Serves 4

Baked Chicken Dijon

1	cube butter
1	clove garlic
5	tsp. Dijon mustard
2	Tbsp. fresh parsley, minced
5	Tbsp. Parmesan cheese, shredded
1 1/2	c. Panko bread crumbs (Japanese bread crumbs)
4	chicken breasts, boneless and skinless
	Parmesan cheese, shredded
	Dijon mustard
	mayonnaise

Make a marinade by melting butter in a saute pan over low heat. Add the garlic and simmer on low for 5 minutes. Blend in the mustard, stirring well. Remove from the heat and let cool enough to touch, but not solidify. Whip vigorously until mixture thickens. Then make a breading by blending together the fresh parsley, Parmesan and the bread crumbs. Dip each chicken breast in butter mixture, coating all surfaces, then in breading mixture, packing crumbs onto chicken to coat well. Place chicken in a single layer in a shallow pan. Cover and refrigerate for several hours to set breading. Place chicken breasts on sheet pan and bake at 350° F for 12 minutes. Chicken should be lightly browned on the outside, moist on the inside. Top with finely shredded Parmesan. Served with Dijon mustard-mayonnaise (1 part Dijon to 2 parts mayonnaise).

Serves 4

Prime Rib of Beef

rock salt
beef prime rib
Lawry's Seasoning Salt
coarse-ground pepper

Cover the bottom of a roasting pan with food-grade rock salt. Place prime rib, bone side down, on the salt. Season with 1 tablespoon seasoning salt and 1 teaspoon pepper for each 4 pounds of roast. Cover prime rib completely with rock salt and place in 210° F oven for 9 to 10 hours, or until internal temperature measures 125° F (depending on the size of the prime rib). Remove from oven and let rest for 30 minutes to set the juices and make roast easier to carve. When ready to serve, remove all salt from rib and carve. Serve with fresh horseradish. (Recipe follows)

Fresh Horseradish

3	c. horseradish, shredded
1/2	c. cider vinegar
1	Tbsp. sugar
1/2	tsp. salt

Scrub fresh horseradish root with a brush under running water. Freeze root to help control aroma when peeling. Peel root, then grate in small shreds. Place shredded horseradish in a colander and pour boiling water over it. Drain. Mix the 3 cups of horseradish with vinegar, sugar and salt. Marinate for 2 hours. Serve with prime rib.

MISSISSIPPI QUEEN

DELTA QUEEN STEAMSHIP COMPANY

MISSISSIPPI QUEEN

A cruise on the mighty Mississippi aboard a paddle wheeler is like time travel, for you roll along with the river in the same manner travelers have since the mid-1800s.

The whole experience is a slice of Americana, as satisfying as a piece of apple pie - or should I say pecan? The Mississippi may alter its course from year to year, cities along its banks may sprout skyscrapers, fancy speedboats may zip in and out of your wake, but for all the change that 150 years have wrought in this country, a cruise down the second longest river in the world is little different than when Mark Twain worked on this river in his youth.

For this alone you should book passage on the Mississippi Queen® or the Delta Queen®, the two giant pleasure boats that ply America's greatest waterway.

From New Orleans to Minneapolis/St. Paul (or vice versa), plus side trips up the Ohio and onto the Tennessee and Cumberland Rivers, the Queens re-enact a period in American history with the same elegance and grace as their famous steamboat forbearer, the Rob't E. Lee.

We boarded in St. Louis on a Friday and sailed out under the famous and awesome arch, heading for a leisurely ten-day trip to New Orleans. Along the way we saw antebellum mansions and famous battlegrounds of the Civil War, we saw how our ancestors lived in the last century and we learned how vital the river was - and is - to the industrial lifeblood of our country, and as importantly, how the myth and mystery of Old Man River is interwoven into our national character.

All of this on one short cruise!

MISSISSIPPI QUEEN

PORTS OF CALL

The places we tied up to shore while aboard the Mississippi Queen® were appropriate to river history. These were the stops of the old riverboats, the towns and cities established by the pioneers who used the river as their transportation, not only for themselves, but for their goods. The cotton, sugarcane, lumber, grain and cattle transported via the Mississippi River made fortunes for many - including the riverboatmen themselves.

* We pulled into Memphis on Monday after two lovely, lazy days on the river. Memphis has been a Mississippi River cotton port for more than a century and a half and is now among the top five vacation cities in the country. But it isn't cotton that's bringing in the tourists, it's Elvis.

Memphis is where Elvis Presley chose to buy his home after he made his fortune. He purchased a lovely but relatively modest colonnaded, brick house and named it Graceland. Since Elvis' death in 1977, Graceland has seen an increasing number of visitors - up to 4,000 a day the summer of 1988. It has become one of the most visited landmarks in the world. For Elvis fans, it's a knockout - you can walk through parts of the house and see where he ate dinner, entertained friends, recorded music; you can view his trophies, his awards and his gold records, his car collection, his private jet and the Meditation Garden where he and other family members are buried.

But other sites in Memphis vie with Graceland, especially if you're not an Elvis nut. I think Mud Island is the best of the Memphis attractions.

What was for decades a scrubby island off Memphis is now a park/museum dedicated to the river that put Memphis on the map. Mud Island is an exceptionally well-done tribute to the

MISSISSIPPI QUEEN

Mighty Mississippi. And the best part of the complex, which includes eighteen galleries representing every aspect of the river, is the River Walk. This five-block-long, to-scale depiction of every bend and sandbar of the lower river from Cairo, Illinois to New Orleans, Louisiana, including every major city, town, bridge and dam along the river's course, will wow your socks off. In fact, you may, like us, take your socks off so you can wade from St. Louis to New Orleans. It's wonderful, one of the highlights of any trip I've taken anywhere in the world. Superb engineering and an ingenious idea.

Another interesting spot in America's fifteenth largest city, one rich in the South's cultural and musical heritage, is Beale Street, one of the country's most famous streets. Here a man named W.C. Handy gave birth to the Blues, and here is where you'll hear them, day and night.

The Chucalissa Indian Village is a working reconstruction of a thousand-year-old Choctaw Indian village; the Memphis Brooks Museum of Art houses fine art from the thirteenth century to the present; the Magevney House, the oldest middle-class house in Memphis, was built in the 1830s and gives an accurate glimpse of how ordinary people lived 150 years ago; the Lorraine Motel, soon to be the National Civil Rights Center, site of Martin Luther King's assassination in 1968, will, by 1991, be America's first pure dedication to the civil rights struggle in this country. This particular attraction gave me such a feeling of solemnity and mysticism, I will never forget it.

* The next stop was Greenville, a quiet, rural town much the same as it was a century ago, despite the ravages of war, flood and yellow fever over the decades. Although its industries thrive, Greenville maintains a gentle way about it. The Indian burial mounds are of special interest.

MISSISSIPPI QUEEN

* Vicksburg was the sight of the turning point of the Civil War. News stories of July, 1863, said the Mississippi "ran red" with blood from the battle. The Old Courthouse Museum contains the largest single collection of Confederate memorabilia in the world. Out of its war-torn past, Vicksburg revived itself to its prewar status - a lovely southern town.

* Natchez may be the Southern Belle city of the South, partly because it was spared any Civil War devastation. More than 500 antebellum homes stand in good repair, many of them so luxurious and sumptuous you'll be awed. The Natchez Garden Club conducts tours through three of the classiest mansions and then through the historical market district, giving a running detail of the history of this cotton center of the past, including racy stories of "Natchez Under the Hill," the waterfront area of roustabouts, gamblers, pirates and prostitutes.

The Carriage House is worth a stop for a bite to eat. A former plantation now a hotel/restaurant, the Carriage House is not only a beauty but serves the best fried catfish I've ever eaten.

Natchez, named after the Natchez Indians, is famous for its Indian heritage, for the pecan, a delicacy of the natives that is now grown and cultivated in the area, and for the small but respected Old South Winery. Here you can buy very hearty, musky wines that go well with extremely spicy foods which often overpower California and French wines.

* St. Francisville, Louisiana, is a regular stop for riverboat traffic, but an unseasonably low river prevented our docking. You may be more fortunate. Near St. Francisville is the Rosedown Plantation and Gardens, a fully restored 1835 cotton planter's home. The live oaks were planted at the turn of the century - the nineteenth, not the twentieth.

* Baton Rouge, capitol of Louisiana, is one of the world's most inland major seaports. It is also to this point that the French influence spread from New Orleans. Hereabouts is where many of the exiled Acadians settled after they were run out of Nova Scotia. One of the tours, which takes you through the back roads to Bayview Tavern on Colyell Bayou, explains the migration of the Acadians to this swampland of Louisiana. I really enjoyed this tour, especially the Cajun food they fed us while we were entertained by Cajun music and dancers.

Another tour visits the downtown area, the Pentagon Barracks, built in 1819, Magnolia Mound (a Creole colonial home) and Louisiana State University.

* New Orleans - the Big Easy. This is where we debarked, so we went on our own to visit the French Quarter - Jackson Square and St. Louis Cathedral, and hear the music, eat the food and wander through one of the most cosmopolitan cities in the Western hemisphere.

SHIPBOARD

Life aboard a Mississippi paddle wheeler is not frenetic and packed with things to do, although there are plenty of activities if you can't sit still to watch the majesty of the passing scene.

Each morning we awoke to the weather forecasts on the ship's radio. Since the weather is a big topic of conversation in America's midsection, we felt that we were starting our day like the locals do. Then we stumbled up to the Riverview Health Club to get our pumpers working, showered and made it to breakfast to gain back the pounds we'd just sweated off.

From there we would join Matthew, the Riverlorian (someone who knows river lore), for information on the Mississippi. We did this every day, eager to find out what Matthew had to say. He was an encyclopedia of information, and also a showman of sorts, so the "lecture" was as much entertainment as lesson.

Matthew taught us how to read the mile markers and the river charts, which made me, at least, feel like an authority - I could figure out where we were, how far we'd come, how far we had to go. He told us tales of river pilots, who are the ones who know the river and how to read it from hour to hour and day to day. Their experiences with the constantly changing waters is like a love affair with a capricious woman, always exciting, sometimes dangerous, endlessly fascinating.

Matthew explained how the Army Corps of Engineers has added to the navigability of the river and worked to maintain flood control. We stayed to watch films of the building of dams and levies and listened to a fellow tell his tale of swimming the length of the Mississippi in 1930. These lectures alone were worth the trip. I felt as if I wanted every school kid in America to hear them.

Our captain, Commodore Harold DeMarrero, gave a talk one morning on Mississippi River navigation from the viewpoint of a steamboat man, from the training of a river pilot through the daily excitement of steaming up and down a moody river. It's hardly as simple as one might think and we came away full of esteem for these men who know the Mississippi better than most people know their own back yards.

Commodore DeMarrero's family is a tradition in itself; his grandfather was a riverboat pilot, his father and son also. He's writing three books about the Mississippi, about piloting and about steamboats. He was a gracious and interesting man.

Other activities include cooking demonstrations, craft-making sessions, daily trivia contests, bingo, bridge and shuffleboard, plus two or three excellent movies a day. Kite flying off the fantail was a daily sport also.

We were fortunate to have on board two of the South's most famous chefs demonstrating the arts of Cajun, French Creole and good old down-home Southern-style dishes.

Chef Gary Darling of Copeland's in New Orleans (one of the most famous chefs from one of the most famous restaurants in a town full of famous cooks and famous eateries) demonstrated Creamed Onion and Garlic Soup, Garlic Cheese Souffle Grits (!) and Grillades (grilled meat) in Brown Creole Sauce.

The next day he taught us how to make Andouille Cucumber Salad, Eggs Crawkitty and Tasso Crawfish Hollandaise, and on the last day of our cruise, Rum Raisin Calas, Creole Tomato Sauce, Sweet Potato-Pecan Upside-Down Pancake and B.L.T. Soup.

Joe Cahn, who also gave cooking demonstrations aboard the Mississippi Queen®, created and opened the New Orleans School of Cooking in 1980. With his wife, Karen, Joe teaches the secrets of Creole food at their Jax Brewery location in New Orleans. Adjacent to the cooking school is the Louisiana General Store where Creole and Cajun ingredients can be found. This school is proof of how seriously New Orleans takes its cooking. A few of Joe's recipes follow at the end of this chapter.

For anyone who likes to cook, these demonstrations were akin to attending Le Cordon Bleu in France. I was in heaven.

Midweek, a Mardi Gras Party claimed nearly everyone on board from dawn to dusk. It was time to make costumes, join the parade and then attend the Mardi Gras Ball. If you can't visit the real thing in New Orleans the week before Ash Wednesday, this is the next best substitute. Many passengers come prepared with costumes, but if this isn't in your baggage plans, the cruise director has ample supplies so you can create something appropriate. This may even be more fun, like rummaging around in your mother's attic when you were a kid. The impromptu costumes were hilarious.

Although the movies will change with the cruises, let me give you an idea of the fare available to us: "Singin' in the Rain," "Yankee Doodle Dandy," "The African Queen," "Shenandoah," "Innocents Abroad." Besides the excellent documentary movies shown in the morning about the river itself, these classic films fit perfectly into the nostalgia of the trip.

MUSIC

On shipboard and in the ports of call, we found that the music of the Mississippi is as much a part of the atmosphere and mood as the sites. We were never far from Dixieland, Jazz, Rhythm and Blues, Rock 'N Roll. It was so indelibly a part of everything we did that I'll remember my Mississippi voyage as a trip set to music. All of these music types are indigenous to America, and all of them have similarities. But they're also highly distinguishable. That they all were spawned along the Mississippi is no longer a mystery to me, because Old Man River is a poetic thing, an inspiring bit of this earth that deserves credit for the joy and pathos of these musical forms.

Entertainment aboard the Mississippi Queen® concentrates on these music forms, on singing and instrument playing as opposed to more elaborate reviews and acts. Banjo players were everywhere and the calliope, which ran off the steam used to propel us downriver, shook the wharfs each time we pulled out of a town. Traditionally, riverboats played a farewell refrain to the ports. The real entertainment, despite the organized activities, is watching the world go by. The difference between ocean cruising and river cruising is that on a river the passengers can always see the shore. Because of this you get a perception of the slowly passing scene - it is enervating, relaxing and, in a too busy world, very satisfying once you get the hang of it. It takes ten days to get from St. Louis to New Orleans - a little over a thousand miles. When's the last time it took you ten days to get anywhere? Let alone a mere thousand miles?

THE LOOK OF THINGS

Our cabin on the Mississippi Queen® was small compared to other cruise ships we have been on, but to make up for it we had a veranda. We loved this private area, furnished with two chaises and a table, and spent a lot of time there watching the towns and countryside.

The Mississippi Queen® was commissioned in 1976 and is quite grand - 382 feet long, sixty-eight feet wide, seven stories high. To think she only draws six to seven feet of water is amazing. Although her exterior look is pure nineteenthth century, inside, the Mississippi Queen® is very modern. The Delta Queen®, built in the 1920s, retains the authentic look of former eras - polished mahogany, lots of stained glass, public rooms that typify Victorian upper-class hotels.

Amenities offered by the Mississippi Queen® include elevators, room-to-room phones, air conditioning privately controlled by the passenger, Jacuzzi/pool, sauna/exercise gym, theatre/conference center, gift shop, beauty/barber shop, library. There are two main bars and two lounges, a huge dining room and the Grand Saloon.

CLOTHING AND WEATHER

We traveled on the Mississippi in August, one of the hottest and most humid months on the river. And although my hair went right into insta-perm and I felt my eyelashes curl all by themselves, I was never uncomfortable. Probably because I did so little! But be prepared for hot, muggy weather in the spring, summer and fall. And rain at any time.

MISSISSIPPI QUEEN

Dress is much more casual on a riverboat than on an ocean liner, so don't bring an elaborate wardrobe because you often won't need to do much more than comb your hair and brush your teeth before you sit down for dinner.

BOOKING YOUR CRUISE

Delta Queen Steamboat Co.
30 Robin St. Wharf
New Orleans, LA 70130
Telephone 504-586-0631
Telex 5101007509
Fax 504-524-7626
or call your travel agent.

FOOD

We were so pleased by the food. What they say about Southern-style cooking being "bodacious" is true. It is mouth-watering. And very caloric. When we learned that fried chicken, pecan pie, angel food cake and chocolate brownies were first served aboard steamboats on the Mississippi, we had to try their version - in the interests of culinary research, of course.

Breakfast is traditional American - juices, fresh fruits, cereals, cinnamon rolls and "hot cakes" or eggs with breakfast meats. All entrees are served with either grits or hash browns, and biscuits are always on the menu.

Lunch is essentially light, but two or three hot entree choices are available for midday heavy eaters. London Broil, Fried Chicken Fillets, Veal Crepes, Shrimp and Sausage Brochette were among the hearty offerings. We were more inclined to eat light, not only to save ourselves for dinner, but because of the hot weather. Two of my favorites were Curried Chicken Salad served with fresh fruit and chutney and Spicy Lemon Shrimp Salad served with Creole Cole Slaw.

For dinner, the Baked Stuffed Catfish was superb. This is a traditional Southern dish - pond-raised catfish filleted and stuffed with crabmeat and spinach, then baked. The French entrees were also excellent, the Oyster Vieux Carre being a combination of French and Southern styles - a casserole of oysters in heavy cream with green onion.

Desserts are big in the South and we banished the agony of diets in order to agonize over choices - Authentic New Orleans Bread Pudding with Rum Sauce, Homemade Peach Pie, Fresh Baked Apple Cobbler and Old South Praline Parfait.

RECIPES

Crabmeat au Gratin Appetizer

3	green onions, finely chopped
2	Tbsp. butter
1/4	c. heavy cream
1/2	lb. crabmeat
2	oz. bread crumbs
1	oz. Parmesan cheese, grated

Preheat oven to 400° F. Saute green onions slightly in butter. Add heavy cream and crabmeat, continue cooking for 5 minutes. Remove from heat, ladle into buttered casserole dishes (6 oz.), sprinkle with bread crumbs and grated cheese. Place in preheated oven and cook until casserole tops are golden brown.

Serves 2

MISSISSIPPI QUEEN

Baked Stuffed Mushrooms

2	Tbsp. butter
25	medium mushrooms (reserve stems for stuffing)
4	stalks celery, minced
1	medium onion, minced
1	Tbsp. fresh garlic, minced
1	tsp. salt
1	tsp. pepper
2	oz. burgandy wine
3	lbs. cream cheese
1	tsp. Worcestershire sauce
	grated Swiss cheese

In a large saute pan, melt butter. Mince mushroom stems and add to celery, onion and garlic. Saute for 3 minutes and add next 5 ingredients until cream cheese is soft and ingredients are thoroughly blended. Stuff mushroom caps with the mixture and top with grated Swiss cheese. Bake in 350° F oven approximately 10 minutes until mushrooms are tender and cheese is melted.

Makes 25 mushrooms

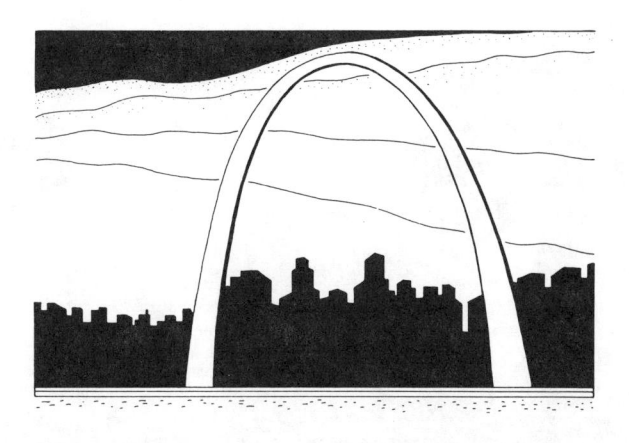

MISSISSIPPI QUEEN

Oyster and Artichoke Soup

1	white onion, chopped
1	lb. butter
8	oz. flour
1/2	gallon shucked oysters and their liquid
1	gallon water
30	artichoke hearts, quartered
1	oz. salt
1/2	oz. white pepper
1	tsp. thyme
2	stalks celery, chopped
2	bay leaves
1	Tbsp. chicken base
	chopped green onions for garnish

Saute onion in butter until translucent. Add flour and cook for at least 5 minutes. Add oysters, water, artichoke hearts, salt, pepper and thyme. Cook for 15 minutes. Add celery, bay leaves and chicken base. Cook for an additional 30 minutes, stirring constantly. Do not boil. Garnish with chopped green onions.

Serves 20

Beer Cheese Soup

1	medium onion, chopped fine
5	stalks celery, chopped fine
2	Tbsp. granulated garlic
1	lb. margarine
1	lb. flour
1	gallon chicken stock
1	tsp. Tabasco sauce
1	tsp. cayenne pepper
1/2	lb. butter
1	c. heavy cream
3	lbs. cheddar cheese, grated
2	12-oz. beers

Saute onion, celery and garlic in margarine. Add flour to make a roux. Cook for 10 minutes. Add chicken stock and bring to a boil. Continue cooking for 20 minutes and add seasonings. Turn down heat and add butter, heavy cream and cheese, stirring constantly. Finish soup by adding beer before serving.

Makes 1 1/2 gallons

Pepper Dill Dressing (or Steamboat Dressing)

1 1/2	c. sour cream
1 1/2	c. mayonnaise
1/4	c. onion, finely chopped
1/4	c. buttermilk
4	Tbsp. white vinegar
1	Tbsp. black pepper
2	Tbsp. dill weed
1/2	Tbsp. garlic powder
1/2	Tbsp. Worcestershire sauce
1/2	Tbsp. dry mustard

Combine the above ingredients and chill overnight.

Makes 1 quart

Crawfish Etouffee

4	oz. bacon drippings
12	oz. all-purpose flour
3/4	c. celery, chopped
3/4	c. bell pepper, chopped
3/4	c. white onion, chopped
2	lbs. crawfish tails, cooked
1	qt. crawfish stock (reserved from boiling crawfish, reduced and strained)
1	tsp. cayenne
3	cloves garlic, chopped
1	tsp. salt

Crawfish Etouffee (Cont.)

In a heavy skillet or Dutch oven, bring bacon drippings to smoking stage, add flour and stir constantly. Reduce heat and cook flour and fat mixture (roux) until golden brown, avoiding lumping. In another pan, cook remaining ingredients, except crawfish tails, in crawfish stock for 15 minutes over medium heat. Add stock mixture to the roux and stir constantly. Cook together for 1 hour over low heat, stirring constantly. Fifteen minutes prior to serving, add crawfish tails, bring to serving temperature and adjust seasoning if necessary. Ladle 1/6 portion over 3 oz. cooked rice. Accompany with hot French bread.

Serves 6

Soft-Shell Crabs

3	eggs
1/4	c. milk
1	tsp. garlic powder
1/2	tsp. cayenne pepper
1	tsp. salt and black pepper
	tsp. onion powder
1	c. corn flour
4	soft-shell crabs, approximately 3-4 oz. each, well cleaned peanut oil for deep frying

Whip together the eggs and milk. Combine seasonings and corn flour. Soak crabs in the egg mixture and then dust in the corn flour mixture. Deep-fry the crabs in 350° F peanut oil for 2 1/2 to 3 minutes. Serve with Creole Tartar Sauce (recipe follows).

Creole Tartar Sauce

1	dill pickle, finely diced
1/2	c. mayonnaise
1/4	tsp. garlic powder
2	tsp. tomato, chopped
1	tsp. white vinegar
1/4	tsp. cayenne pepper

Combine all ingredients and chill.

Serves 4

Grilled Chicken with Herbal Marinade

1	qt. olive oil
4	tsp. fresh garlic, minced
1	tsp. basil
1	tsp. oregano
1/4	c. white onion, chopped
1/4	c. soy sauce
1/2	oz. salt
1/2	oz. pepper
1	whole chicken, cut in serving pieces

Combine first 8 ingredients. Place chicken in marinade and allow to rest overnight. Remove chicken from marinade and cook on a high-temperature grill until tender.

Serves 4

Grilled Snapper & Crawfish Hollandaise

4	6-oz. snapper fillets
1/2	tsp. salt
1/2	tsp. pepper
	melted butter

Sprinkle snapper fillets with salt and pepper. Brush with melted butter and grill on each side for 2 to 3 minutes. Serve with Crawfish Hollandaise (recipe follows).

Serves 1

Crawfish Hollandaise

8	egg yolks
1/2	oz. white wine
1	tsp. crawfish stock
1/4	tsp. cayenne pepper
1/2	tsp. lemon juice
3	lbs. butter, clarified
1/4	lbs. crawfish tails, cooked

Combine egg yolks, wine, crawfish stock, cayenne and lemon juice in a bowl and blend well. Cook this mixture in a double boiler until frothy. Remove from heat. Slowly add clarified butter, stirring constantly, causing mixture to emulsify. Pour sauce over grilled snapper and garnish with the crawfish tails.

Serves 4

Chicken and Andouille Gumbo

1/2	c. onion, coarsely chopped
1/2	c. celery, coarsely chopped
1/4	c. green pepper, coarsely chopped
1/2	c. andouille sausage,* chopped
1	gallon chicken stock
1/4	tsp. thyme
1/2	tsp. garlic
1/2	tsp. basil
1/2	tsp. black pepper
1/2	tsp. cayenne pepper
1	tsp. Worcestershire sauce
1/2	lb. dark roux (1/4 lb. pork fat sauteed with 1/4 lb. flour)
1	lb. chicken meat, cooked
1	Tbsp. file powder*

Saute onion, celery and green pepper with andouille sausage. Add chicken stock and bring to a boil. Add seasonings and continue to boil, slowly adding roux. Add chicken and file, then cook for at least 1 hour. Adjust seasoning. Continue cooking for at least 1 more hour.

Makes 1 1/2 gallons

* see glossary

JOE CAHN'S RECIPES

Oyster Artichoke Soup

24	oz. quartered artichokes
1	qt. strong chicken stock
1	c. green onions, chopped
	salt and cayenne to taste
1	tsp. thyme leaves
1/4	c. melted butter
1/4	c. flour plus 1 Tbsp.
1	qt. heavy cream
2	dozen oysters (1 qt.) shucked
1	c. green onions
1	Tbsp. parsley, chopped

Combine first 5 ingredients and bring to boil. Combine butter and flour for light roux. Add to boiling soup. Stir in heavy cream and simmer for 10 minutes. Add oysters and simmer for 5 more minutes. Garnish with green onions and parsley.

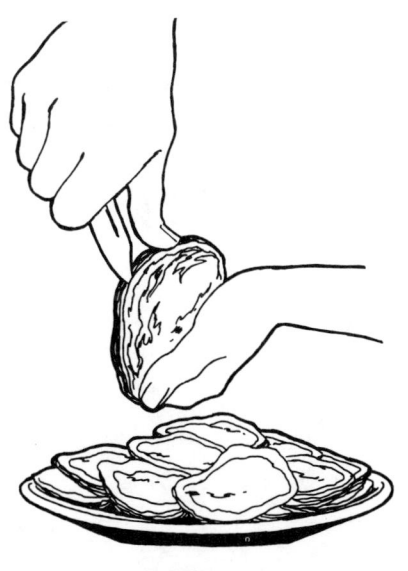

Serves 6 to 8

Shrimp Creole

3	lbs. shrimp, peeled
8	Tbsp. butter
8	Tbsp. flour
2	c. onions, chopped
1	c. celery, chopped
1	c. green pepper, chopped
1	Tbsp. garlic, chopped
3	c. shrimp stock or water with fish bouillon
1	14- to 16-oz. can tomato sauce
1	Tbsp. thyme
1	Tbsp. basil
3	bay leaves
1	Tbsp. brown sugar
4	thin lemon slices
	salt and cayenne to taste
1	c. green onions, chopped
1	c. parsley, chopped
	cooked rice

Saute shrimp in butter for 2 to 3 minutes and remove. To the butter add flour and stir over medium heat until lightly browned. Add onions, celery, green pepper and garlic and saute until transparent. Add stock, tomato sauce, thyme, basil, bay leaves, brown sugar, lemon slices, salt and cayenne. Simmer 15 minutes. Add green onions, parsley and shrimp for the last 5 minutes of cooking. Serve over rice.

Serves 8

Blackened Chicken

1	Tbsp. sweet paprika
2 1/2	tsp. salt
1	tsp. granulated onion or onion powder
1	tsp. granulated garlic or garlic powder
1	tsp. ground red pepper (preferably cayenne)
3/4	tsp. white pepper
3/4	tsp. black pepper
1/2	tsp. dried thyme leaves
1/2	tsp. dried oregano leaves
	melted butter
6	8- to 10-oz. chicken breast fillets

Heat a large cast iron skillet over very high heat until it is beyond the smoking stage and you see white ash in the skillet bottom (the skillet cannot be too hot for this dish), at least 10 minutes. Heat the serving plates in a 250° F oven. Thoroughly combine the seasoning-mix ingredients in a small bowl. Dip each chicken breast in melted butter so that both sides are well coated. Then sprinkle the seasoning mix generously and evenly on both sides of the meat, patting it by hand. Place in skillet and pour 1 teaspoon melted butter on top of each fillet (be very careful as the butter may flame up). Cook uncovered over high heat until the underside looks charred, about 2 minutes (the time will vary according to the meat's thickness and the heat of the skillet). Turn the meat over and pour 1 teaspoon more butter on top. Cook until chicken is done, about 2 more minutes. Repeat with remaining fillets. Serve while piping hot.

Serves 6

MISSISSIPPI QUEEN

Pralines

1 1/2	c. sugar
3/4	c. light brown sugar, packed
1/2	c. milk
3/4	stick butter (6 Tbsp.)
1 1/2	c. pecans, roasted
1	tsp. vanilla

To roast pecans, bake them on a sheet pan at 275° F for 20 to 25 minutes until slightly browned and smell permeates. Combine all ingredients except vanilla and bring to boil. Cook to soft ball stage (238-240° F), stirring constantly. Remove from heat and add vanilla. Stir until mixture thickens and becomes creamy and cloudy and pecans stay suspended in mixture. Spoon out on buttered wax paper.

Makes approximately 50 pralines, depending on size

Bread Pudding

1	10-oz. loaf stale French bread, broken
4	c. milk (or 1/2 milk, 1/2 heavy cream)
2	c. sugar
8	Tbsp. butter, melted
3	eggs
2	Tbsp. vanilla
1	c. raisins
1	c. coconut, shredded
1	c. pecans, chopped
1	tsp. cinnamon
1/2	tsp. nutmeg

Combine all ingredients; mixture should be very moist but not soupy. Pour into buttered 9" x 9" baking dish. Place on middle rack of oven and cook at 350° F for 1 1/4 hour until top is golden brown. Serve with following sauce.

1/2	c. butter
1 1/2	c. powdered sugar
1	egg, yolk or whole
1/2	c. bourbon

Cream butter and sugar over medium heat until all butter is absorbed. Remove from heat and blend in egg yolk. Pour in bourbon gradually, stirring constantly. Sauce will thicken as it cools. Serve warm over bread pudding.

Serves 20

CEDAR GROVE MANSION IN VICKSBURG'S RECIPES

Vicksburg Mint Julep

1	jigger Jim Beam bourbon
2	jiggers club soda
1 1/2	tsp. powdered sugar
1	Tbsp. cherry juice
	dash of peppermint extract
	sprig of fresh mint

Combine ingredients. Pour over crushed ice and serve in a silver goblet.

Serves 1

MINT

COPELAND'S RECIPES

Corn and Oyster Soup

2	Tbsp. butter
1/4	c. bell pepper, finely chopped
2	ears corn, corn sliced off cob
1/2	tsp. garlic, minced
1/4	c. green onion, finely chopped
2	Tbsp. parsley, minced
1	Tbsp. flour
1	c. oyster stock
	salt and pepper to taste
2	c. cream
2	dozen oysters, shucked

Melt butter, add bell pepper and saute for 3 minutes. Add corn and saute for 2 minutes. Add garlic and saute for 2 minutes. Add green onion and parsley and saute for 1 minute. Add flour and cook for 2 minutes. Add stock and bring to a boil. Add salt and pepper to taste and cream and bring to a boil. Add oysters and cook for 3 minutes.

Makes 1 quart

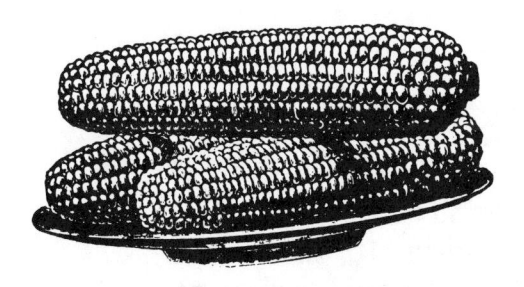

Cajun Cucumber Stirfry

2	Tbsp. tasso,* cut in shoestrings
4	Tbsp. clarified butter
1/2	tsp. dill seed
12	oz. cucumbers, cut into shoestrings
	salt to taste
1/4	c. cilantro, chopped

Saute tasso in butter until slightly browned. Add dill seed, then cucumbers. Saute 1 minute. Add salt to taste. Add cilantro.

Serves 6

* see glossary

Soft-Shell Crab Belizaire

6	jumbo soft-shell crabs

Spice Blend:

1	Tbsp. cayenne pepper
1	Tbsp. black pepper
1	Tbsp. white pepper
3	Tbsp. salt
1	Tbsp. paprika
1	c. flour
2	c. egg wash*
1/2	c. clarified butter
1	qt. heavy cream
24	oz. crawfish tails
6	slices eggplant, 1/2" thick
2	c. Italian seasoned bread crumbs

Soft-Shell Crab Belizaire (Cont.)

Clean crabs and lightly season under flaps with spice blend, then season entire crab with spice blend. Dust crab in flour, dip into egg wash, then back into flour. Brown crabs on both sides in butter and place in warm oven. Over medium heat reduce cream by half. Add crawfish tails and spice blend to taste. Season eggplant with spice blend, then dust in flour, dip in eggwash, then into seasoned bread crumbs. Brown both sides in clarified butter. Place eggplant slice on warm plate. Place soft-shell crab onto eggplant. Ladle crawfish cream sauce over crab and eggplant.

Serves 6

* see glossary

Shrimp and Crawfish Diane

1	Tbsp. butter
2	dozen 2-oz. shrimp
1/2	tsp. Cajun seafood spice
2	oz. crawfish tails
1/4	c. Gewurztraminer wine
6	oz. whipping cream
4	oz. angel hair pasta, cooked
1	tsp. green onion, chopped

Over medium-high heat melt the butter. Add shrimp and seasoning and saute 3 to 4 minutes until the shrimp curls and turns pink. Add crawfish tails and saute for 1 minute. Remove the shrimp and the crawfish from the pan and return pan to heat. Add wine to pan. Deglaze the pan and reduce the wine to half volume. Add whipping cream and bring to a boil.

Shrimp and Crawfish Diane (Cont.)

Add shrimp and crawfish. Bring back to boil and allow to boil for 1 minute. Add angel hair pasta and bring back to boil. Sprinkle green onion over pasta.

Serves 1

Jalapeno Sweet Potato Pancake

24	oz. sweet potatoes, baked and mashed
1	Tbsp. jalapeno peppers, diced
1/2	c. green onion, diced
1	c. butter, clarified, softened
1	c. whole wheat flour
1/2	c. corn tortilla flour
	butter or sour cream garnish

Combine sweet potatoes with the jalapeno, onion and butter. Mix thoroughly. Add enough wheat flour to pull mixture together, forming 4-oz. patties. Dust patties in corn tortilla flour and brown on both sides. Top with butter or sour cream.

Serves 6

MISSISSIPPI QUEEN

Banana's Foster

4	Tbsp. butter
1	c. brown sugar
1/2	tsp. cinnamon
2	oz. banana liqueur
4	bananas, quartered
2	oz. rum
	vanilla ice cream

Melt butter, add sugar, cinnamon and banana liqueur. Mix well (sugar should melt). Add bananas and cook until soft. Add rum and heat well, tipping pan toward flame to ignite rum. Allow flame to burn out on its own. Serve over ice cream.

Serves 4

VINEYARDS ESTABLISHED CIRCA 1868

GLEN·ELLEN

CALIFORNIA
CHARDONNAY
PROPRIETOR'S RESERVE

VINTED & BOTTLED BY GLEN ELLEN WINERY & VINEYARDS, SONOMA, SONOMA VALLEY, CA
ALCOHOL 12.5% BY VOL.   CONTAINS SULFITES

A medium-straw color is apparent in each glass of Glen Ellen's Chardonnay. Its aromas are reminiscent of Bosc pears with hints of apricot. The flavors are a classic varietal definition of Chardonnay...pear and apple-like, layered with accents of cinnamon, spice and oak.

This is a most versatile Chardonnay. It easily makes the transition from a before meal drink to its place at the dinner table. Seafood and poultry dishes, especially those prepared on the outdoor grill, create an ideal pairing.

BRITANNIA

KD GERMAN RHINE LINE

BRITANNIA

A trip on the Britannia, a KD German Rhine Line ship, is a cruise unlike all others. I can only describe it as quiet elegance, for there is no planned activity aboard except meals, so you merely relax, collect your thoughts, read a book and socialize as you wend your way along one of the most beautiful and history-laden river valleys in the world.

The flat-bottomed luxury ships of the KD line accommodate from approximately 140 to 200 passengers, a comfortable number. There is never a feeling of getting lost in the shuffle. And the crew outdoes themselves in taking care of their multi-national customers.

The Britannia's five-night, four-day cruise from Basel to Rotterdam, which we took in late August, was an interlude of serenity in my life that I look back on with fondness and which I recommend to anyone who needs to get away from it all.

Prices are moderate and amenities are up to date. We had a sauna, a pool and a gift shop aboard, plus a roomy cabin that in the daytime was a comfortable sitting room. All cabin windows overlook the river and each room has a private bathroom with shower.

Having been in operation since 1826, this company knows what it's doing. Begun in Cologne as a ferry and freight operation more than 160 years ago and eventually named KD for Cologne- (Koln in German) Dusseldorf, the line shifted its emphasis to passenger traffic after the railroads took over the heavy work in the 1850s, and then expanded into a pleasure cruise line.

Now, a thousand people work for the cruise line, many of them third and fourth generation. Two and a half million day passengers alone are taken care of in comfort and luxury by KD, thousands more on overnight cruises.

PORTS OF CALL

We were picked up at our Zurich hotel by KD and taken to Basel to board the Britannia. That first evening we cruised toward Strasbourg after being served an extremely beautiful buffet - gravlax in pate or in aspic, venison, carpaccio (thin slices of beef with capers) and my favorite creamed herring. We then went to bed. No midnight frivolities here, no late movies, bingo or dancing till the wee hours. We awoke to a hearty breakfast and then sat and relaxed in the glassed Observation Lounge. We watched the river and the flat, green fields of middle Europe, traversing several locks throughout the morning. People fished from the riverbanks as we passed by.

We then used the tickets, sold at the Pursers office, for our afternoon's excursion in Strasbourg, stopped in to meet the captain at his welcoming reception and then ate lunch. All shore excursions are run by private entities separate from KD enterprises, but arrangements are made on board. Passports are relinquished to the purser in exchange for boarding passes, which means that if you want to spend money in town, cash your traveler's checks before you debark. In Strasbourg, the French franc is used; on board and in the German towns, the German mark, or DM (Deutschmark) is used. American money and traveler's checks sometimes are not accepted by tradespeople in port.

Also, because Strasbourg is French, you must carry a French visa with you if you tour the town. Apply for this before your trip, before you leave the States.

* Strasbourg was in the midst of celebrating a birthday while we were there - its 2,000th. It was founded by the Romans in about 12 B.C. because of its strategic crossroads location. Since then it has served as a major trading center in Europe, from its Middle

Ages trade fairs to its current position as the second largest city on the Rhine. Strasbourg is also a cultural and academic mecca, the second largest research center in France.

And it's lovely. Well-preserved, a city that obviously reflects the pride and care of its citizenry, Strasbourg is really a place to spend more than an afternoon and evening. But if that's what you have, make the most of it by taking a guided tour. You'll hit the high spots, see the famous cathedral (site of the original Roman camp), the Gymnasium, founded in 1538, and the Old City. The squares and streets are full of entertainment - festivals, feasts, traditional dancers and singers and the local people themselves, observed from a sidewalk cafe.

The Strasbourg waterways are particularly beautiful and the bridges are works of art. The history of this remarkably long-lived city, despite the wars that have been fought over it, lives throughout the town, in its Renaissance half-timbered buildings, in the eighteenth-century Palace of the Rohan Cardinals and in the ultra-modern steel and pink sandstone Council of Europe and the European Parliament.

Strasbourg maintains a definite cosmopolitan feeling, no doubt from the centuries of strangers who came to conquer or to learn and made it their home.

* The Heidelberg excursion is a coach ride to a six-hour tour of this city that is billed as a "romantic university town." And that it is, among other things. It is also an enchantingly beautiful city on the Neckar River with a history to match. This sixth oldest city in Europe may turn out to be one of your favorites on the tour, as it was ours.

The castle for which Heidelberg is famous has a thirteenth-century foundation and a Renaissance style - the ruins of the castle I should say. In 1689 and again in 1693, the French partially destroyed the classic sandstone fortress, but still it dominates the scene from its perch on the wooded heights of the Konigstuhl.

The university, the first one in Germany, is less than 500 years old, a new kid on the block compared to the town itself. It was modeled after the higher learning center of Paris and is still considered to be one of the prestigious universities of Europe.

* Cologne is another Roman city, its location chosen by the advancing legions because of the Rhine. Cathedral spires that reach 515 feet high dominate the skyline as you approach the yet-unseen city from the river. The cathedral looks as if it were built of liquid red sand, poured over a frame like frosting dripping from a mammoth cake and left to set in the gentle light of the area. The ornateness of the exterior cathedral continues right on into the cavernous, high-vaulted main room with its massive pillars, elaborate stained glass windows of scenes from the Bible, shrines and sculptures from the twelfth century. The Dom (cathedral in German) was begun in the thirteenth century and completed 600 years later!

The cathedral is a must-see, but so is the Domplatz, the shopping area, and a stroll along Hohe Strasse - High Street, which is what it's been called since Roman times. Toward the river lies the Alter Stadt or Old City, narrow, winding, medieval streets, reconstructed and preserved gabled houses. The busy roadway that once ran along the river has been put underground, so that pedestrians can walk along the well-landscaped river that is now a part of Alter Stadt. The city is full of flowers.

* Lorelei Rock is not, strictly speaking, a port of call, but the boat passes it and the myths that surround it are very universal.

High above the river, so the story goes, above the pretty town of Koblenz where the confluence of the Moselle and the Rhine create a great sweep of waters, lived a temptress famous throughout the world. Lorelei was her name and many a sailor she lured to his death with her lovely, seductive song and her flowing, gauzy robes. This treacherous stretch of gorge, with the waves dashing the cliff and the wind howling on a bad night, is a natural place for ships to have met their sad fates. Lorelei came alive through the imaginations of men whose friends and brothers had died at that spot, and Lorelei lives on in song and story.

* All along this part of the river, the going is narrow and winding and neatly spaced with castles, the likes of which took me back to my childhood days of princes and princesses and happily-ever-after tales. I spent a lot of time oohing and ahing or just sitting in a kind of breathless amazement at these fantastic "homes." The castle of Thurnberg, once the mightiest castle on the Rhine, took more than 300 years to complete. It is now ruins, rent asunder in just a few days during the French Revolution. But even the ruins are impressive.

Just south of Koblenz is the site of the Marksburg, the only fully preserved castle on the Rhine. Since before the Romans this has been a mining area and remains so. Smokestacks line the horizon next to medieval turrets.

We passed by vineyards that marched up the increasingly steep and hilly slopes, and the villages that have been the vintners' market towns for centuries, places and scenes that have barely changed for 2,000 years. The charms and beauties of the Rhine, heralded worldwide, must be seen to be believed. It's difficult to do justice with words to a place that takes your breath away.

* Dusseldorf was forty-five percent destroyed during World War II by Allied bombing. All the bridges and shipping area are new. In fact, the rebuilding created a lovely, modern town with one of the premier shopping areas in the world. Dusseldorf rivals Milan or Paris or Rodeo Drive for goods - expensive goods, I must say, but you can find it here if you can find it anywhere.

I recommend the night tour through Dusseldorf - it is a dazzler. Spectacular lights, gorgeous city.

* Rotterdam was our debarkation city.

SHIPBOARD

Life on board a Rhine cruise is a time of quiet elegance. The age range was thirty-five to sixty years, the passengers cultured and somewhat reserved. We were just a few of the Americans on our cruise, the majority being Germans and a few French, but we had no trouble at all communicating. The staff speaks English and most Europeans have at least a smattering of our language in their repertoires. German, however, is a relatively easy language for English-speakers to understand, at least when reading it, for English is closely related. Most instructions are printed in German, French and English.

Several evenings aboard we were invited to "light-hearted" dancing after the second-seating dinner (which was 7:30 p.m.). This was fun but sedate.

In what they call the "boardshop," you can buy perfume, tobacco, paperbacks, postcards, stamps, gifts and souvenirs. Stationery and envelopes are free at the Purser's Office. The Reading Room contains a selection of daily newspapers, games, books and magazines.

We took advantage of the sauna, but not the pool, as we hit a cool spell. But most of our time was spent on the deck chairs watching the fairy-tale world of the Rhine pass by.

OTHER CRUISES

KD offers more than 350 cruises during the regular season, which runs from early April to late October: "Traditional Connoisseur" and "Heart of Europe" cruises on the Rhine, short "Rhineland Explorer" cruises, Moselle River cruises and special cruises.

Traditional 600-mile Rhine River cruises follows the river through Switzerland, France, Germany and Holland. Three-country cruises from Amsterdam to Strasbourg or Cologne to Basel take five days. Cruises are available not only on the Rhine but on the Main from Frankfurt and on the Moselle, a narrow, twisting tributary of the Rhine. The special cruises vary - wine seminars, studying the subject with talks and tastings aboard and ashore; Christmas and New Year's cruises.

CLOTHING AND WEATHER

Take a raincoat and umbrella. The weather is similar to our Midwestern weather, which means you can expect hot and cold, dry and wet. Be prepared and you'll feel comfortable. As with all cruises, take a few dressy things and never forget to pack your most comfortable walking shoes.

GRATUITIES AND CUSTOMS

No service charges are made, but it is customary to tip your stewards, waiters and attendants at the end of the voyage - if the service has been satisfactory. The amount is up to you, but a rule of thumb in Europe is four to five percent of the fare, divided between the restaurant help, the cabin help and anyone else who has been of assistance.

Europeans are more formal than Americans and are sometimes startled to be addressed by their first names too soon in a relationship or friendship. Oftentimes they will not call you by your first name unless you give them permission to do so.

Guests are allowed aboard when the Rhine cruise ship docks along the river.

BOOKING YOUR CRUISE

for the USA East
Rhine Cruise Agency
170 Hamilton Avenue
White Plains, New York 10601-1788
Telephone 914-948-3600
Telex: 6818192
for the USA West
323 Geary Street
San Francisco, California 94102-1860
Telephone 415-392-8817
Telex: 470409
or call your travel agent.

FOOD

Five meals a day are served on Connoisseur Cruises, four on the other cruises. Breakfast, mid-morning snack, lunch, afternoon coffee and dinner constitute connoisseur service, with a cold buffet served on the evening of embarkation.

The food is good and plentiful but not in the sumptuous league of many ocean cruises. Although there was not enough German fare for me, the food was excellent - mostly Continental.

Each day's menu is printed in German, English, French, Italian and Spanish, which I found great fun to read, comparing the names of dishes well-known to me. "Apple Strudel with whipped cream" translated recognizably into "Apfelstrudel mit sahne" (German), "Stroudel aux pomme avec chantilly" (French), "Strudel di mele con panna montata" (Italian), "Tarta de manzana con nata" (Spanish).

A typical lunch would offer two soups, (my favorite was Potato Soup Schaffhausen Style) a salad, two entrees, a cheeseboard and two desserts. Although the choices are not as varied as on larger ships, I found nothing I didn't like. A lobster soup, "Heligoland style," was particularly good; roast breast of duckling, grilled lamb chops or pork chops - all were simply prepared and tasty.

Dinners offer one appetizer, (try the Butterfly Noodles with Salmon in Herb Cream Sauce) one salad, usually only one entree, always a cheeseboard and either the dessert of the evening or fresh fruit. It was at first surprising, but never presented a problem as far as my not liking the main course. We had Fried Fillets of Perch coated with egg and served with herbal butter; Veal Cutlet Cordon Bleu; Grilled Lamb Steak with Piquant Sauce; Steamed Fillets of Sole in Dutch Shrimp Sauce. Desserts are wonderful but never flamboyant.

The staff goes out of its way to please you, however, so if you have any dietary requirements, all you have to do is speak to them and they will do everything in their power to help you out. If, for example, you can't eat red meat, they will always serve you fish or chicken. They were the most accommodating crew in this respect. And this was one cruise where I never felt guilty about eating nine times a day. It was just right and I felt very good by the time I debarked.

RECIPES

Creamed Herring Housewife Style

2	egg yolks
2	Tbsp. vinegar
1/4	tsp. Worcestershire sauce
1/2	tsp. Dijon mustard
1/2	c. oil
1/4	c. fresh parsley, chopped
4	whole herring fillets
	juice of 1/2 lemon
1	onion, chopped
1	cucumber, chopped
2	apples, chopped
2	cornichons (gherkins), chopped
1	tsp. horseradish
1/4	tsp. Worcestershire sauce
	salt and pepper to taste

In a food processor, process the egg yolks, vinegar, Worcestershire sauce and mustard. With the machine running, slowly pour in the oil until it is all incorporated. Remove from processor and stir in the parsley. Set aside. Cut the herring into 2" pieces. If the herring is very salty, marinate it in lemon juice for a while. Add the herring and the remaining ingredients to the mayonnaise mixture and refrigerate for several hours. If mixture is too thick, thin with a little of the juice from the cornichons.

Serves 4

Butterfly Noodles with Salmon in Herb Cream Sauce

8	oz. butterfly pasta
2	Tbsp. oil
1/2	lb. salmon fillet, cut in 2" cubes
2	small onions, diced
2	cloves garlic, minced
3	Tbsp. flour
1	c. fish stock
1/2	c. white wine
1	c. cream
	salt and pepper to taste
1	tsp. herbs (mixed parsley, chives, tarragon and chervil)
	juice of 1/2 lemon
2	Tbsp. butter

Cook noodles al dente; drain and set aside. In a skillet, heat 1 tablespoon oil and saute the salmon with 1 of the onions and the garlic until salmon is just done. Set aside. In another pan, heat the remaining tablespoon of oil and saute the remaining onion until it's a little bit dry. Sprinkle with flour and stir; add the fish stock, wine and cream and simmer gently for 1/2 hour or until thickened. To this add the salmon, salt, pepper, herbs and lemon juice. Re-heat the pasta in butter. Top each portion of pasta with some of the sauce and serve immediately.

Serves 4 (appetizer-size portions)

Potato Soup Schaffhausen Style

2	Tbsp. oil or butter
1	slice bacon, diced
1	small onion, diced
2	carrots, diced
4	ribs celery, diced
2 1/4	lbs. potatoes, diced
1/2	lb. fresh peas, shelled
4	c. water or beef broth
1/4	tsp. each salt, pepper, marjoram, thyme
1	tsp. dried parsley or 1/4 c. fresh parsley
1	clove garlic, minced
8	oz. cream
1	egg yolk, beaten
4	oz. white cheese, grated

Heat oil or butter in a soup or stock pot and add bacon, onion, carrots, celery, potatoes and peas. Saute for about 10 minutes. Add water or broth, spices and herbs. Simmer until the potatoes and other vegetables are tender. Remove the potatoes and vegetables and puree in a blender or food processor. Return them to the broth. Mix cream with egg yolk and add this to the soup just before serving. Top each portion of soup with grated cheese and, if you like, croutons rubbed with fresh garlic.

Serves 6

Lobster Soup

1	live lobster
2	Tbsp. butter
1	onion, diced
1	leek, diced
1	carrot, diced
1/2	stalk celery, diced
1	c. white wine
3	Tbsp. cognac or Pernod
2	c. fish stock
	salt and fresh ground pepper to taste
1	tsp. chives, minced
1	tsp. parsley, minced
1	c. cream
1	egg yolk, beaten
4	Tbsp. whipping cream

Fill a large stock pot with about 4 quarts water (enough to cover lobster). Bring to a boil and drop in the lobster. Cook covered for about 10 to 15 minutes. Remove the lobster and, when cool enough to handle, cut in large pieces. In another pan, heat the butter and saute the onion, leek, carrot and celery for about 5 minutes. Add the lobster, wine, cognac or Pernod and the stock; then add salt and pepper to taste and the herbs. Simmer for about 1 hour. Remove the lobster and cut the meat into smaller pieces. Strain the rest of the mixture, reserving the liquid. Add the lobster meat to the liquid. Blend the cream with the egg yolk and gently mix in. Add 1 tablespoon whipping cream to each portion before serving.

Serves 6

Pepper Dressing

1	c. milk
1	c. cream
1	egg
1	c. oil
2	Tbsp. vinegar
	juice of 1/2 lime
1	clove garlic, minced
1	Tbsp. green peppercorns, ground

Blend all ingredients in a food processor or blender.

Makes 3 cups

Butterfish

4	fillets butterfish (pompano)
	salt and pepper to taste
	juice of 1 lemon
1/2	tsp. Worcestershire sauce
1	Tbsp. butter

Sprinkle the fillets with salt and pepper. Marinate them for several hours in lemon juice and Worcestershire. Melt the butter in a saute pan and cook fillets gently until just done.

Serves 4

Quail Ridge

Napa Valley
Chardonnay

Cellared and Bottled by Quail Ridge Cellars & Vineyards
Napa, California
Alcohol 13.4% by Volume

Rich, velvety, yet balanced and elegant.

Perfect with pasta in a non-tomato sauce. Delicious with all fish or fowl, particularly those with rich, creamy sauces.

CROWN ODYSSEY

ROYAL CRUISE LINE

Napa Valley
FUMÉ BLANC
Dry Sauvignon Blanc

ALCOHOL 12.5% BY VOLUME

PRODUCED AND BOTTLED BY

ROBERT MONDAVI WINERY

OAKVILLE, CALIFORNIA

The original Fume Blanc and still the natural choice with fish, seafood, poultry and other light dishes.

CROWN ODYSSEY

Royal Cruise Line went into business in 1971, a youngster in the field of cruise ships. It came on the scene with the express purpose of providing top-of-the-line sailings, the very height of upper crustness. And succeeded.

We sailed on the Atlantic Crossing, billed as "The Great Trans-Atlantic High Society Cruise," the year the Crown Odyssey was launched - 1988. We fell easily into the lap of luxury. We discovered that we took right to the life of the idle rich and could handle it without stress. What a trip.

Because we were sailing straight from Southhampton to New York, we were for the first time on a cruise that wasn't stopping at ports for sightseeing, which made it a unique experience, one that was gratifyingly isolated from the real world. Although crossings are not yet popular enough to warrant many steamship lines jumping in to compete, I have a feeling it will be the way to travel in the future whenever possible. So many people either fear or loathe flying - the crowded terminals, the cramped seating, the mediocre food and the inevitable jet lag. A crossing is so relaxing. I arrived home ready to go to work, not beat for a week because I was so disoriented.

The Crown Odyssey is surely as fancy as a ship can get. It is masses of marble, chrome, brass, mirrors - extremely plush, expansive and grand. The plan for this second ship in the line was that it be as elegant as possible in a combined classical and art deco tradition, as modern as tomorrow and as comfortable as one's home.

They succeeded with the help of such touches as Royal Doulton bone china, custom-designed Brinton carpets, Van Havere fabrics, Cannon bed linens and Italian Frette table linens, Hepp Pforzheim silver plate from Germany, French Grosfillex deck furniture and interior furniture by famed European craftsmen including Poltrona Frau, Saporiti, Tino Sana, Colber Alfa Arredamenti and so on. Walkways, lounges and the Galleria are hung with reproductions of original masterpieces found in the museums of Athens, Cairo, Rome, Paris, Vienna, Berlin, London and New York; specially designed sculptures grace public rooms; and extensive stained glass windows, including a magnificent dome above the Grand Staircase, sparkle from the most surprising places.

The cruise line claims that the resources and references for the Crown were ancient theaters, Italian villas, Roman baths, museums and winter gardens combined with the style of the art deco period. The ship's interior design will quite simply take your breath away. It's practically a floating Versailles.

Although the price of the ticket is not cheap it's definitely worth it. The staff are particularly solicitous - every time I sat on a deck chair and a steward came along and tucked the blanket around my tootsies, I felt like the Queen of England.

SHIPBOARD

Because of the nature of the particular cruise we were on, we were surrounded by celebrities, who, we found, are just as much fun as we are. We talked with Glenn Ford and Linda Ellerbee and shook hands with Helen Hayes. Jack LaLanne was aboard with his wife Elaine, and we saw Ann Blyth, Helen O'Connor and Frankie Laine.

Our stateroom was roomy, very modern, clean and pretty, decorated in pumpkin and yellows, with mirrors on all the doors and throughout the bathroom. We had a vanity, which was nice, tie racks and shoe racks. All the furniture was solid hardwood and we had original Greek paintings on the walls.

No matter where we went in the ship the staggering attention to detail and good taste was delightful. On the Horizon Deck is the Top of the Crown, the top-floor observation deck designed for a

360-degree view. In the afternoon it is a cocktail lounge and in the late evening a disco - with a sunken dance floor made of glass and illuminated from underneath. Spectacular. But not as lovely as the view of the stars through the two glass domes set in the ceiling.

The Penthouse Deck houses the Penthouse Bar & Grill next to the outdoor pool and whirlpools. A white granite bar adds that touch of luxury so much a part of this ship's image, and a fetching mosaic tile mural of "Ladies by the Seaside" is imbedded behind the bar.

The Coronet Theatre on the Lido Deck is two stories high and a nostalgic piece of work for anyone who used to go to the big movie houses in New York and Los Angeles. The Coronet is art deco, its lobby lined with mirrors and pink marble columns. Going to the movies in style is almost impossible these days, what with four theatres in one building and a push toward the utilitarian. We saw "The Last Emperor" in the Coronet and both the movie and the theatre were events.

The Yacht Club on the Odyssey Deck is a coffee shop, a bar and a late-night dance club. The walls are hung with famous black and white photos of the America's Cup winners. It's a nice room.

The Monte Carlo Court is like a hotel lobby in the grand old tradition. From here you can get to the shopping area or downstairs to the purser or the library or drop in next door at the casino for a hand of blackjack or a spin of the roulette wheel. The slot machines take quarters.

ACTIVITIES

Not a minute to waste on the Crown if you're the let's-get-out-there-and-do-things kind of person. From Sunrise Stretch to midnight disco, the active soul will have a ball. Low impact aerobics is popular, as well as bingo, gambling, bridge, chess, table tennis, dance classes, muscle toning with rubberbands (!), arts and crafts, creative writing classes, aquatic exercise, fashion shows, lectures on various topics (including seabirds and stargazing, gourmet cooking, television reporters), cribbage tourneys, Greek language lessons, slide shows on former famous luxury liners, white elephant auction, interviews with famous people and, of course, what would a cruise be without shuffleboard?

The ship is equipped with an outdoor pool, an indoor pool, a gym/sauna that is a replica of the days of Roman emperors except that it's equipped with the latest Universal machines - what a beautiful setting with its pink columns and mosaic tile pools, a walking path, a massage room, a beauty salon right out of Hollywood.

You can go to the latest first-run movies or to classics like "Kismet." You can watch sports on the big screen in the Lido Lounge, dance to rock 'n roll or Big Band, listen to jazz or first-rate comedians. The captain throws a cocktail party which is wonderfully fancy - your best clothes here. And the mandatory costume party is really fun. We had folks dressed up as very strange things: as "Open Seating" - several people in union suits with the flap down showing off a painting of a rear (not the real thing). Very amusing. Another group came as "Royal Flushes" - with toilet seats on their heads as crowns. Such imagination.

One of the ingenious ideas promoted aboard Royal Cruise Line ships that has no doubt been adopted by other lines is the Host Program.

On each cruise, distinguished-looking single men over fifty act as unofficial shipboard "dates" to single women. This program is successful and popular and rightly so, for the majority of passengers on any cruise are single, older women. For them to be able to dance a couple of times in an evening, have a male join in the bridge game and someone to escort them on port tours - it's a natural. I'm surprised someone didn't think of it sooner. This program is very aboveboard - strict admonitions are given that no romantic involvement is to occur and the gentlemen must spread their charms among all the women, not just a few or those in one group. These fellows are stringently interviewed, receive no pay, but likewise, do not pay for their cruise. They are recommended to Royal Cruise Line by reputable travel agencies and then screened and personally interviewed by ship authorities. According to these executives, selections are based on general congeniality, respectability, travel experience and enthusiasm for card-playing and nightly dancing. It's a great idea.

Another innovative program launched by Royal Cruise Line is called "New Beginnings." This is a series of onboard lectures, activities and classes supporting travelers eager to revitalize themselves physically, emotionally and psychologically.

Royal Cruise Line invites on board leading nutritionists, psychologists, exercise physiologists, fitness experts, medical doctors and motivational specialists. Topics include stress reduction, improving self-esteem and overcoming loneliness, eating light, a healthy heart and physical well-being. Future topics include pain-reduction clinics, talks on second careers and volunteer opportunities for mature adults, seminars on financial planning and retirement adjustment.

CROWN ODYSSEY

BOOKING YOUR CRUISE

Royal Cruise Line Ltd.
One Maritime Plaza, Suite 660
San Francisco, CA 94111
Telephone 415-956-7200
or call your travel agent.

OTHER CRUISES

The Crown Odyssey travels the world, so if you want more than a crossing, consider other itineraries.

The Crown Odyssey travels between Ensenada and Honolulu on the "Pacific Hawaiian Odyssey;" between Honolulu and Tahiti on the "Polynesian Paradise;" between San Juan and San Diego on the "Cruise of the Americas and the Panama Canal;" between San Juan and Rio de Janeiro on the "South American Odyssey;" from San Juan to Lisbon on the "Blue Riband;" from Athens to San Juan on the "Magnificent Odyssey;" between Lisbon and Athens on the "Gala Mediterranean;" and between Lisbon and Venice on the "Mediterranean Highlights;" from London north and back on the cruise labeled "Scandinavian Capitals and Russia." These are subject to change.

The Golden Odyssey plies between Bangkok and Hong Kong on the "Treasures of the Orient & Java Seas;" from Singapore to Athens on "The Route of Marco Polo;" between Athens and Venice on the "Seas of Ulysses & Black Sea;" roundtrip from Athens through the Adriatic on the "Golden Greek Isles" tour; between Venice and Nice on the "Best of Italy, France and the Greek Isles."

For the long cruise experience several itineraries may be combined to create an extended cruise of nineteen to thirty-five days.

FOOD

The Yacht Club serves "eye-opener coffee" at 6:30 a.m., a breakfast buffet at 7:45, morning bouillon at 10:45, a luncheon buffet at noon, afternoon tea at 4:00 p.m. and a late evening light buffet between 11:30 p.m. and 12:30 a.m.

The Lido Lounge serves soup, salad and sandwiches between noon and 1:30 p.m.; the Penthouse Grill, weather permitting, serves outdoor grilled specials at the same time.

The Seven Continents Restaurant, the main dining room on the ship with two seatings for each meal, is a knockout of a room - lacquered woods, beveled glass, stained-glass domes, art deco wall sconces, variegated pastel colors. It seats 600 for good food and kindly service. The waiter was more than happy to direct the chef to fix my fish the way I wanted it.

Lunches offered "starters" and salads - relish tray or sardines, tomatoes with feta cheese or just plain lettuce salads with dressing. Usually a cold and a hot soup were offered, really excellent soups ranging from Bavarian Lentil to Cold Apple Soup and including Cream of Artichoke, Vichyssoise, Chilled Minted Consomme. Lunch entrees included items such as Poached Salmon, Barbecued Ribs, Croissant Sandwich, quiche, pasta, fruit salads, burgers, always served with vegetables such as eggplant or spinach puree, and potato choices such as French fries, mashed, escalloped. Fresh fruits and cheeses were always available and choices of desserts - pie, ice cream, cake, pudding, baked apple. Lunch was thorough, not elegant

Dinner was a different matter. Beluga caviar, smoked salmon, goose liver pate for starters. Shrimp Bisque for soup, lobster and prime tenderloin of beef, or rack of lamb for entrees, Cherries Jubilee for dessert... just one meal. One evening the dinner was announced as "12 Tastes from 12 Countries" and we dined on Greek lamb, American sirloin, Italian veal and eggplant, Spanish prawns, British grill (veal, beef, lamb, liver, sausage and tomato), French fillet with mushrooms, German pork and scallops, Japanese teriyaki chicken, Indian spiced chicken, Korean swordfish and Turkish kebabs.

Another innovative Royal Cruise Line first, labeled "Dine to Your Heart's Content," is approved by the American Heart Association and serves food that's good for you - low fat, low sodium, low cholesterol. It's delicious. Using fresh herbs in place of salt and butter and eliminating rich sauces, the recipes pass for the richest French cuisine. Each day's menu offers to the watchful eater a selection titled "To Your Heart's Content," dinners such as Artichoke with Baby Scallops, Swordfish, Fillet of Salmon (marinated in apple cider, olive oil and fresh herbs), Little Italy (sauteed vegetables and fresh pasta with marinara sauce); lunches such as Pacific Crab Salad, Skewered Scallops, Vegetarian Lasagna (wonderful taste, recipe follows).

RECIPES

"TO YOUR HEART'S CONTENT" RECIPES

Little Italy

4	oz. fresh vegetables (broccoli, etc., anything in season)
8	oz. cooked, fresh fettucine
2	tsp. margarine
1	whole tomato, peeled
2	Tbsp. tomato paste
1	oz. onion, chopped
1/2	clove garlic, minced
	pinch each fresh oregano, basil, thyme

Saute the fresh vegetables and fettucine in half the margarine. Add the marinara sauce (recipe follows). Toss all together with fresh herbs and spices.

Marinara Sauce

Saute onion and garlic in the remaining margarine. Dice the whole tomato, add to the saute. And tomato paste and cook very slowly. Add salt to taste. If too thick, thin with tomato juice.

Serves 4

Discover America

	large portions of assorted greens such as romaine, iceberg, leaf lettuce, spinach, chicory
	radishes
	mushrooms
	green onions
3	oz. large shrimp, cooked

Toss the greens and vegetables together and place on a plate. Garnish with shrimp. Dress with Lemon-Mustard Dressing. (recipe follows)

Serves 1

Lemon Mustard Dressing

1	tsp. mayonnaise
1/2	oz. olive oil
1	tsp. Grey Poupon mustard
	juice of 1 lemon
2	drops Tabasco sauce
	pinch of fresh herbs: oregano, thyme

Mix all the above ingredients together. If too thick, thin with lemon juice.

Serves 1

South Pacific

1	whole fresh pineapple
7	oz. raw skinless chicken breast
	red bell pepper strips, or beets

Broil the chicken breast. Let it cool and then cut in julienne style into strips. Core and slice the pineapple lengthwise, into 6 long pieces. Arrange the chicken breast and pineapple on a plate and sprinkle with tiny strips of red bell pepper or beets. Serve with Honey Creamy Dressing. (Recipe follows)

Serves 1

Honey Creamy Dressing

1	oz. low-fat plain yogurt
1	Tbsp. honey
1/2	banana, pureed
1/2	oz. fresh lemon juice
1/2	oz. fresh orange juice
1/2	tsp. cumin

Mix first 5 ingredients in a bowl. Serve in half a hollowed-out orange (or use a bell pepper) and sprinkle with cumin.

Serves 1

Odyssey Treat

7	oz. fresh raw salmon
3	fresh apricots, chopped
	juice of 1 lemon
1	clove garlic, crushed
1/2	tsp. fresh ginger, chopped
1	tsp. fresh herbs: rosemary, oregano, thyme
3	whole peppercorns, crushed
	pinch of salt
1/2	oz. olive oil
	garnish: grated fresh lemon rind, orange rind and cilantro

Place salmon in bowl. Mix remaining ingredients and marinate salmon in the marinade overnight, covered. The following day, remove salmon and reserve marinade. Broil the salmon slowly and brush with the marinade while you are broiling it. Serve with fresh steamed vegetables and garnish with grated fresh lemon rinds, orange rinds and cilantro.

Serves 1

The Midwest

6	oz. lean beef (tenderloin fillet, NY strip), cooked rare
	assorted greens: romaine, iceberg, chicory
	radishes
	green onions
	slices of green, yellow or red peppers

The Midwest (Cont.)

Slice the beef and place it on the bed of assorted greens and vegetables. Garnish with slices of green, yellow or red peppers. Top with Sesame Oriental Dressing (recipe follows).

Serves 1

Sesame Oriental Dressing

1/2	oz. soy sauce
	pinch fresh ginger, chopped
1/2	tsp. sesame seeds
1/2	oz. sesame oil
1	tsp. fresh-squeezed lime juice
	pinch pepper

Mix thoroughly and pour over salad.

Serves 1

Southwest Special

5	oz. chicken fillet (all white meat), skinless
4	oz. fresh garden vegetables: broccoli, bell peppers, cauliflower, zucchini, etc.
2	tsp. margarine
	spices: powdered ginger, sage, cayenne pepper
	salt and pepper
	steamed rice

Southwest Special (Cont.)

Cut chicken into strips and cut vegetables into bite-sized pieces. Saute all ingredients in margarine over a very low fire, until cooked. Season to taste very lightly with salt and pepper. Take a small bowl of rice and turn it over on the plate. Arrange the vegetable-chicken mixture around it and serve.

Serves 1

A Bite to Remember

2	pieces (1 oz. each) fresh swordfish, diced
2	large raw prawns
2	chunks pineapple, diced
1	cherry tomato
	pinch paprika
	salt and pepper to taste

Skewer the ingredients like a shish kebab. Marinate overnight (recipe follows). Remove from marinade, sprinkle with a pinch of paprika, salt and pepper. Broil until cooked, brushing with the reserved marinade. Serve with fresh vegetables or plain steamed rice or pasta.

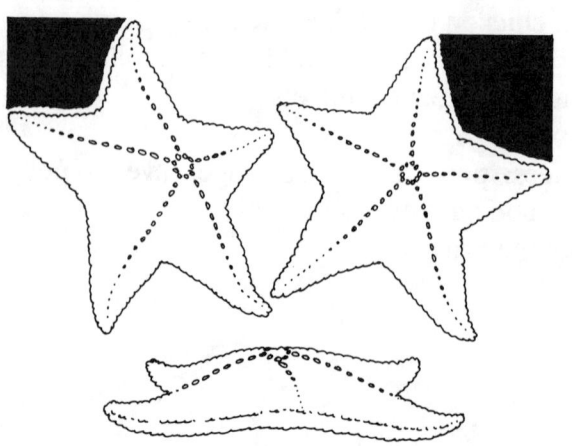

Serves 1

Marinade

1	clove garlic, crushed
1	oz. lemon or lime juice
1/2	oz. olive oil
2	bay leaves
	pinch each oregano, sage
4	whole peppercorns, crushed

Blend all ingredients together. Mix well.

Serves 1

Lasagne (vegetarian)

12	oz. dried lasagne noodles
4	medium zucchini, thinly sliced
4	medium carrots, thinly sliced
	low-fat margarine, melted
1/4	c. fresh basil, chopped or 1 Tbsp. dried
	freshly ground pepper to taste
1/4	c. low-fat margarine
2	Tbsp. all-purpose flour
1/2	c. skim milk
	salt and freshly ground white pepper
1/2	c. skim milk mozzarella cheese, shredded
2	lbs. tomatoes, peeled and seeded
4	tsp. fresh basil, chopped
4	tsp. fresh lemon juice
	freshly ground pepper

Lasagne Cont.)

Add noodles to large amount of rapidly boiling, salted water, stirring to prevent sticking. Cook until just tender but still firm to bite. Drain. Place in bowl of cold water. Steam zucchini and carrots until tender, about 5 minutes. Cool. Preheat oven to 350° F. Lightly coat 6" x 10" x 2" baking pan with melted low-fat margarine. Drain noodles and line prepared pan with 1/4 of noodles. Arrange 1/3 of zucchini and carrots over this. Sprinkle with 1/3 of basil and pepper. Arrange another layer of noodles; cover with second 1/3 of vegetables; season with 1/3 of basil and pepper. Repeat with another layer of noodles, vegetables and seasoning. Top with final layer of noodles. Brush with melted margarine. Melt 1/4 cup margarine in small saucepan over medium-low heat. Whisk in 2 Tablespoons flour and stir 2 minutes. Whisk in skim milk and simmer until thickened, stirring constantly, about 5 minutes. Season with salt and white pepper. Pour over lasagne. Top with mozzarella cheese. Bake until cheese is bubbling and lasagne is heated through, about 35 minutes. Meanwhile, prepare tomato sauce: Combine tomatoes, basil, lemon juice and pepper in blender and puree. Cook over medium heat until thickened. Cut lasagne into squares to serve. Pass tomato sauce separately.

Serves 4

REGULAR RECIPES

Paros Eggplant

1	c. salad oil
1	eggplant, peeled and cut in half
1	c. onions, finely sliced
3	cloves fresh garlic, finely chopped
2	Tbsp. olive oil
1/2	c. crushed tomatoes
1/2	tsp. cumin
	salt and pepper to taste
1	Tbsp. parsley or cilantro, chopped
1/2	c. chicken broth, as needed
	pinch each pepper, sugar, salt
2	slices Monterey Jack or mozzarella cheese

Heat salad oil in heavy skillet. Saute eggplant halves until golden brown; reduce heat and continue cooking. In another pan, saute onions and garlic in olive oil until transparent. Add tomatoes, cumin, salt and pepper. Add parsley or cilantro and simmer for about 10 minutes. Add chicken broth as needed if mixture is too thick. Flatten eggplant halves with a spatula; remove from heat and cool slightly. Sprinkle with pepper, sugar and salt. Press center of each eggplant half with back of spoon to make an indentation. Fill indentations with the tomato-onion mixture. Bake at 350° F for 10 minutes. Add a slice of cheese on top of each eggplant half and return to oven for 1 minute or until cheese is slightly melted. Remove from oven and serve immediately.

Serves 2

Odyssey Lamb

2	onions, pureed
2	c. salad oil
2	stems fresh mint, chopped
4	bay leaves
1	Tbsp. fresh rosemary
1	Tbsp. whole peppercorns
2	cloves garlic, crushed
1	rack of lamb, trimmed of fat
1/2	c. sourdough bread crumbs (no crusts)
1	tsp. thyme
1	tsp. garlic, finely chopped
	pinch each ground fresh pepper, oregano, paprika

Combine the first 7 ingredients in a bowl. Add the lamb and marinate for 24 hours. Remove lamb from marinade and place in pan. Mix together the sourdough bread crumbs, thyme, garlic, pepper, oregano and paprika. Sprinkle the lamb with bread crumb mixture and bake at 350° F for 25 minutes. Serve with Mint Sauce (recipe follows).

Serves 2

Mint Sauce for Lamb

2	Tbsp. fresh mint, chopped
1/2	c. chopped garlic
1	whole vanilla bean, chopped
1/4"	slice fresh ginger
2	c. water
1	Tbsp. raspberry vinegar
1	tsp. sugar
1	Tbsp. chardonnay
3	Tbsp. mint jelly
2	Tbsp. fresh mint, chopped

Put fresh mint, garlic, vanilla bean pieces and ginger in a 6"-square of cheesecloth. Tie securely and put in pan along with the water, vinegar, sugar and chardonnay. Boil for 15 minutes; remove cheesecloth bag and reduce heat. Add mint jelly and fresh mint. Serve sauce with lamb.

Makes 3 cups

Stuffed Shrimp Imperial

6	large prawns
	pinch each cayenne pepper, oregano
1	tsp. butter

Stuffing:

3	Tbsp. butter
1/4	c. onions, diced
1	c. Dungeness crabmeat
3/4	c. white wine
1	tsp. thyme
1/2	c. bechamel sauce*
1	Tbsp. capers
1/2	c. sourdough bread crumbs (no crusts)
1	Tbsp. fresh parsley, chopped
	salt and pepper to taste

Topping:

1/2	c. sourdough bread crumbs (no crusts)
1	tsp. thyme
1	tsp. garlic, finely chopped
	pinch each fresh ground pepper, oregano, paprika
	fresh parsley or cilantro, chopped

Butterfly prawns with their shells on. Lift up shells (don't remove) and sprinkle with cayenne pepper and oregano. Butter a casserole and place prawns in it. Set aside. In a large frying pan, melt 3 Tablespoons butter and saute the onions. Add crabmeat and saute. Add wine, thyme and bechamel sauce; stir to blend. Add capers and simmer for 3 minutes. Add 1/2 cup bread crumbs to thicken the mixture, then add 1 tablespoon parsley, salt and pepper. Simmer for 3 minutes, then cool. When mixture is cool, stuff prawns with it and sprinkle them with the topping mixture of sourdough crumbs, thyme, garlic and spices. Top with parsley

Stuffed Shrimp Imperial (Cont.)

or cilantro. Bake at 350° F for 10 minutes. Serve with Creamy Lemon Sauce (recipe follows).

Serves 2

*see glossary

Creamy Lemon Sauce

1	Tbsp. shallots, finely minced
1/2	clove garlic, finely minced
2	Tbsp. sweet butter
2	Tbsp. lemon juice
2	Tbsp. white wine
1/2	c. whipping cream
1	tsp. cornstarch, blended with
1	Tbsp. cold water or
1	Tbsp. roux*
	salt and pepper to taste

Saute shallots and garlic in butter slowly. Add lemon juice and wine and simmer 2 minutes. Add cream, shaking pan constantly for 5 minutes. Add the cornstarch mixture or the roux and stir until thickened. Add salt and pepper to taste. Serve with Stuffed Shrimp Imperial, either on the side or pour on dinner plates and place the prawns on top of sauce.

Makes 1 cup

*see glossary

Jordan

ESTATE BOTTLED

Cabernet Sauvignon
Alexander Valley

GROWN, PRODUCED & BOTTLED BY JORDAN VINEYARD & WINERY
ALEXANDER VALLEY, HEALDSBURG, CALIF   ALCOHOL 12.8% BY VOLUME

This wine has a fresh, berry aroma with undertones of cherry, and the taste is soft and round with ample, rich tannins and a lasting finish. The characteristics exhibit dominant cassis flavors. The full fruit flavors and soft tannins makes Jordan's Cabernet Sauvignon a delicious wine to drink at a youthful age, yet the complex structure of this classic wine assures development and enjoyment for many years to come.

SS MONTEREY

ALOHA PACIFIC CRUISES

SS MONTEREY

Pulling Together.

Over one thousand years ago, Polynesians crossed vast, uncharted ocean distances in outrigger canoes. Such amazing feats could only be accomplished when every member of the community supported their courageous voyagers. And every paddler pulled together as one man.

Today, Hawaiian Airlines still follows these ancient Polynesian traditions. We take pride in joining with others, striving together for a common goal.

Our congratulations and best wishes to all who have made this event possible by pulling together.

Hawaiian Airlines. First in the Hawaiian skies.

HAWAIIAN®
The Colors of Paradise.

Call your Travel Agent. Or call us in Hawaii: 1-800-367-5320.

1 9 2 9   1 9 8 9

SS MONTEREY

We cruised aboard Aloha Pacific Cruises' SS Monterey during its maiden season, the fall of 1988, when the crew and staff were still ironing out little wrinkles in the fabric of their operation - but it didn't alter the exceptional friendliness and attentiveness we received. This was one of the most sincerely considerate and exuberant crews we sailed with.

The SS Monterey first slipped down the ways in 1952, and now, fully refurbished and re-outfitted - to the tune of more than 40 million dollars - she is a liner with the latest technology amid mid-century spaciousness. Many of the cabins are larger than today's norm and the public areas are roomy and airy. The ship contains a new swimming pool, ballrooms, dining rooms and lounges. Three hundred cabins, a 2,260-square-foot conference center and a 107-seat theater with the best in audio-visual equipment will capture the convention trade.

The intent of the American-flagged Aloha Pacific SS Monterey is to offer not only the romance of being at sea, but all the luxury of a top-flight hotel, fine restaurants, plus shore-side trips to Kauai, Maui and Hawaii. The ship is American-owned and staffed by an all-American crew.

PORTS OF CALL

The SS Monterey departs Honolulu every Saturday evening at eight, a lovely time to watch the lights of the city fade to twinkling stars as the Pacific sun sinks into a red and purple sea. By sunrise Sunday morning, we were docked at Nawiliwili on the island of Kauai.

* Kauai, geologically the oldest island in the Hawaiian group, is called the Garden Isle, so we decided to opt for the Fern Grotto shore excursion. This is an eight-hour trip. The verdant, luxurious rain forest is as hauntingly lovely as the brochures said. The place is so overgrown with vegetation we could barely see the

sky. There were chirping birds and we could hear rushing water - a real "Green Mansions" setting.

On our way back to the ship we stopped at Hanalei Bay - there's no doubt about it, the Hawaiian Islands have the most beautiful beaches in the world. This is where parts of "South Pacific" were filmed, and down the way, at Ke'e Beach, scenes from "The Thornbirds" were filmed.

Other excursions on Kauai include the Waimea Canyon and Kilohana Estate sugarcane plantation. The Waimea Canyon is dubbed the Grand Canyon of the Pacific. It is ten miles long and 3,400 feet deep, with red clay and volcanic rock walls chiseled by rain and wind - remarkably similar to the Grand Canyon of the mainland.

At the Kilohana Estate, restored to its 1935 heydays, you can tour the tudor mansion, ride in a horse and buggy drawn by Clydesdales, and shop for Hawaiian arts and crafts.

One excursion titled "Picnic U-Drive," you explore on your own equipped with a map of Kauai, helpful brochures and a picnic lunch. This was billed at $30 per person based on two per automobile, but the gasoline was extra, so be prepared.

A fifty-minute flight aboard a Piper Chieftain gives you the bird's-eye view of the important sites of Kauai - the exclusive Poipu Resort, Waimea Canyon, Hanalei beach and the wettest spot on earth, Mount Waialeale. It also flies you over the small island of Nihau, called the Forbidden Isle. Nihau is privately owned and home to 230 full-blooded Hawaiians who practice the island life as it was lived for centuries before the Europeans came.

Three adventures for the brave include Kauai by kayak on the Huleia River (where some of "Raiders of the Lost Ark" was filmed); Waimea Canyon by helicopter, which also includes pas-

SS MONTEREY

ses over the secluded Na Pali Coast and a swoop over the dormant volcano, Waialeale Crater; or the Zodiac Expedition, a trip on a motorized rubber raft that will bounce you along Kauai's Na Pali Coast and give you time to swim in secluded coves, snorkel and watch migrating humpback whales.

The ship stayed overnight in Kauai and set sail Monday at sunrise past the northern side of Oahu, past Molokai and slipped into Lahaina, Maui at sunrise on Tuesday.

* Maui, called the Valley Isle, is the second biggest island in the chain. There is a saying, "Maui no ka oi," which means "Maui is the best." Many people think so. We spent Tuesday and Wednesday on Maui, so there was time to do several of the shore excursions.

The best by far - and one no respectable island visitor should neglect - was the Lahaina Luau. The roast pig is succulent and wonderful, prepared in the "imu," the underground oven full of hot lava rocks and ti leaves. You should try the poi, poke, the haupia and kulolo, but other side dishes are more familiar - sweet potatoes, chicken long rice, teriyaki beef, fresh fruits and salads. As the sun sets, the traditional Hawaiian hulas are performed. This was really an enjoyable evening.

The "grand overview" tours include Haleakala Crater by motorcoach; drive guides of Maui (a guide plans a tour to your interests and specifications); a helicopter tour over waterfalls that plummet 4,500 feet; and a Zodiac Expedition that in the summer allows snorkeling near a shipwreck and in the winter an opportunity to see close at hand the migrating whales.

If you're in great shape, try the Bike Haleakala tour. This is for the seasoned bicyclist. You're taken to the 10,023-foot, twenty-one mile-wide crater, outfitted with a bike and a guide and then you cruise down the thirty-eight miles from the mouth of the crater to the Pacific Ocean. The guide knows a lot and you'll be full of information by the time you hit sea level. Wear warm clothing as it is freezing cold at the crater in the early morning.

Horseback riding and parasailing excursions are available, both offering unique perspectives of Maui. And you might simply want to spend a day in Lahaina exploring. This is a casual and interesting village, the first capitol of the Kingdom of the Hawaiian Islands.

* On Thursday you spend the day in Hilo on Hawaii, which is called the Big Island because it's twice the size of the other islands combined. This is the volcano island - actively. Since January of 1983, Kilauea has erupted more than forty times.

Because time is short, the best way to see things here is to take a helicopter tour over the volcanoes. Another way to see the island is to rent a car or go in a motorcoach and leave the driving to someone else. Or you can just wander around Hilo, a charming capitol city that hangs onto its past.

* Friday at sunrise the ship lands in Kona where we went snorkeling - it was exciting, relaxing, fun - everything island vacationing should be. The crew was great here, teaching, guiding, always in good humor. This was a lovely day.

We also went helicoptering on the Kona side. This is so much fun and always ends too quickly.

Saturday 8:00 a.m. we slid into our berth in Honolulu, alas. Either coming or going, you can take a half day island circle tour - it's about four and a half hours and acquaints you with the island of Oahu, its history and scenic wonders.

Other shore excursions will appeal to the golfers and tennis players. The golf program offers passengers the opportunity to pick from world-famous courses and play four of them during the cruise. Do these names entice you? Westin Kauai, with two new eighteen-hole courses designed by Jack Nicklaus; Kapalua Golf Club, Maui, home of the annual Isuzu International Golf Tourney; Wailea Golf Club, Maui, on the slopes of a dormant volcano, with ocean views; a golf course built on black lava; and the Robert Trent Jones Waikoloa Village course on the Big Island. All tee-off times are arranged and carts are provided, as is transportation from boat to clubhouse to boat.

Tennis aficionados will play early mornings only at the Coco Palms Resort on Kauai, Kapalua Tennis Garden and Royal Lahaina Resort on Maui and the King Kamehameha Hotel in Kona.

This kind of shore excursion bonus may persuade non-cruising types to make plans for a luxury liner trip.

SHIPBOARD

Life on board the Monterey offers activities, like all cruise ships, but there isn't an overabundance of them, partly because the shore excursions are so inviting. I found, also, that I enjoyed being a real vacationer and sitting on the deck doing nothing but basking in balmy breezes and wondering why I lived in the mountains where snow ten feet deep is common.

We did take ukulele lessons, enter a few trivia contests (I won a bookmark) and listen to a few entertainers. By the time we'd finished dinner each evening, however, I was ready to fall into bed.

Catholic Mass is offered on Saturday evening; an interdenominational church service is available on Sunday. The shore excursion talks are interesting and may help you decide what to do with your time; the captain's party is always fun on any ship - fancy and classy; the movies on the Monterey were either classics or current releases; exercise classes, beach volleyball, paddle tennis, golf driving, card games, books to borrow, dancing, lei making, bingo, hula classes - a nice variety but never so overwhelming you can't make up your mind.

The swimming pool is big and comfortable; two Jacuzzis and health spas provide the pampering factor, along with a hair salon. There is, of course, a doctor's office and medical facilities, a TV room, a designer boutique and a photo shop.

THE LOOK OF THINGS

Everything is brand spanking new and is kept looking that way - no slack-off of maintenance on the Monterey. It is indeed like a first-class hotel in that respect. The formal dining room holds two seatings and is spacious. The Veranda is an open-air cafe and there are two lounge bars, the Palm Terrace and Captain Cook's. The Seven Pearls is a multi-leveled, authentic-looking art deco show room.

The interior was decorated by Platou Ship Design of Norway, famous for some of the most beautifully decorated ships afloat. The staterooms are unusually large and contain a great deal of storage area. On the bathroom counters sit the shampoo, body lotion and powder just like you get in a big hotel. Each cabin has its own phone, hair dryer and private bath. Laundry and dry-cleaning service is available - and, a really handy touch - twenty-four-hour room service.

CLOTHING AND WEATHER

In December it was eighty-six degrees, so take your summer togs. We did, however, have stormy weather a couple of days, so take your brolly and slicker. If you plan to snorkel, take along a pair of tennies you're willing to wear in the water. You can't wear your thongs and if you're the least bit tenderfooted, you'll be sorry you don't have something for your feet. Of course, take your swimming suits and shorts, but keep in mind that dinner is formal and you must dress. You don't need a lot of clothes for this cruise. Pack light and you'll be happy with yourself. And remember, the laundry services can keep your wardrobe on a quick turnaround.

BOOKING YOUR CRUISE

Aloha Pacific Cruises
510 King Street, Suite 501
Alexandria, VA 22314
Telephone 703-684-6263
Fax 703-684-0126
Reservations 1-800-544-6442

SHIP'S FACTS

The U.S.A.-registered Monterey is 563 feet long and can travel at twenty knots. It has a total crew of 277 and can accommodate 638 passengers. There are four suites, 255 deluxe staterooms and forty standard cabins. It displaces 21,051 tons.

FOOD

Menus change nightly in the dining room and offer at least one island dish along with more traditional and new American cuisine. Most of the island dishes contain fish and are exceptionally good, for example: Steamed Opakapaka with Papaya, Red Onion and Red Pepper Coulis; Grilled Marlin with Green Peppercorn Butter Sauce; Baked Kamanu with Black Bean Papaya Salsa; Poached Butaguchi with Lemon Sauce and Steamed Vegetables (the most flavorful of Hawaiian fish); Baked Ulua with Macadamia Nut Butter (a sweet-tasting fish). Desserts are on the rich side, but the menu always offers fruit and cheese.

SS MONTEREY

Breakfasts are traditional with a tad of fancy - Freshberry Pancake with Macadamia Nut Butter is a good example. They also serve regular old ham and eggs and oatmeal.

Lunches are light as a rule, although you can get a grilled steak or red snapper. Each day at poolside you can order hotdogs and burgers and not have to dress for lunch inside. Late at night you can get buffet items - from 11:00 p.m. to 12:30 a.m. There is also a breakfast buffet between 6:00 and 9:30 a.m.

RECIPES

Cream of Shiitake Soup

1	lb. shiitake mushrooms
2	oz. whole butter
4	oz. onion, diced
1	oz. dried shallot
2	bay leaves
3	c. chicken stock
2	c. heavy cream
3	oz. dry sherry
	salt and pepper to taste
	chopped chives

In a non-corrosive skillet, saute mushrooms in butter with onion and shallot, until the mushrooms are wilted and the onions are translucent. Do not brown. Add bay leaves and stock and simmer for 15 minutes. Strain and puree the solid portion. Combine the mushroom pulp with the stock and the cream and simmer 20 minutes. Add sherry and cook another 10 minutes. Add seasoning and serve immediately, garnished with chives.

Tortilla Soup

1/2	c. olive oil
12	cloves garlic, crushed
3	medium onions, julienned
4	stalks celery, chopped
1	c. carrots, chopped
2	Serrano chiles
1	Tbsp. cumin powder
1/2	c. cilantro
4	c. tomatoes, peeled, seeded, diced
6	c. chicken stock
3	8" flour tortillas
3/4	lb. cheddar cheese, grated
3	c. avocado, diced
	sour cream to garnish
1	flour tortilla julienned and fried crisp

In a heavy saucepan heat olive oil. Place garlic, onions, celery, carrots and chiles in pan and stir continuously, caramelizing the ingredients, approximately 20 minutes. Add cumin, cilantro and tomatoes and continue to cook slowly for another 20 minutes. Remove and puree the ingredients, placing them back in the saucepan. Add the stock and 3 tortillas and cook until the texture is consistent and the tortillas have broken apart. Season to taste. Serve immediately and garnish with cheese, avocado, sour cream and julienned tortilla.

Serves 6 to 8

Eggplant and Red Pepper Soup

6	red peppers
4	medium eggplants
1/2	c. olive oil
12	cloves garlic, crushed
2	yellow onions, julienned
1/4	c. fresh basil, chopped
8	c. chicken stock
1/4	c. balsamic vinegar
	salt and pepper to taste
	sour cream to garnish

Lightly oil peppers and eggplant. Preheat oven to 450° F., place peppers and eggplant on a cookie sheet and roast approximately 30 minutes. Continually check and rotate the vegetables so they cook and brown evenly on all sides. Remove eggplants, peel and discard skins, saving pulp. Place peppers in a paper bag and let sit approximately 20 minutes to allow skins to pull away from flesh. Remove skins and seeds from peppers and mix together with eggplant. In a stockpot heat oil until smoking. Add garlic and onions and brown. Add peppers, eggplant and basil and mix well. Puree in batches and add back to pot. Add stock and balsamic vinegar to pulp and simmer slowly. Adjust seasoning and serve immediately, garnished with sour cream.

Serves 10

Salmon Chowder

1/4	lb. smoked bacon, diced
4	stalks celery, diced
2	white onions, diced
4	cloves garlic, minced
1	Tbsp. thyme leaves
1/2	c. flour
5	c. fish stock
3	c. cream
1/4	c. sherry
3	c. salmon, diced into 1/2" cubes
	salt and pepper to taste
	Tabasco to taste
	Worcestershire sauce to taste
	butter pats

In a saucepan, over low heat, saute bacon until just crisp. Drain most of the bacon grease. Add celery, onions, garlic and thyme. Stir and cook until translucent. Add flour and continue stirring until mixture becomes paste-like and dry, approximately 5 minutes. Add stock slowly while mixing rapidly to prevent lumps. Cover and simmer for 20 minutes. Add cream and cook covered another 20 minutes, slowly skimming any fat that may rise to the top. Add sherry and salmon and mix well so that the salmon pieces separate from each other to cook uniformly. Season with salt, pepper, Tabasco and Worcestershire sauce. Simmer approximately 10 minutes and serve immediately with a pat of butter in each soup bowl.

Serves 10

Roast Kamanu w/ Macadamia Nut Butter

6	6-oz. kamanu* fillets
	salt and pepper
1/4	c. white wine
1/2	c. fish stock
1	shallot, peeled and chopped
1	Tbsp. lemon juice
1/2	lb. butter, in 1-oz. cubes
1	c. macadamia nuts, toasted and ground to the size of small pebbles
	olive oil
2	stalks lemon grass, broken in 4" shards
12	cloves garlic

Season kamanu with salt and pepper and set aside. Combine white wine, stock, shallot and lemon juice in a non-corrosive pan and heat slowly, reducing by 3/4. Slowly add cubes of butter so that it blends evenly with the stock to form a clear butter sauce. Add 3/4 of the nuts. Set the sauce aside in a warm area so the butter will not congeal and break the sauce. In a heavy skillet large enough to hold the fish, or 2 standard-sized skillets, add olive oil and heat until just smoking. Add lemon grass and garlic and brown slightly. Immediately add fish skin side up and cook approximately 5 minutes on one side or 3/4 of the way, so that you develop a crisp side that retains the juices within the fish. Lightly brown other side. Serve the crisp-side up and cover with half the sauce. Garnish with remaining nuts.

Serves 6

*see glossary

Grilled Mahi Mahi with Black Bean Papaya Salsa

3	c. black beans
6	c. water
1	bay leaf
	salt and pepper to taste
6	6-oz. mahi mahi fillets
1	c. red peppers, diced
1	c. yellow peppers, diced
3/4	c. red onion, diced
3	c. papaya, diced
1	tsp. Serrano chiles, diced
1/4	c. cilantro, chopped
2	Tbsp. walnut oil
1/4	c. rice wine vinegar
	whole cilantro leaves

Soak beans in water for 24 hours, rinse and add 6 cups of water. Simmer slowly with bay leaf, salt and pepper until tender, approximately 45 minutes. Remove, rinse with cool water and set aside. Season fish lightly with salt and pepper. Lay skin-side up on charcoal grill and in intervals of 2 to 3 minutes, depending on the heat, circulate the fish around so that no pattern forms on the fish and it is golden brown and crisp. While the fish is on the grill, mix together peppers, onion, papaya, chiles, cilantro, oil and vinegar; season to taste. Lay 3 to 4 ounces of the mixture on 6 heated plates. Remove the fish from the grill and lay with the golden brown side facing up. Garnish with whole cilantro leaves.

Serves 6

Roast Rack of Lamb with Mint Pesto

12	French-cut lamb chops
3	c. olive oil
2	bunches rosemary
20	cloves garlic
2	bunches mint (approximately 3 cups)
1	c. macadamia nuts
2	c. beef broth or stock
1	c. olive oil

Marinate lamb chops in olive oil, rosemary and garlic for 24 hours. Puree mint, nuts, beef broth and olive oil in blender 5 minutes. Season to taste. Roast lamb chops in oven at 325° F for 25 minutes. Remove and set aside for 3 minutes. Spoon even amounts of pesto on each plate and place lamb chop atop.

Serves 6

Chocolate Mousse

1	lb. semisweet chocolate
4	oz. water
16	oz. heavy cream
5	egg yolks
6	oz. sugar
5	egg whites
18	oz. sugar

Chocolate Mousse (cont.)

Melt chocolate and water together. Whip heavy cream. Whip yolks and 6 oz. sugar. Whip whites and 18 oz. sugar to stiff peaks. Fold yolks into chocolate, then fold in whites, then whipped cream. Chill and serve.

Serves 6

Cafe Latte Custard

1	qt. heavy cream
10 1/2	oz. milk
9	oz. sugar
2 1/2	oz. cold coffee
17	egg yolks

Heat cream, milk, sugar and coffee. Do not boil. Slowly mix and whip mixture into yolks. Strain and pour into ramekins. Bake in waterbath* at 300° F approximately 1 hour.

Serves 8

*see glossary

PREMIUM SELECTION

Grand Cru
VINEYARDS

CARNEROS
CHARDONNAY

Produced and Bottled by Grand Cru Vineyards
Glen Ellen, California USA Alcohol 13.0% by Volume

Lightly toasted aromas of pineapple and vanilla. Nicely balanced fruit, wood and acidity. You would describe this wine as lean, fresh and crisp.

Food pairing: Shellfish, salmon, veal - dishes with rich sauces.

SS COSTARIVIERA

COSTA CRUISES

SS COSTARIVIERA

Costa Cruises, Inc. runs three ships in the Caribbean - the MTS Daphne, the MS CarlaCosta and the SS CostaRiviera. We took the Riviera, the largest of the three, on a seven-day cruise from Ft. Lauderdale westbound to Ocho Rios, Grand Cayman, Cozumel and Playa del Carmen/Cancun, returning to Ft. Lauderdale. We had two days at sea.

Costa is an Italian-registered line and the atmosphere exuded by crew, decor and cuisine swings along in exuberant Italian friendliness. The Italian zest for life, ever apparent on the CostaRiviera, is the best thing about the ship, and you'll feel well taken care of, maybe even loved, for the crew is sincere in their friendliness and regard for their passengers.

Midpriced, the Riviera's Cancun trip ranges, according to off season or high season, luxuriousness of staterooms, size and location, from about $1000 to close to $2000. It's a nice-looking ship with its best feature being the common rooms, many of which are designed with alcoves, terraces and intimate areas. On the Riviera Deck is a charming Italian piazza with street lamps, park benches and shops. A decided Italian look to it all, this area is especially pretty.

PORTS OF CALL

* After a day at sea out of Ft. Lauderdale, we landed in Ocho Rios, Jamaica, just around noon and since we had to be back on board by 5:30 p.m., took a guided tour of the famous fern gardens of Carinosa. This area is a preserve of rain forest so dense the sun barely permeates the giant umbrella-like ferns, but a plethora of flowering things are easily spotted because of their brilliant colors - hanging orchids and bromelia, ginger lilies, cannas and water lilies, hibiscus and anthuria. There is also a "seaquarium" of exotic tropical fishes here, a 25,000-square-foot aviary with seventy-five kinds of colorful birds and many ponds and waterfalls. You can dine alongside a forty-foot waterfall, opting for

SS COSTARIVIERA

Smoked Bay Marlin or Seville Chicken Julienne. This is indoor/outdoor dining - covered roof, no walls - a seductive spot.

Other guided tours included rafting on the Martha Brae, a tour of Prospect Plantation and the 600-foot drop of Dunn's River Falls, and, a fourth tour, a ride past Ocho Rios highlights and Dunn's River Falls.

Spots to watch for: Noel Coward's estate, Firefly; Golden Eye, near the village of Orcabessa where James Bond's creator, Ian Fleming made his home; the White River Bridge.

Or you can spend the day browsing the shops of the rambling resort town of Ocho Rios, or lying on the white beaches. Or you can go along to Dunn's River Falls on your own and play in the water - it's cool and it's beautiful; something children might like to do.

* At 9:00 a.m. the next morning we anchored in George Town, Grand Cayman, one of three of an island group called the Caymans belonging to the British West Indies. A continuous tender service takes you to the pier whenever you're ready to go, but the final tender leaves the island at 3:30 p.m., so you may want to get going as early as possible.

This was my favorite stop on this cruise. George Town is clean, neat, orderly, the shops are quality, there is little huckstering and the locals are easy-going and friendly.

Grand Cayman is the wealthiest island in the Caribbean, no doubt because its laws are conducive to privacy (secrecy, if you wish) in banking. Five-hundred banks headquarter here, making this island the largest offshore banking center in the Western Hemisphere and a tropical cousin of the famous Swiss banking system.

The history here is lively - these islands were once the haven for the infamous Blackbeard and the piratical Sir Henry Morgan. Sunken treasure, buried treasure - all the legends persist on the island, and its clear, deep waters are considered the best diving in the world. I'm not sure, however, if it's for the clarity or for the possible treasure lying in the deep that lures so many water babies here.

Tours include a general "explorer" tour, an island tour, a submarine tour or a snorkel cruise. Or you can just walk around George Town, spend some time on Seven-Mile Beach (the whitest, prettiest beach we'd ever seen) or hire a cab to take you to the Cayman Turtle Farm, Hell Post Office, Bodden Town and Pedro's Castle, a former pirate haunt from the 1700s.

* At noon on Wednesday we anchored at San Miguel on the island of Cozumel, Mexico. Again, all-aboard, weigh-anchor call is at 5:30 p.m., so time is short. Guided tours include a land tour, a cruise around the island, a snorkeling tour or a tour of the carefully restored Mayan site of Chichen Itza, by plane.

Or... once again, you can relax in the town, relax on the beaches (some of the least crowded in the Caribbean) or take a taxi tour. Points to look for: Punta Molas - ruins in a swamp; the ruins of San Gervasio and Santa Rita, interior of the island; El Cedral or Tumba de Caracol, Buenavista, Punta Morena or Santa Pilar, more ruins; the Celarain Lighthouse, with a spectacular view. Mexican history goes back thirty centuries and in these many ruins you can explore a bit of that past grandeur. The Mayans devised a calendar more accurate than the one we use; their doctors were as advanced as ours are today, practicing brain surgery many centuries ago; their buildings were intricate, architecturally sound and aesthetically lovely. They did, however, practice the sacrifice of maidens.

The western side of the island is calm, tropical, with sheltered coves and great snorkeling; the eastern side is beautiful also, but in a rugged and turbulent way. This side is more for looking at, the western for lying about on.

* We steamed into Playa del Carmen, an island twelve miles off the coast of Mexico, at 7:00 a.m. and had all day to explore. Two excellent Mayan ruins tours depart at 8:00 a.m., one to Chichen Itza and the other to Tulum Xelha. Tulum, also well-restored, offers a really unprecedented view of a highly evolved culture whose people mysteriously disappeared around 900 AD. Theory abounds, from famine to extra-terrestrial kidnapping, but archaeologists have yet to solve the puzzles of this brilliant and sophisticated Mayan civilization that disappeared and left behind its accomplishments.

If you missed the Cancun highlight tour of the previous day, you can take one today, from Playa del Carmen. You can also rent a taxi for the entire day at the dock and the driver will stop where ever you wish.

SHIPBOARD

Costa doesn't jam its days with activities, but there is plenty to do if you prefer not to go ashore. Beginning with a two-mile walk around the ship at around 7:00 a.m. to get your heart pumping, you can spend the day fully active. The "sunrise celebration," coffee and pastries in La Dolce Vita, is nice, as is the regular main dining room seating, or, if you're really self indulgent, a continental breakfast in bed (this was great once or twice, but the days are so lovely you hate to be indoors).

On the Riviera you can bike, row or join a fitness class. You can build your triceps or your chest or powerwalk with weights or join the Dance-to-Health group. You can practice your golf on the Amalfi Deck, skeet-shoot, play basketball or learn to disco.

SS COSTARIVIERA

Play bingo, bridge, horse racing, super quiz series or practice lip-syncing so you can perform along with your favorite tune.

Demonstrations will vary according to cruise, but, for example, on ours in late January, we had a mixology demonstration, a gourmet cooking demo, Italian wine tasting, a fashion show, a great perfume seminar, hair and beauty care instructions, a financial lecture.

Ping-Pong and shuffleboard tourneys attract a lot of attention, but you can laze it up if you want to. Lively - and good - music by the pool is a definite charmer - calypso and reggae are most popular, I suppose because you're in the tropics.

Catholic Mass is said daily and an ecumenical service is held on Sunday. Movies are current and the casino is plush, but the library was rather skimpy.

The shops are good. Duty-free goods from five small stores might really entice you - you can take back into the States $400 worth of merchandise. Famous perfumes are about thirty percent less than at home, Italian leather goods are inexpensive and of course you can save quite a bit on liquor and cigarettes, although you can't consume them until you debark the ship in Florida.

Massage is available - what a delight this is - and sauna and hot tubs. I had a body wrap one afternoon after a long day of sightseeing, and it made a new woman out of me - I could have danced all night.

Speaking of which, the dancing is nightly and it's great fun.

OTHER CRUISES

In the Caribbean, Costa also cruises for seven days from Ft. Lauderdale eastbound to St. Thomas, St. Croix and Nassau and back to Ft. Lauderdale. This is on the CostaRiviera.

Aboard the MS CarlaCosta, the seven-day southern Caribbean cruise takes you from San Juan to Curacao, Caracas, Grenada, Martinique and St. Thomas.

The MTS Daphne offers a seven-day southern Caribbean resort cruise from San Juan to St. Maarten, Martinique, Barbados, St. Lucia, Antigua and St. Thomas.

The Daphne also takes a trip through the Panama Canal. This is a sixteen-day cruise that leaves San Juan, stops in St. Thomas, Caracas, Cartagena, goes through the canal, then stops at Caldera, Acapulco, Mazatlan and finally, drops you off in Los Angeles. The eastbound cruise is the same in reverse.

The Daphne is also recruited for the Alaska and Inside Passage cruise, a seven-day trip that begins in Vancouver and takes you through the Inside Passage, stops at Ketchikan, Endicott Arm, Juneau, Skagway, Davidson and Rainbow Glaciers, Wrangell and back to Vancouver.

In the Mediterranean, the Danae (an identical twin to the Daphne) gets in on the act also, taking passengers on eleven-day cruises. Venice to Venice offers stops at Katakolon, Greece; Istanbul and Kusadasi, Turkey; Rhodes, Santorini, Mykonos, Athens and Dubrovnik, Yugoslavia.

The ten-day Egypt/Israel itinerary aboard the ts EugenioCosta begins in Genoa, Italy, and stops in Naples, Catania/Taormina,

SS COSTARIVIERA

Alexandria and Port Said in Egypt, Ashdod in Israel, Limassol on Cypress, Rhodes and Kithera in Greece and back to Genoa.

The seven-day Spain/Canary Islands on the ts EnricoCosta voyage begins in Genoa, proceeds to Barcelona, Spain, then to Casablanca in Morocco, on to Tenerife in the Canary Islands, to Funchal, Madiera; stops in Malaga, Spain and returns you to Genoa.

CLOTHING AND WEATHER

An average eighty-two degrees will keep you comfortable, but bring a sweater or jacket and an umbrella. For touring, don't forget your most comfortable walking shoes. Aboard ship, you can wear sandals and swim suits or shorts, but ashore you'll feel better in slacks or a skirt. Bring a couple of fancy things - the Captain's cocktail party is worthy of dressing up, as is the welcome dinner. Dressing to the nines for dinner is not mandatory, but it certainly is fun - a very shipboard-y thing to look forward to.

BOOKING YOUR CRUISE

Costa Cruises, Inc.
World Trade Center
80 S. W. Eighth St.
Miami, FL 33130
Telephone 305-358-7325
Reservations 800-462-6782
or call your travel agent.

ENTERTAINMENT

Aside from the dancing and the wonderful music all the time, almost everywhere, evenings offer Show Time in the La Scala Showroom. One night it was a welcoming review, the next an Italian festival of song and dance, a country and western revue, a Broadway tribute (something many cruise ships do because it is so popular), a '50s/'60s party and a grand finale of a bacchanal and toga party. Maybe because of their heritage, the Italians aboard the CostaRiviera knew how to throw a proper bacchanal. The crew handed out sheets on the afternoon of the party with the admonition, "no sheets, no eats."

Because of that, 99.9% of the passengers showed up in sheets; we had underwear in sheets, slacks in sheets, T-shirts in sheets, the greatest array of sheet costumes I had ever seen. Even a Lawrence of Arabia style sheet draping with a towel headdress bound with a headband. He could have ridden straight out of Scheherazade.

The cabaret room offers good vocalists and small bands and an occasional stand-up comedian. The bars and lounges have music - the RendezVous Bar and the Grand Prix Bar on the Riviera Deck, the Lido Bar on the Lido Deck aft.

All in all, it's a lively and happy ship.

FOOD

The food is always beautifully presented, particularly at the midnight buffets. There is lots of sculpturing of ice and butter and fruits and sandwiches - really, it's amazing what a creative Italian chef can dream up to do with a piece of bread.

The fruits are fresh and succulent - no bruised or tired or mushy anything.

Going backward from the midnight buffet, where by the way, you can get just about anything from caviar to lox and bagels to a plain roll with butter, the evening's dining offers plenty of selections.

A typical menu would list, from appetizer through dessert: Italian prosciutto and chilled honeydew, artichokes vinaigrette, white celery hearts and cherry peppers, Minestrone alla Ligure (thick vegetable soup with pasta), Cohchigliette alla Pugliese (pasta shells with broccoli in white sauce topped with Parmesan cheese even as I write this I want this once again - excellent); followed by entrees such as Fillet of Flounder in Butter Almond Sauce, Broiled Spring Chicken, Pot Roast of Beef with Mushrooms, Oven-Baked Leg of Veal Boulangere; and desserts from Lemon Meringue Pie to Almond Tartlets, fresh fruit and, always, an assortment of distinctive and delicious Italian cheeses.

Each evening is a theme evening, which involves not only the entertainment but the food. On Italian night, for example, you'll bless the Italians for what they've done for this world: Melanzane Sottolio (grilled eggplant in garlic and oregano), Manicotti di Ricotta Golfo dei Poeti (fresh stuffed pasta in creamy basil sauce), Saltimbocca alla Romana (veal piccata with bondiola and sage), Tartufo alla Amaretto (chocolate amaretto truffle).

Lunch can be taken in the dining room via the menu, good things like Chickpea Soup, club sandwich, omelettes, always a pasta dish, Beef Stroganoff, halibut. Or you can go the Pizzeria, which we did often. Costa offers four pizzas of their own, creations out of this world, or you can decide your own from a list of ingredients that's about a block long.

Breakfast, as I mentioned earlier, comes in a variety of guises, from continental in bed to the Lido buffet or sit-down in the dining room.

Afternoon tea is a nice tradition - good pastries, tasty little sandwiches. And happy hour is fun just for drinks and nibbles. Each day, the bars serve a different special, but the Costa Special is a humdinger. (At $5.50 it should be! Although, to be fair, you do get to keep the fifteen-ounce glass.) It contains three kinds of rum, orange, lemon, pineapple juices, melon liqueur and grenadine. One a day will do you.

You'll never starve aboard a cruise ship, especially a Costa. The reason they have to have so many exercise classes aboard this ship, as I'm sure you've figured out after reading this food section, is because there is so much food and it's around almost constantly. You have to be a stronger person than I to resist all that they have to tempt you with.

RECIPES

Risotto ai Funghi (Risotto with Mushrooms)

1/2	medium onion, chopped
3	oz. butter
2	Tbsp. olive oil
3	oz. dried porcini mushrooms, minced, soaked for 15 minutes in lukewarm water
1/2	pt. white wine
16	oz. rice, preferably arborio or other short grain
5	pts. beef broth, heated
3	oz. Parmesan cheese, grated

In a large casserole, brown the onion with half the butter and the olive oil over low heat until onion is softened. Add the drained, minced mushrooms and stir; add the wine and let reduce slightly. Add the rice and mix well. Let simmer a few minutes then add 2 ladles of hot beef broth and stir until broth is absorbed and mixture is dry. Continue adding hot broth and stirring the rice mixture until all broth is absorbed and rice is dry, about 20 minutes. Add remaining butter and the Parmesan. Let the risotto sit for 2 or 3 minutes before serving.

Gamberi alla Marinara (Shrimp Marinara Style)

1	medium onion, chopped
6	oz. olive oil
3	cloves garlic, minced
2	Tbsp. fresh parsley, chopped
4	medium tomatoes, peeled and cubed
	salt and fresly ground pepper to taste
2	lbs. large raw shrimp, shelled and deveined
4	oz. dry white wine.

Brown the onion in 5 ounces olive oil and let simmer a few minutes. Add the garlic, parsley, tomatoes and salt and pepper. Let this cook for about 15 minutes. Meanwhile, in a separate pan, saute the shrimp in the reserved olive oil. Add the wine and cook for 4 to 5 minutes. Add the tomato-onion mixture to the shrimp, mix gently and serve immediately.

Serves 4 to 6

Gnocchi de Patate alla Ligure (Potato Dumplings Ligurian Style)

For the gnocchi:

20	oz. Idaho potatoes
7	oz. flour
2	eggs
2	Tbsp. Parmesan cheese, grated
	salt and pepper to taste

Gnocchi de Patate alla Liqure (Cont.)

Wash and boil the potatoes until tender when pierced. Peel them while still hot and rub them through a sieve or use a potato ricer or fork. Pour the flour on a counter or work surface and make a well in the center. Put potatoes in center of well and incorporate into flour. Add eggs and Parmesan the same way. Season with salt and pepper. Knead the dough for about 5 minutes and divide it into 4 or 5 equal portions. Using the palm of your hand, roll the dough out on a floured surface into ropes about 1" in diameter. Cut these into 1" pieces then roll them across a cheese grater gently, making an indentation with your thumb as you roll. When you're ready to cook them, boil the gnocchi in salted water until they float to the top. Remove with a slotted spoon and serve imediately.

For the sauce:

2	cloves garlic, minced
4	bunches fresh basil, washed and trimmed
1	Tbsp. pine nuts
	salt to taste
3	Tbsp. Parmesan cheese, grated
3	Tbsp. Romano cheese, grated
1	pt. olive oil

Using a food processor or blender, combine the garlic, basil, pine nuts and salt. Add the cheeses a little at a time until well incorporated. Blend in the oil until you've obtained a smooth texture. To serve, dilute the pesto with a little of the hot water from boiling the gnocchi and pour over the prepared gnocchi.

Serves 4 to 6

SS COSTARIVIERA

Agnolotti con Gamberi e Zucchini (Ravioli with Shrimp and Zucchini)

4	oz. olive oil
1	medium onion, chopped
2	cloves garlic, minced
1	lb. Italian zucchini, cubed
1	lb. raw shrimp, shelled and deveined
1	pinch fresh marjoram leaves
	salt and pepper to taste
5	oz. ricotta cheese
2	eggs, beaten
1	lb. flour
4	eggs, beaten
4	oz. butter
1 1/2	pts. heavy cream

Heat the olive oil and saute the onion, garlic, zucchini, shrimp, marjoram and salt and pepper. Cook over a low flame until zucchini is tender. Let cool then blend in a food processor or blender until completely mixed. Pour out and add the ricotta and the 2 beaten eggs and mix thoroughly. Set aside. To make the pasta, pour the flour onto a counter or work surface and form a well in the center. Add the 4 eggs to the well and mix into a dough. Season to taste with salt and pepper. Knead the dough until smooth and elastic. Using a rolling pin, roll out 2 sheets of dough as thin as you can. On 1 sheet, put 1/2 of the zucchini/shrimp mixture in spoonfuls equal distances from each other. Cover with the other sheet of pasta and cut out the ravioli with a ravioli cutter or stamp. Cook in boiling salted water for about 10 minutes or until al dente. While they are cooking prepare the sauce. Melt the butter in a large pan and add the cream and the reserved

Agnolotti con Gamberi e Zucchini (Cont.)

zucchini/shrimp mixture. Stir until creamy and heated through. Served over the drained ravioli.

Serves 4 to 6

Tagliatelle Verdi al Salmone (Green Tagliatelle with Smoked Salmon)

5	oz. butter
10	oz. smoked salmon strips
2	pts. heavy cream
16	oz. white flour
3	eggs
2	oz. olive oil
3	oz. water
8	oz. spinach, pureed
	salt and pepper to taste

In a pan over a low flame, melt the butter and add the sliced smoked salmon. Add the cream and let cook until reduced slightly. Meanwhile, make the pasta. Place the flour in a mound on the table or work surface. Form a well in the center and add eggs, oil, water and spinach puree. Mix together until well blended. Form into a ball and knead until smooth and elastic. If dough is too soft and sticky add more flour; if too dry add more water. Roll the dough out as thin as you can. Let dry for a few minutes, then cut into 1/2" strips. Cook the pasta in boiling water, with a little oil in it, for just a few minutes. Drain and serve with the hot salmon cream sauce. Season to taste with salt and pepper.

Serves 4 to 6

SS COSTARIVIERA

Legumi Ripieni alla Italiana (Stuffed Vegetables Italian Style)

3	medium Italian zucchini
12	slices white bread, soaked in milk
2	eggs, beaten
1/2	pt. olive oil
1	Tbsp. oregano
2	oz. dried porcini mushrooms, softened in warm water and minced
	salt and pepper to taste
2	Tbsp. Parmesan cheese, grated
3	medium onions, cut in half, insides scooped out
3	medium red bell peppers, cut in half
3	large tomatoes, cut in half and scooped out
	melted butter

Cut the zucchini in half lengthwise; with a spoon, scoop out centers. Remove the bread from the milk and squeeze until nearly dry; mix this with the zucchini pulp, eggs, olive oil, oregano, porcini and salt and pepper. Add 1 tablespoon of Parmesan and mix well. Fill the zucchini shells and the onions, red bell peppers and tomatoes with this mixture and place in a greased baking dish. Sprinkle with the remaining Parmesan and a little butter. Bake for 20 minutes at 365° F.

Serves 4 to 6

Scallopine di Vitello al Limone (Veal Scallopine with Lemon)

12	2-oz. veal scallops
1	Tbsp. flour
4	oz. butter
	juice of 1 lemon
1	Tbsp. fresh parsley, chopped
	salt and pepper to taste
2	lemons, sliced

Pound the veal scallops flat, and flour on both sides. Saute in 3 1/2 ounces butter until browned on both sides; remove from heat and keep warm. Deglaze the pan with the lemon juice, add the remaining butter and parsley and season to taste. Cook until sauce thickens slightly but doesn't look creamy. Pour over the veal, garnish with the lemon slices and serve immediately.

Serves 4

FREEMARK ABBEY

VINTAGED
NAPA VALLEY

CHARDONNAY

PRODUCED AND BOTTLED BY
FREEMARK ABBEY WINERY, ST. HELENA, CALIFORNIA, U.S.A.
Alcohol 13.0% by volume

Bold, dramatic, full-bodied wine! Excellent bottle bouquet. Intense fruit flavors.

Delicious with seafood, salads, poultry and pastas.

CARIBBEAN PRINCE

AMERICAN CANADIAN CARIBBEAN LINES, INC.

The Caribbean Prince, a homey, comfortable ship, shuns the bigger-is-better concept. American Canadian Caribbean Line, Inc. bills themselves as "the small ship cruise line." The Caribbean Prince boards up to eighty passengers only, and cruises nonchalantly through the Lesser Antilles and the Windward Islands, weighing anchor right on the beach of little-known and uninhabited paradises.

This is an informal cruise. For the captain's cocktail party, we didn't have to fluff out the brand new fancy dress and don the heels and hose; we combed our hair and put on shoes. It was lovely. I could cruise this way the rest of my life if they'd let me. The brochures said it would be very much like traveling on a private yacht, and they were not far from wrong. It was friendly - within three days we knew everyone on board; it was relaxing - we spent most of our time swimming, sunning on a beach or snorkeling among the coral reefs; it was inexpensive - we did very little port-hopping so there was no urge to shop, and all excursions were part of the price of the cruise except for two city tours and one taxi cab ride.

PORTS OF CALL

We flew on a Friday from Miami to Antigua, where the ship departs, and were met by the crew after a short taxi ride which is included in the price of the cruise. Falmouth Harbor is clean, there is no smog, it is the kind of place I envision Americans wanting to retire to. Antigua is known as a stop-off point for yachters, and you see the biggest and the most luxurious here, from every port in the world. English Harbour is a popular attraction on this island as it is home to Nelson's Dockyard, named after Admiral Horatio Nelson and built in 1725. The main buildings here are the Admiral's House, which is now a museum, the Naval Officer's Quarters and you will also find the Copper and Lumber Store, refurbished in 1984 to a hotel with fourteen suites. Each suite is named after one of the ships that fought at Trafalgar and is furnished with antiques and period pieces.

Antigua is a limestone and coral island in the island group known as the Lesser Antilles. St. John's is the capital city. Most restaurants are informal and inexpensive in Antigua and the food is spicy.

On Saturday we slid out of Falmouth Harbor at 10:30 a.m., and by one o'clock were making a bow landing at Deep Bay. Here we swam for two hours, admiring the coral, the beach, the sun, the pure pleasure of it all.

By 3:00 p.m. we were back on the boat and on our way to Great Bird Island. The next morning - by 9:00 a.m.! - we were jumping off the back of the boat to snorkel in the pristine waters off Great Bird.

We left there at noon and in a couple of hours arrived at the essence of the Caribbean - Darkwood Beach - a crescent beach of white sand with palm trees in perfect order on the perimeter as if someone had planted them so we could say, "Ah, how perfect." A flat reef with no jagged edges made for great snorkeling, and the millions of brilliantly beautiful fish seemed almost to be performing for us as we watched them in their intricate dances. This is what people envision when they think of getting away from it all.

We spent the night anchored at Darkwood Beach and left the next morning at 3:00 a.m., heading for Guadaloupe, and if you were up, you could spot the Southern Cross constellation low in the sky. What is called the "crossing," the trip from Antigua to Guadaloupe, is rough, but the captain told us this one was the smoothest he'd ever made.

* The island of Guadaloupe is actually two small landmasses bisected by the slim Riviere-Salee, a narrow channel with a drawbridge that connects the island of Grande-Terre to the east and the island of Basse-Terre to the west. At the town of Basse-Terre, we went ashore to visit. This is the administrative capital of Guadaloupe and claims a seventeenth century cathedral, French provincial ambience, fine-goods shops and fresh fish and produce markets. At Parc Naturel you will find a waterfall and rain forests. Above it lies the 4,813-foot volcano, La Soufriere. Beaches are plentiful and some are topless. Local products include rum, spices, handicrafts and coffee beans. Restaurants feature French, Asian, African and Hindu cuisine. Columbus landed on this island in 1493, on his second Atlantic crossing.

* Next stop, the Saints Islands (Iles des Saintes), where we anchored overnight. This cluster of eight islands is considered among the most lovely in the entire Caribbean. Inhabitants are fishermen, not plantation workers, and the life is slow and easy. Prince Rupert Bay on the island of Dominica (dom in EE ka) was our next stop. Dominica is known as the nature island of the Caribbean, truly lush - wild orchids, wild birds, barely touched by civilization, a rain forest clime. It is also quite poor, quite undeveloped. But it is here that we found the starfish on the beach. We toured to Trafalgar Falls - spectacular. The Botanical Gardens are lovely, but you look down on impoverishment, lean-to huts as houses. Dominica's native Carib Indians held the fort, so to speak, as other Caribs on other islands did not, and neither the French nor the British were willing to claim the island because of the Carib resistance. There is now a Carib reservation on the island where the original landowners, the Caribs, practice their age-old craft of basket-making.

* We left Dominica sometime in the wee hours of the morning and arrived at Martinique, Fort de France, at 9:30 in the morning. Martinique is thoroughly French and engagingly European and cosmopolitan. (Empress Josephine was born here.)

This is the "island of flowers," appropriately, for orchids grow wild, bougainvillaea is profuse and lilies abound. The island of Martinique also sprouts mangrove, coconut palm, tree fern, banana, tree bamboo and mahogany.

There are bars and restaurants, casinos and supper clubs, and 4,000 tourist rooms. The French-Creole inhabitants make this a happenin' place, and with four or five major cruise-line ships in port, Fort de France jumps with action for the folks off the boats.

French and Creole are spoken on Martinique, and some English. The currency is the franc and the prices for goods are steep. Fort de France Bay is crowded with yachts, a very pretty sight. The Parisian opera company visits Martinique each February, and the Grand Ballet de la Martinique performs throughout the year.

* We left Martinique early and stopped off at Castries on St. Lucia (LOO-sha) to shop. St. Lucia is famous for its batik designs and they are indeed beautiful. We couldn't resist buying shirts at Bagshaws and parading around town in them. Just like tourists.

St. Lucia, a volcanic island, was the most fought-over island in the Caribbean when the French and the British were battling one another in several parts of the world in the eighteenth century. English, French and Creole are spoken, but there is a subtle French predominance in the names of things and in the food. The capital city of St. Lucia is Castries and its port is a flooded crater of an extinct volcano. The food market is a sight to behold. Some scenes from the movie "Dr. Doolittle" were filmed on St. Lucia.

In the afternoon we cruised to the southern end of St. Lucia to swim and snorkel at Soufriere Beach. This was the best snorkeling since we left on Saturday, absolutely beautiful waters, coral reefs and beach. On the west coast you will find fishing villages, a drive-in volcano, Diamond Falls and mineral baths.

We then moved down the coast a ways and made a bow landing at the Piton, twin volcanic peaks that rise out of the Caribbean Sea. There an elephant greeted us on the beach. He was offering rides and we had great fun with the gentle giant. "Bupa" the Elephant was one of the animal stars left over from the "Dr. Doolittle" movie.

* Friday morning soon after breakfast we arrived in Kingston on the island of St. Vincent. Until very recently this island was relatively unknown to tourists. It is only eighteen miles long and eleven miles wide, and it is one of the most picturesque of the Windward islands.

In the capital, charming with a mixture of French and English architecture, English is spoken. St. Mary's Cathedral is considered an architectural oddity because it combines so many styles - Roman arches, Gothic spires and a maze of balconies, turrets, battlements and courtyards. The oldest botanical gardens in the Western Hemisphere, founded in 1765, are in Kingston, and within the gates grows a breadfruit tree planted by Captain Bligh on his return trip from the South Pacific on the *Bounty*.

* In the afternoon we ventured on to the island of Bequia, second in the string of the Grenadines stretching from St. Vincent to Grenada. This area offers some of the best sailing in the Caribbean. Quaint fishing villages dot the coasts and inland the planters grow arrowroot and coconut. After Bequia come Mustique (privately owned, visited by the likes of Mick Jagger and Princess Margaret), Cannouan, Petit St. Vincent, Mayreau, Palm Island and Union Island. Saturday, Sunday and Monday we wound our way through these gems of the Caribbean, stopping to swim or snorkel. This was so relaxing.

* After spending the night anchored off the tiny and lovely island of Carriacou, at noon on Monday we arrived in St. George's on Grenada, the southernmost island in the Antilles. I know I'm

repeating myself, but this island, too, is one of the most beautiful in the West Indies. And the aromas - ah, I will never forget them. Intoxicating, sensuous, the smells come from the mace, cloves, vanilla, bay leaf, coffee, cinnamon, cocoa, ginger and, the most important crop, nutmeg. Grenada is the "spice island" of history and myth.

St. George's historical points of interest include the National Museum, Fort Matthew, Fort Frederick and the Dougaldston Estate where you can tour a spice factory and see how spices are prepared and sorted.

Grenada's history is interesting. Founded by Columbus in 1498, it changed hands several times between the feuding British and French until it finally wound up as a British possession. It was a prosperous island and served as the headquarters of British West India until 1958. In 1979, after a brief revolution, the Grenadians got rid of their parliament and instituted a revolutionary government, which in 1983 fell to a coup. That was when the U.S. entered the scene to make sure order was kept. Everything's peaceful now, and likely to remain so, for they now have an elected representative government.

And so, the end of our idyllic voyage. Twelve days is a nice long trip, but the beauty and serenity of this particular cruise made us long for more of the same. Next year....

SHIPBOARD

The Caribbean Prince has three decks and three cabin classifications: Sun Deck rooms are 9' by 10' with two lower berths, picture windows; Main Deck rooms are 7' by 11' with two lower berths and picture windows; Lower Deck staterooms are 7' by 10' and are a good deal moneywise.

The atmosphere aboard ship is casual and friendly. Captain Roy and First Mate Dixie, the married duo that ran our trip so effortlessly, were easy to be with and kept their crew happy. Curtains on the windows of the common rooms added the homey touch and the main gathering spot, the lounge, was like someone's living room, with a piano, TV, VCR, comfy chairs and plenty of up-to-date magazines, games and books.

In the dining room we played an occasional "arranged" game of Trivial Pursuit with the other passengers, or plunged into a hot game of shipboard bingo. This was old fashioned kitchen bingo, where we played for quarters. The big prize for the evening was $12.

One of the interesting features of an American Canadian Caribbean Line cruise is that you bring your own booze. Antigua is the place to stock up, for many of the islands don't have much of a selection. We kept our bottles in the lounge with our names on them and everyone was on the honor system. It was fun, and one of the things that made the trip so intimate, so personal.

Other things the line suggests you bring for yourself: beach towels, binoculars, hair dryers, old tennies for walking on the coral, enough clothes for the duration because there are no washers or dryers aboard. Clothing should be comfortable and casual - and don't forget a couple of bathing suits - for the majority of the trip is spent on the beach, on the deck or in the water. Men should bring a jacket and ladies will need one nice dress, but don't get fancy.

We brought our own snorkeling gear but the boat carries more than enough for everyone, and also lifejackets. They also provide one-or two-man sailboats for qualified sailors if you feel like getting away from your fellow passengers. Many people brought their own fishing gear, which the brochures encourage. The fishing was wonderful, and if you caught something worthwhile, the chef might be persuaded to fry it up for supper.

Take cigarettes and extra film. Both are available at certain points - but not all points.

There is no doctor aboard, but the boat can put into dock almost immediately and seek medical assistance.

This line also discourages children, requiring that if they come they be at least fourteen years old. Dispensations can be made by applying to the general offices in Rhode Island. For retired folks whose kids are long gone and who are unaccustomed to the energy level of youngsters, this is a great idea, and maybe almost a must, for the size of the ship disallows getting away from other people except in one's cabin.

MONEY ETIQUETTE

Everything is paid for in your ticket on this cruise. Of course, if you go shopping, it's your credit card. This cruise line has no policy on tipping. It is left entirely to the discretion of the passengers. Whatever is received from a cruise is divided among the crew. 6% of the cruise fare is suggested.

CLOTHING AND WEATHER

Bring plenty of shirts, shorts, swim wear, tennis shoes that you can wear in the water, a town touring outfit or two and one mildly dressy outfit for the captain's cocktail party. This cruise was very close to a "barefoot cruise." Don't forget to bring a beach towel.

BOOKING YOUR CRUISE

American Canadian Caribbean Line, Inc.
P. O. Box 368
Warren, RI 02885
Telephone 401-247-0955 Rhode Island Only
800-556-7450 for the rest of the USA
or call your travel agent.

ENTERTAINMENT

The passengers and crew meeting one another and developing friendships is what constitutes the entertainment aboard the Caribbean Prince. The fishing, snorkeling, swimming and lazing in the sun are the daytime activities; in the evenings we'd have an occasional bingo game or watch a movie on the VCR, but as a rule we were in bed early and up with the chickens. The Cruise Director plans a program for each night that is loose and informal.

OTHER CRUISES

American Canadian Caribbean Line, Inc. offers other distinctive and relaxing cruises. Their two ships, the Caribbean Prince and the New Shoreham II, fill up quickly, so plan well in advance.

The Belize trip cruises from Belize City to the Guatemalan jungle, rivers and lakes, highlighting snorkeling and tarpon trolling. This is not a well-traveled tourist area, so you'll have beaches to yourself and also be able to see Mayan ruins and get to meet primitive but friendly, English-speaking natives.

The Virgin Islands twelve-day cruises start in St. Thomas, mecca of duty-free shopping. But unlike the big cruises, you then stop at little-known islands and coral reefs for the promised snorkeling, shell-seeking and bird-watching that American Canadian delights in.

The Bahamas cruise also begins in a cosmopolitan city - Nassau - and then takes you off to the paradise islands, cays and bays of untraveled, non-commercial routes.

Besides the Lesser Antilles trip we went on, American Canadian offers "Caribbean Potpourri," which is a similar trip but from Antigua to St. Maarten, and the "St. Maarten Circle," which takes you from Philipsburg through the islands of Marigot, Grand Case, Ilet Tintamarre, St. Barts and back to St. Maarten.

The Erie Canal-Saguenay/Canada trip is unusual, historic and, especially in the fall, spectacular with brilliantly colored autumn leaves. This is a trip inaccesible to large vessels - just the ticket for the New Shoreham II with its shallow draft. You'll cruise Narragansett Bay, the Hudson River and the Erie Canal. Then on through the eastern tip of Lake Ontario to the St. Lawrence Seaway.

The Eastern Seaboard cruise is a fifteen day trip from West Palm Beach, Florida to Warren, Rhode Island along the inland waterways of some of America's most lovely scenery. This route - either way - takes you through canals, rivers, marshes and bays that touch on the very beginnings of this country, its history, commerce and beauty.

The Florida cruise takes you from east to west along the Lake Okeechobee, the beaches, the Everglades, the Shark River, the Marquesas Keys and the Dry Tortugas. This is a twelve-day cruise.

The Belize/Cancun cruise is a Christmastime delight, twelve days in the sun, exploring Mayan ruins or lazing on isolated beaches.

FOOD

All meals are family style and you eat what's served or you can request dietary food, kosher, or if you can't eat meat, for example, you can request fish. But the food is so good, very simple but absolutely wonderful, that you'll probably be like us and eat everything in sight. We had a chef on board who loved to bake, so we had exceptional breakfast sweets, fresh-baked homemade rolls for lunch and dinner and scrumptious desserts.

A typical day's menus would run something like this: breakfast - assorted fruit strudels, hotcakes, sausage links, hot Cream of Wheat. On Sunday we had scrambled eggs, sliced ham and English muffins, or on another day cheese and mushroom omlettes, croissants and hot Maypo cereal; lunch - Beef Barley Soup, BLTs, homemade cookies, and another day's fare was Cream of Spinach Soup, seafood salad, cottage cheese and pasta salad, with butterscotch brownies for dessert. On Tuesday we were served Corn Creole Soup, French Leek and Tomato Pie, Salad Nicoise and chocolate ice cream. One of my favorite lunches was Chili con Carne, fruit salad and Grasshopper Pudding; dinner - Cream of Mushroom Soup, Arroz con Pollo, peas and Spanish rice, homemade whole wheat rolls, Cherries Jubilee. On Wednesday we had Baked Oysters with Guyere, Filet Mignon, Baked Stuffed Shrimp, Potato Stars, Zucchini with Tomato Coulis and French Silk Pie which was probably the all time favorite of all of the passengers.

The second evening of our cruise, the captain held a cocktail party featuring Rum Punch and exquisite hors d'oeuvres - shrimp and chicken wings and smoked salmon.

The menus are not set in stone, either, for if at a port something looks especially good or the catch of the day is particularly appealing, that's what we'll have for dinner. There is a nice spontaneity not only about the food but about the whole cruise. On one island, local fisherman were selling lobster that we were going to buy and have the chef cook for all of the passengers, but we couldn't strike a proper deal.

RECIPES

Banana Nut Bread

1	c. shortening
2 1/8	c. sugar
1	c. beaten eggs
4 1/2	c. bread flour
2	Tbsp. baking powder
1/2	tsp. baking soda
1 1/2	tsp. salt
2 2/3	c. ripe bananas, mashed (6 to 8 bananas)
1 1/2	c. walnuts, chopped

Cream shortening and sugar thoroughly. Add eggs and beat. Sift together flour, baking powder, baking soda and salt. Add 1/3 amount of dry mixture and 1/3 amount of bananas. Mix well. Repeat until all ingredients are added and mixed well. Add nuts last. Bake at 350° F for 45 minutes to 1 hour.

Makes 3 loaves

Basil Vinaigrette

2/5   c. basil or marjoram
3   Tbsp. salt
1 1/2   c. sugar
1/6   c. whole garlic, crushed
13   oz. vegetable oil
13   oz. cider vinegar

Mix all ingredients in a mixer or food processor. Don't whip too long. Pour into a dry jar.

Makes 1 quart

Beef Macaroni Soup

4   oz. butter or margarine
1   lb. ground beef
2   c. green peppers, chopped
1   c. onions, chopped
1   46-oz. can crushed tomatoes
3   qt. beef stock
1/2   Tbsp. garlic, chopped
1   tsp. oregano
1   tsp. black pepper
8   oz. elbow macaroni
2   Tbsp. Romano cheese, grated

In butter, saute ground beef, green peppers and onions until soft. Add tomatoes, beef stock, garlic, oregano and black pepper. Bring to rolling boil. Add elbow macaroni and cook until al dente. Top with grated cheese.

Cream of Nothing Soup

8	oz. butter or margarine
8	oz. flour
1/2	gallon chicken stock, hot
2	carrots, diced
1	large onion, diced
10	stalks celery, diced
1/2	gallon milk, warm
1	c. cheddar cheese, shredded
2	c. chicken meat, diced
1	tsp. white pepper
2	oz. sherry
3	tomatoes (canned), drained and diced
2	Tbsp. parsley, chopped

Melt butter, add flour and stir continuously for 2 to 3 minutes. Add stock and cook until thick. Add carrots, onions and celery. Simmer until tender. Add milk, cheese and rest of ingredients. Simmer until smooth, top with parsley.

Makes 1 gallon

Cream of Mushroom Soup

1 1/2	lbs. large mushrooms, cut in half
2	Tbsp. shallots, chopped
1	qt. heavy cream
5	oz. butter
4	oz. flour
1	qt. chicken stock, heated
1/2	tsp. white pepper
2	Tbsp. Harvey's sherry
2	Tbsp. parsley, chopped

Poach mushrooms and shallots in cream until mushrooms are firm. Melt butter. Add flour and whisk constantly for 2 to 3 minutes. Add hot chicken stock. Cook until thick. Add poached mushrooms, cream and shallot mixture. Add white pepper and sherry. Simmer 5 minutes more. Garnish with fresh parsley.

Serves 8

Herbal Tomato Soup

1	#10 can whole tomatoes
8	stalks celery, diced
1	large onion, diced
4	carrots, diced
2	Tbsp. sugar
4	tsp. basil
8	sprigs fresh parsley, chopped
2	tsp. marjoram
8	bay leaves
1	c. butter
6	c. water
1/2	c. plus 2 Tbsp. chicken base
1	c. cornstarch
4	c. cold milk
12	c. milk, warmed
2	tsp. paprika
2	tsp. white pepper
2	c. sour cream

Place first 4 ingredients in a food processor. Pour into a saucepan and simmer until vegetables are soft. Add next 8 ingredients to vegetable mixture. Blend cornstarch and cold milk together. Add to soup mixture. Cook until slightly thickened, then add warm milk, paprika and white pepper. Cook for 45 minutes over medium flame, stirring occasionally. Watch for scorching. Blend in sour cream with whisk.

Makes 1 1/2 gallons

Chile con Carne

1	lb. ground beef
4	oz. bacon fat
2	green peppers, seeded and chopped
1	bunch celery, diced
2	medium onions, diced
1/2	c. bacon, cooked and chopped
1/2	lb. Italian sausage, cooked and sliced
1/4	lb. pepperoni
1	46 oz. can crushed tomatoes
1	46 oz. can chili sauce
2	Tbsp. sugar
1	Tbsp. fennel seeds
2	tsp. cayenne
3	Tbsp. chili powder
3	tsp. ground cumin
1/2	gallon beef stock
1	46 oz. can kidney beans, drained

Saute ground beef in bacon fat. Add green pepper, celery, onions and cook until almost soft. Add bacon, sausage, pepperoni. Add crushed tomatoes, chile sauce and spices. And beef stock and simmer down until desired flavor is reached, about 30 minutes. Add drained kidney beans. If hotter taste is desired, add diced hot peppers.

Makes 1 gallon

Pat's Caribbean Chicken

4	pieces chicken breasts and legs
1/2	c. flour
1/3	c. vegetable oil
1	tsp. salt
1/4	tsp. pepper
1	lb. plus 4 oz. pineapple chunks
1	c. sugar
2	Tbsp. cornstarch
3/4	c. cider vinegar
1	Tbsp. soy sauce
1/4	tsp. grated ginger
1	tsp. chicken base
1/2	green pepper, julienned
1/2	red pepper, julienned

Wash chicken, pat dry, roll in flour. In large skillet, heat oil, then add chicken pieces one at a time, browning both sides. Place chicken skin-side up in roasting pan. Add salt and pepper. Set aside. Preheat oven to 350° F. Drain pineapple, saving juice. Add enough water to juice to make 1 1/4 cups total. In saucepan, combine sugar, cornstarch, pineapple juice, vinegar, soy sauce, ginger and chicken base. Bring to boil, stirring constantly. Boil 2 minutes. Pour over chicken. Bake uncovered 30 minutes. Add pineapple chunks and red and green peppers. Bake 30 minutes longer or until chicken is tender.

Serves 4

Seafood Newburg

6	oz. butter
1	Tbsp. paprika
5	oz. flour
1	qt. heavy cream or milk, heated
2	Tbsp. Minor's lobster base or fish bouillon
1	qt. water
1	lb. scallops
1	lb. shrimp, peeled
1	lb. snow crab
1	tsp. white pepper
2	Tbsp. Harvey's sherry

Melt butter with paprika, add flour and cook 3 to 4 minutes. Add warm cream or milk and cook until very thick, about 2 minutes. Dilute lobster base or fish bouillon in boiling water. Blanche separately the scallops and then the shrimp in boiling stock until just barely done. Add to cream sauce. Add snow crab and simmer together. Add white pepper and sherry. If too thick add water; if too thin simmer down; if not rich enough add undiluted base. Serve over rice or toast points.

Serves 8

French Leek and Tomato Pie

1	10" pie shell
1	beaten egg
1	jumbo onion, peeled and sliced
3	leeks, cleaned and julienned
1	oz. butter
1	tsp. sugar
1/4	tsp. garlic, chopped
1	46-oz. can whole tomatoes, chopped
6	eggs
4	oz. heavy cream
	salt to taste
1/8	tsp. white pepper
1/8	tsp. nutmeg
1/4	tsp. cayenne pepper
1/2	c. Swiss cheese
1/2	c. cheddar cheese

Brush uncooked pie shell with beaten egg. Bake shell at 400° for 6 minutes. Saute onion and leeks in butter and sugar until transparent. Add garlic and chopped tomatoes and cook 2 minutes more. Mix together the eggs, cream, salt, pepper, nutmeg and cayenne. Place a layer of Swiss and one layer of cheddar into pie shell. Then add leek, onion and tomato mix. Add rest of cheese and top with quiche mix. Bake at 350° F for about 40 minutes or until custard is set.

Serves 6

Veal Piccata

2	4-oz. veal cutlets
1	c. flour
1/4	tsp. each salt and white pepper
2	Tbsp. olive oil
4	Tbsp. beef consomme
1 1/2	Tbsp. lemon juice
3	large mushrooms, sliced
1	oz. butter
2	cloves garlic, chopped
1/2	tsp. parsley, chopped

Pound veal on both sides until thin and flat. Dredge veal in seasoned flour; add olive oil to a hot skillet. When oil is very hot, add floured cutlets. Quickly saute on both sides until brown. Remove veal to warm platter. Drain off grease and add half stock and lemon juice. Bring to a boil and scrape bottom of pan. Add mushrooms, butter and garlic. Boil 1 minute and add veal. Boil until reduced and thick. Garnish with parsley. Serve with crusty French bread.

Serves 2

Grasshopper Pudding

1	small package vanilla pudding, whip-and-chill variety
8	oz. milk
8	oz. marshmallow fluff
1	oz. green creme de menthe
1	oz. white creme de cacao
	whipped cream
	shaved chocolate

Mix vanilla pudding with milk. Add an equal amount of marshmallow topping, then add creme de menthe and creme de cacao. Garnish with whipped cream and shaved chocolate.

Serves 4

Caribbean

French Silk Pie

1 1/4   c. coconut
2   oz. unsweetened chocolate
2   Tbsp. brandy
2   Tbsp. Sanka or instant coffee powder
1   c. sweet butter, softened
1   c. sugar
2   eggs
1/2   c. ground hazelnuts
1/2   c. ground almonds

Line the bottom and sides of an 8" pie plate with coconut and bake in a preheated oven (250° F) for 1 hour, or until golden. Place on rack to cool. In top of double boiler, melt chocolate with brandy and Sanka. In a bowl, cream together butter, sugar and eggs, one at a time, beating well after each egg. Add chocolate mixture and nuts. Put filling in pie shell and chill 3 hours.

Serves 8

Deep Dish Apple Pie

1 3/4   c. flour
1/4   c. sugar
1   tsp. cinnamon
1/2   tsp. salt
1/2   c. plus 2 Tbsp. butter
1/4   c. water or apple cider
8   McIntosh apples
1 3/4   c. sour cream
1   c. sugar
1/3   c. flour

Deep Dish Apple Pie (Cont.)

1	egg
2	tsp. vanilla
1/2	tsp. salt

Preheat oven to 450° F. Combine flour, sugar, cinnamon and salt. Cut in butter. Add water or apple cider and toss with 2 forks. Roll on floured board to about 10" in diameter. Combine filling ingredients and spoon into crust. Bake 10 minutes. Turn oven down to 350° F and bake until filling is slightly puffed and golden brown.

topping

1	c. ground walnuts
1/2	c. flour
1/2	c. brown sugar
1/3	c. granulated sugar
1	Tbsp. cinnamon
1/2	tsp. salt
1/2	c. butter, room temperature

Combine nuts, flour, sugar, cinnamon and salt in a bowl. Blend in butter until crumbly. Spoon over pie and bake 15 minutes longer.

Serves 6 to 8

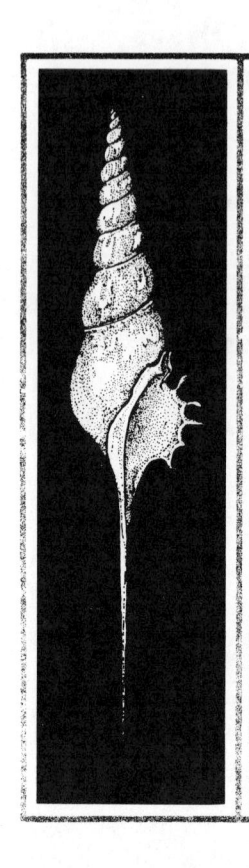

SEA RIDGE

SONOMA COAST
PINOT NOIR

PRODUCED AND BOTTLED BY
SEA RIDGE WINERY • CAZADERO • CALIFORNIA
TABLE WINE • CONTAINS SULFITES

The Sea Ridge "Sonoma Coast" Pinot Noir is a blend of grapes from vineyards in the cool coastal regions of Sonoma Country, California. The wine has a luminescent ruby glow. The aromas combine overtones of cinnamon and cherries with a subtle toasty, earthy character from French oak aging. The flavors combine the snap of lively natural acidity, soft ripe tannins and a depth of fruit to give a wine with substance but not overbearing heaviness.

This Pinot Noir marries perfectly with pork, rich fowl such as duck or turkey, prime beef of leg of lamb. The crisp acidity also makes it an ideal complement to barbequed salmon.

MS CARIBE I

COMMODORE CRUISE LINE

MS CARIBE I

Since Commodore Cruise Line came on the shipping scene in 1966, one of their ships has been known as the "happy ship." We found the nickname apropos for the MS Caribe I, the present "happy ship," because the crew was exceptionally accommodating. They were quick to help us whenever we asked and always sincerely cheery.

The 23,000-ton, 900-plus passenger ship was built in Scotland for trans-Atlantic travel for the wealthy when only the wealthy traveled back and forth between America and the continent. In 1983, the Caribe I was refitted and refurbished for the Caribbean cruise market. The latest in navigational gear, diesel engines and power plant equipment were installed, but the luxuries of the original design remain - the Old World library, the covered promenade, the polished mahogany, teak and other expensive woods used throughout.

Two whirlpools were added, a gymnasium (a necessity for our love affair with keeping in shape) and a large dance floor in the Mermaid Lounge. In 1987 and 1988 all the common rooms were redecorated and the movie room was redesigned as the Mirage, still a movie house by day, but a dazzling lounge by night - two bars, two dance floors, a state-of-the-art sound system. All the staterooms were redone at this time also, so the whole ship is a comfortable combination of late twentieth century chic blended with the aristocratic elegance of half a century ago.

For mid-level prices, the MS Caribe I offers real luxury. And with twenty-three years of Caribbean cruising behind them, Commodore Cruise Line is definitely experienced in the blue waters they regularly ply.

EMBARKATION

Miami is the home port of the Caribe I. Commodore's "Flying Start Air/Sea" program includes free airfare from more than

MS CARIBE I

ninety major U.S. cities. To take advantage of this deal, you have to make arrangements at least forty-five days in advance. Many travelers like to fly into Miami a day early and stay in a hotel before boarding ship. Some airlines permit this, others do not. Also, some airlines allow post-cruise stopovers with a special three-day, two-night rate for Walt Disney World and Epcot Center at nearby hotels. Your travel agent can inquire about these variations on your cruise plan.

PORTS OF CALL

On the "happy ship" eastern Caribbean cruise, you'll stop in Puerta Plata in the Dominican Republic, Old San Juan on San Juan, the island of St. John in the U.S. Virgin Islands and St. Thomas, across the channel from the tiny St. John.

* Puerta Plata, on the Dominican Republic's north coast, means port of silver. This port has a volatile history as a pirate port in the 1500s, a free port in the 1700s and a coffee port in the 1800s. The Dominican Republic itself occupies two-thirds of the island of Hispaniola. The other third belongs to Haiti. Columbus discovered this island, the French and Spanish fought over it for several centuries, it began the fight for its independence in 1844, and since 1961, when the dictator Raphael Trujillo was ousted, it has come a long way as a tourist attraction.

The beaches here, especially Sosua Beach, are superb. The scuba diving and snorkeling are outstanding. It's easy to go ashore and take your own tours, wander the streets of Puerta Plata and find your own beaches, but as you have from only 11:00 a.m. to 4:30 p.m., one of the following shore excursions might allow you to see more than you would on your own.

The town tours include an explanation of historical sites (the oldest fort in the Western Hemisphere, for example), a buffet lunch at the internationally famous resort of Corfresi with a folkloric show, then shopping. Although this covers all the bases, some folks who took this tour said it did not offer as much as they'd assumed it would.

A slight variation offers a bus tour to the Brugal Rum Factory and the Amber museum. The Dominican Republic is one of the few places in the world where amber is found. You'll have an opportunity to purchase black coral, local pottery, woodwork and Haitian art.

The "Horseback Riding Tour," however, brought raves. The Dominican countryside is tropical island at its best, and you'll ride through the mountains, stopping at vista points to ooh and ah about the ocean down below. The horses are sure-footed. This is a leisurely and unusual way to see the Caribbean.

Sosua Beach is fifteen miles outside Puerta Plata, and the tour bus will drop you off there for snorkeling, swimming, scuba diving, wind surfing, water skiing or the most popular: lazing in the sun. Pop, beer, snorkeling gear, instructions and the trip to and from the boat are included in the price of this tour. Beautiful beach.

A cable car ride to the top of the mountains is an inexpensive but inspiring trip. Not only the beauty of the lush forests, but the views of the coastline, the chance to roam through the botanical gardens and the maze of nature trails and the spectacular sixty-foot figure of Christ, reminiscent of the famous statue outside of Rio de Janeiro, make this an easy trip. And you can shop for souvenirs at the top also.

The least expensive tour is the "Mink Factory" jaunt. Unless, of course, you decide to buy a mink coat, even though the prices are half what they are in the States. Skins from Scandinavia and North America are shipped to the Dominican Republic for drying, curing and assembling because the labor is cheaper in the

Caribbean. You'll see the entire process a skin goes through before it's ready to grace the shoulders of the lovely models who parade for you in the showroom. This is an interesting tour, but obviously not the place for you if you disbelieve in the raising of animals for their fur.

* Puerto Rico has been a United States self-governing commonwealth since 1951. Discovered in 1493 by Columbus, Puerto Rico was governed by Ponce de Leon, played a major role as the gateway to Spain's Latin American empire and is today the most prosperous country in the Caribbean.

The first tour to leave the ship is the "Rain Forest Tour," which lasts about four and a half hours. If you're interested in shopping in San Juan, one of the most famous shopping islands in the Caribbean, don't buy onto the rain forest trip because you'll have very little time to shop when you're returned to the city. If, however, you're a nature lover, this is the trip for you. More than 240 species of trees grow in El Yunque, the only tropical U.S. National Park. It gets 100 billion gallons of rain every year! For a person from Nevada to hear this sounds like gross exaggeration, but the lush jungle is proof. From the observation tower at the top of the 3,526-foot-high park, you'll see as much of Puerto Rico as is possible from one spot. Truly a fun excursion, with plenty of stops to take photos of waterfalls and breathtaking views.

The "Old and New City Tour" is a great way to see the past and present of a very busy and cosmopolitan city - from the quaint and lovely cobblestoned old town to the ultramodern, high-rise new town. It takes only two hours and drops you off in Old San Juan, about two blocks from the ship, and right in the middle of the shopping district. Earlier that morning, if you're smart, you'll attend the information lecture aboard ship on where to go for the best bargains in Bacardi rum, jewelry, watches, linens, crystal and so forth. This mini-talk will allow you to make the most of your time in the shopping district.

The "Beach and City Tour" offers relaxation on the sand with endless rum punches plus a brief tour of San Juan. If you're no shopper nor sightseer, this tour will take care of your lazy nature while giving you the rudiments of info on this particular port.

The "Bacardi Rum Factory Tour" is very interesting. Puerto Rico is the world's largest producer of rum and Bacardi is the biggest rum plant in the world. The quality is supervised by the government, and they offer you samples as you tour the plant. The bus drops you off in Old San Juan to shop, two blocks from the Caribe I.

The evening flamenco show in San Juan is worth the trip. Since the Caribe doesn't sail until 1:00 a.m., fit this one in. Those dancers do things with their hands and feet, they move them so fast, that you'll be spellbound. This show is held at the El San Juan Hotel, which is one of the most beautiful, prestigious and well-known hotel/casinos in the entire world. Just seeing the place is a delight, from the gardens to the elegant parlors and lounges. Quite a place.

Another evening excursion offers a Las Vegas-style review at the Sands Hotel. Casino gambling, too.

* St. John at 7:00 a.m. is breathtaking. This twenty-one-square-mile island supports one of the Rockefeller resorts, Caneel Bay. Laurence Rockefeller, who finished the resort in 1956, also deeded 5,000 acres of St. John island to the U.S. government for what is now the Virgin Islands National Park.

We took the catamaran tour to Honeymoon Beach. This was the most enjoyable tour we took the entire trip. The scenery was lovely, but the snorkeling off the back of the cat was perfect. There are, believe it or not, tamed sting rays that hang around Honeymoon Beach. We also saw what was pointed out to us as a "tame" barracuda, which I avoided no matter what they said. And although we searched the beach grasses for the sea turtle, said to hang around to greet tourists, we never found him. Towels, snorkeling gear and refreshments are a part of this tour. Take money with you, if for no other reason than to tip your guide -- he's knowledgeable and fun.

There is also a private yacht tour to Honeymoon Beach.

The trip to Trunk Bay for snorkeling is also a big success, for Trunk Bay is touted by National Geographic as one of the top ten beaches in the world. An underwater snorkeling trail is a pleasure, and offers you the best look at the rainbow of fish and coral of the Off Shore Reef.

The "Island Beach Tour" takes you on a guided, narrated trip through the Virgin Islands National Park, a natural park with only indigenous flora and fauna.

The helicopter fly-over of St. John and St. Thomas was just a kick. The pilot swooped us down into the jungly canyons and up the mountain tops. It was like riding a roller coaster or a ferris wheel. I loved it and the view from up there is beyond describing - it's a seeing-is-believing experience. This was expensive but well worth the money. I can't say enough good things about this excursion.

You can see St. Thomas if you opt for the "Coral World and City Island Tour", which points out the main touristy interests in St. Thomas, like Bluebeard's Castle, Skyline Drive or Drake's Seat. Then you go on to Coral World, an underwater marine observatory (one of only three in the world), that is three stories deep and reveals to you what you might have missed had you been scuba diving on your own.

The "Looking Glass Submarine" is another underwater trip that allows you to remain dry and see the beauty of St. Thomas's harbor town, Charlotte Amalie, from the fish-eye vantage point.

A shopping tour of St. Thomas is a must for some people - the best shops are discussed by the ship's cruise director on the previous day, a really good idea so you can hit the high spots. St. Thomas is known for its inexpensive liquors, linens, jewelry and leather goods. After shopping, you're whisked to a sailing yacht for a trip to Buck Island, where you can snorkel over a WWI shipwreck or lie on the beach and drink rum punches.

SHIPBOARD

On the port-of-call days, shipboard life went on, but few folks remained aboard. You could eat lunch there, of course, and most of us had our breakfast on board, but except for access to the library, the bars and so forth, there really wasn't much action. If you wanted privacy and a chance to wander the ship alone, this would have been a good opportunity.

The daily fitness class, at 9:00 a.m., was early enough on most days to take advantage of it before joining a shore excursion. And the daily trivia quiz was fun to keep track of also.

I found that attending the informative talks on the ports coming up was very helpful for me in deciding what I wanted to do and which tours I felt I'd enjoy.

Shuffleboard (called on this ship an "ancient nautical sport") is as popular aboard Caribe I as all the other ships I've been on. And chess, checkers, Scrabble, backgammon, skeet shooting, golf practice . . . there really is something for everyone, or for every mood.

Hours for the beauty shop/barber shop are posted; the gym is open 6:00 a.m. to 6:00 p.m.; the pool and whirlpools are open all day, the lounges all day, the casino until the last player hits the hay. The gift shops are open morning and late afternoon-early evening. The library is open in the afternoon.

ACTIVITIES

Lifeboat drill is always the first activity you participate in. And since it's mandatory, it doesn't matter if you like it or not. It does give you a sense of security, however, knowing where to go and what to do in case of emergency. The Bingo Hour is popular, and the prizes are cash - if you're lucky you might finance part of a shopping trip in San Juan.

The first evening's get-acquainted party is a good excuse to talk to strangers - shipboard friends are great, for there is no history, no complications from before. The Caribe also throws a singles-only party, which is a good idea, and welcomed by the non-couple passengers.

Casino tournaments go on at various times - blackjack and roulette. Flying kites off the fantail is fun. You can jog or walk around the miles of deck. Movies are shown daily, current and old-timers. Tours of the bridge can be arranged, and with special wheedling and coaxing, a tour of the kitchen - which is immaculate stainless steel. You could also attend a camera clinic, a perfume seminar, bet on the horses at a major daily double event in the Grand Lounge, try your elbow at the beer-drinking contest, attend Mass or go to Seder.

The Caribe I's Aquanaut program is unusual, something I'd not seen on other cruises. Here you can take beginner scuba diving or get your certification as a scuba diver. In these classes you will learn the fundamentals of snorkeling, if you've never attempted it before. With guides, you tour the underwater wonderland of the Caribbean, and at the end of the cruise, if you've dived enough, you will receive your certificate: Resort Diver. This is a very good program, a natural for the cruises through the best diving waters in the world. You can even rent underwater cameras

LOOK OF THINGS

As I mentioned, the Caribe has been entirely refurbished and updated - without losing its "grand tour" charm of yesteryear. We were billeted in one of the nicest cabins I've seen in all my travels, a spacious room - and I mean spacious - with two bathrooms, two single beds, a sofa bed, a comfortable living room chair, a desk, two closets, a TV and a VCR. We had large windows out to the deck, but they were done in one-way glass, so we could see out but the passersby could not see in. It was interesting watching folks fix their hair and put on their lipstick at our windows - kind of like we were watching a peoplequarium.

The common rooms are done in good taste, and the vestiges of opulence from the old days are lovely. There are eight decks and twelve public rooms, including the library, the gym, the Mermaid room, the Mirage room, the Grand Lounge.

The staterooms are plain but neat.

OTHER CRUISES

Commodore Cruise Line also sails in the western Caribbean, to Ocho Rios, Grand Cayman, Cozumel and Playa del Carmen. All of these cruises leave Miami and return to Miami. On these cruises you'll enjoy the scuba diving and snorkeling and beaching as well as the tours through Mayan ruins, partying on a Kon Tiki party raft, rafting on the Martha Brae River, hiking to 600-foot waterfalls.

This line also offers special cruises throughout the year. For example, 1989 offered a Mardi Gras cruise, an NFL party cruise, and cruises specializing in Barber Shop Quartet, Country & Western, an Oktoberfest, an arts and crafts cruise, and the gala Christmas and New Year's cruises.

Commodore Cruise Lines is a subsidiary of Effjohn, a Scandinavian-based corporation with cruise fleets traveling throughout Scandinavia, to Germany, on the English Channel and to Leningrad.

CLOTHING AND WEATHER

The Caribbean is subtropical, so the days are in the seventies and eighties. It rains often, but usually not for long. It is very humid. Bring swim gear, tennis shoes, light jackets or sweaters, casual touring clothes and a few fancy clothes for dinners.

BOOKING YOUR CRUISE

Commodore Cruise Line
1007 North American Way
Miami, FL 33132
Telephone 305-358-2622
Cable Comline
Telex 441771
Fax 305-371-9980
Reservations 800-432-6793 (Florida)
Reservations 800-327-5617 (Rest of the US)
or call your travel agent.

ENTERTAINMENT

The Caribe I is concentrating on "Remember When" cruises, so many of the entertainers fall under the category of stars we knew when we were young. A year's worth of entertainers looks like this: The Four Freshmen, Little Anthony, Lesley Gore, The

Imperials, The Crystals, Bobby Rydell, Gary Lewis and The Playboys, The Drifters, The Shirelles, Danny and The Juniors. We had a wonderful time with the really great and electrifying entertainment of The Mamas and the Papas. They were as good as they ever were when I was a kid.

Nightly dancing, piano bar, plus a masquerade ball, and constant Caribbean music on every deck made this an exceptional music cruise.

FOOD

Several travel agents had informed me this was the highlight eating cruise of the Caribbean. I found the food delicious but I didn't overeat. The executive chef was a prize, a wonderful man, professional to the core. He employed approximately seventy people in his eat-off-the-floor domain, many islanders - Haitians, Grenadines, Jamaicans. The servers were polite and smiling but there English was broken. It was definitely an international kitchen. Chef Jean-Christian Souil comes from a French-restaurant family - Le Pied de Cochon in Lyon, one of the ten best restaurants in France. He trained at Maxim's in Paris, as well as at the Hotel Georges V and the Savoy in London. He was a chef in the French Navy, private chef of Winston Churchill and Aristotle Onassis and has taught culinary arts at the University of Tokyo in Japan. This man has a cooking background like I'd never heard of.

We could eat breakfast in bed, if we wanted, order a regular breakfast in the dining room, or graze through the breakfast buffet between 7:00 and 9:30 a.m. - on deck. This was a luxurious feeling, dining alfresco under the balmy skies of the Caribbean.

Early lunch was served in the dining room for anyone leaving ship on a tour. Regular lunch and a buffet lunch were served at noon.

MS CARIBE I

Dinner, two seatings, was served in the Grand Lounge at either 5:30 and 7:45 p.m. or 6:00 and 8:15 p.m., depending on the time ashore for tours.

A midnight buffet was served either on the pool deck or in the dining room. And an occasional evening ice cream fest, late tea or pizza party offered additional opportunities to eat more than you should.

Each evening's meal was labeled, in other words, "Dinner Americana"-roast filet, roast turkey or salmon mousse; "Continental Dinner"-roast loin of pork, roast chicken or grouper Grenoblaise; "International Dinner"-with T-bone, Veal Marsala or baked quail; Captain's Gala Dinner"-with chateaubriand, rack of lamb or pheasant. As you can see, nothing too French, or too gourmet, just very nicely prepared.

The wine list contained a good selection of California whites, roses and reds from Paul Masson, Robert Mondavi, Parducci, Dry Creek, Sebastiani, Caymus, Sterling, Jordan and Kenwood. German and Italian wines were listed and a good assortment of French wines, whites and reds, including the best French champagnes, rounded out the wine menu.

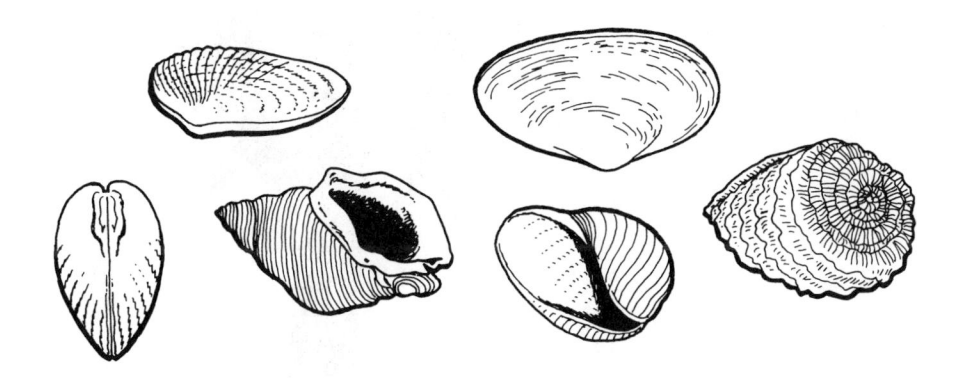

RECIPES

Chilled Cantaloupe with Champagne

1	large cantaloupe, peeled and cut into cubes
1/2	tsp. almond extract
1	tsp. granulated sugar
1/2	bottle extra dry champagne

In a food processor, combine the melon, almond extract and sugar. Puree until smooth, then pour the mixture into a bowl. Stir in champagne and refrigerate for 2 hours. Serve from a glass bowl. (Note: By adding the rest of the champagne, along with a half cup of cognac, you can turn this into a recipe for wonderfully tall drinks.)

Serves 4

Salmon Mousse with Red Bell Pepper Sauce

1	lb. fresh salmon fillet
1/2	tsp. salt
1/4	tsp. freshly ground white pepper
1/2	c. heavy cream
1	c. heavy cream, softly beaten
3	egg whites
1	lb. red bell peppers, cleaned of the inner seeds, cut into cubes
2	c. heavy cream
2	shallots, finely chopped

Combine the salmon, salt and pepper in the food processor and puree until smooth. Add heavy cream and process for 10 seconds. Stop the motor and add the egg whites. Puree again for 1 minute. Pour the mixture into a bowl, add the cup of softly beaten cream. Butter 4 individual ramekins and fill them with the salmon mixture. Arrange the ramekins in a roasting pan. Fill the pan with water around the ramekins and cover the pan with parchment paper. Place in a preheated 350° F oven for 25 to 30 minutes. Unmold onto a dinner plate and cover each with sauce.

To prepare sauce, place the red bell pepper and shallots into a food processor and puree until smooth. Turn off the motor, add 2 cups heavy cream and puree again for 10 to 15 seconds. Transfer the mixture into a saucepan and bring slowly to a simmer (do not boil) before serving over mousse.

Serves 4

Frog Legs Aux Fines Herbes Caribe

6	pairs frog legs (approximately 1 lb.)
1	tsp. salt
1/2	tsp. freshly ground white pepper
1/2	c. milk
1/2	c. flour
1	Tbsp. vegetable oil
2	Tbsp. sweet butter
1/2	stick sweet butter
2	Tbsp. parsley, finely chopped
1/2	Tbsp. fresh chives, finely chopped
3	cloves garlic, peeled and crushed
1/2	c. hazelnuts, crushed

Place the frog legs in a dish and add salt, pepper and milk. Let sit for half an hour at room temperature. Place the flour in a plastic bag. Drain the frog legs and place them in the bag. Shake vigorously and discard the excess flour. Place oil and 2 tablespoons butter in a large skillet. Heat until the mixture foams, then place the frog legs flat in the skillet. Cook over medium heat for 6 to 8 minutes on each side. Arrange the legs on a serving dish. Melt 1/2 stick of butter in a clean skillet. When it starts to foam, add parsley, chives, garlic and hazelnuts. Saute briefly, then spoon the sauce over the frog legs and serve.

Serves 2

Petite Marmite

2	lbs. beef chuck, cut into 2" squares
2	lbs. beef marrow bones
4	qts. cold water
3	cloves garlic, peeled
3	leeks, trimmed and coarsely chopped
1	large yellow onion, quartered
3	stalks celery, coarsely chopped, with leaves on
3	carrots, coarsely chopped
3	ripe tomatoes, quartered
2	bay leaves
1/4	c. fresh parsley
1/2	tsp. thyme
1/2	tsp. salt
2	black peppercorns

In a stock pot, combine the beef chuck, marrow bones and water. Bring slowly to a boil, removing scum as it floats to the top. Add the remaining ingredients and simmer (do not boil) for 3 hours, keeping a lid partially on the pot so that steam can escape. Strain the broth and refrigerate overnight. Then skim and discard any fat that has floated to the top.

Petite Marmite Garnish

1/2	lb. carrots, julienned
1/2	lb. turnips, julienned
2	stalks celery, julienned
1/2	lb. beef chuck, diced

Take 1 quart of beef stock from the Petite Marmite and pour into stock pot. Heat until simmering, then add the above garnish ingredients. Cook until all vegetables are al dente. Serve very hot, with melba toast on the side if desired. (The remaining stock may be frozen in ice cube trays for later use.)

Serves 4

Baked Quail Perigourdine

4	oz. goose liver mousse *
8	oz. cooked rice, warm
4	farm quail (5 to 6 oz. each)
1/2	tsp. salt
1/2	tsp. freshly ground white pepper
1	Tbsp. vegetable oil
2	Tbsp. sweet butter
2 1/2 c.	Madeira wine
1/2	c. dry white wine
1/2	tsp arrowroot
2	oz. black truffles, finely chopped

Preheat oven to 325° F. Cut the liver mousse into small cubes and gently combine with the rice. Season quail with salt and pepper to taste. Stuff quail with the liver mixture and truss by placing a piece of string under each quail at the tail opening, crossing string above the drumsticks and tying securely. Heat the oil and butter in a roasting pan, add the quail and cook for 25 minutes, basting from time to time. When done, remove quail from pan, place on a platter and keep warm in low (160° F) oven. Deglaze the roasting pan with 1/2 cup of the Madeira. Boil the remaining 2 cups of Madeira in a small saucepan for 3 minutes. Add the contents of the deglazed roasting pan and the white wine and remove saucepan from the heat. Add the arrowroot and beat the mixture vigorously. Gently stir in the truffles. To serve, remove the trussing strings and place 2 quail on each dinner plate. Spoon a generous portion of sauce over each serving.

Serves 2

* Can be purchased at gourmet markets

Frozen Souffle au Grand Marnier

2	envelopes unflavored gelatin
1/2	c. fresh lemon juice
4	egg yolks
1/2	c. granulated sugar
1	c. Grand Marnier
8	egg whites
1/4	tsp. cream of tartar
3	c. plain non-fat yogurt

In a saucepan, soften gelatin in lemon juice. Simmer over low heat, stirring frequently, until gelatin is dissolved. Pour into a bowl. Beat egg yolks with sugar for approximately 5 minutes, or until light and fluffy. Pour the Grand Marnier into the top of a double boiler, then stir in the egg yolk and gelatin mixtures. Cook over boiling water, stirring constantly, until mixture thickens. Cool to room temperature (about 45 minutes.) Beat egg whites until soft peaks form, adding the cream of tartar. Fold the egg whites and the yogurt into the cooled Grand Marnier mixture. Pour into a 2-quart souffle dish with a waxed paper collar extending 3" above the rim of the dish. Chill for 3 hours, then remove the paper collar and serve.

Serves 4

MV THE VICTORIA

CHANDRIS FANTASY CRUISES

Several ships of Chandris Fantasy Cruises sail in the Caribbean, along the eastern Mexican coast, to South America and to the Bahamas. The MV The Victoria took us from San Juan, Puerto Rico to St. Thomas in the U.S. Virgin Islands, Martinique, Barbados, Grenada, La Guaira, Venezuela and back to San Juan. Under Panamanian registry, the Victoria is run by Greek officers, and their sense of hospitality is obvious as soon as you board.

Chandris sends out one of the most comprehensive and plainly intelligible booklets long before you leave for your cruise. "What To Know Before You Go" tells you what to wear, suggests the little extras you might not think to bring -- your tennis racket or golf clubs, extra prescription glasses, a full supply of any prescription medicine, or extra diapers if you're traveling with babies. It also lists telephone numbers and telex numbers to leave with your family in case of emergency.

EMBARKATION

The overall feeling when I walked aboard the Victoria was that everything was well done - the layout of the ship, the decor and the abundance of public rooms with cozy conversation groupings. The buffet awaiting us was beautifully presented and gave me the feeling I was indeed a special person simply by being aboard. We were able to board at three in the afternoon, even though the ship did not sail until 11:45 p.m. The first edition of "Seascape," the daily bulletin of ship's activities, awaited us in the cabin and gave us a handy map of the ship, with clues on how to get from one place to another via which stairs or elevators. It also included the entire seven-day itinerary of our trip, with arrival and departure times at each port of call.

PORTS OF CALL

* St. Thomas, U.S. Virgin Islands, was our first stop, on our second day out, at 7:30 a.m. St. Thomas was a Danish possession from

the mid-seventeenth century, established as a sugar producing center. In the 18th century, Charlotte Amalie, the capital city of St. Thomas, thrived as a major slave-trading market and free port. The U.S. purchased St. Thomas from the Danes for $25 million in order to establish a naval base in the Caribbean.

The St. Thomas shore excursions were listed on the front of "Seascape" for easy reference. They included a tour along Skyline Drive above St. Thomas; a tour of the coral reefs; a trip across the channel to the tiny island of St. John; a tour combining shopping with swimming at Magen's Bay; a sailboat tour; a glass-bottomed submarine ride; a snorkeling excursion; a scuba diving trip.

Since I had been to St. Thomas before and experienced the shopping and sightseeing of historical places, I took the "Looking Glass Submarine Tour" of the harbor. From the ship we walked along the pier to board the Mad Hatter, a tender that whisked us through the luxury yachts tied up at the port city of Charlotte Amalie, to the submarine - which we passed over as it lay beneath the surface.

Watching the sub emerge thrilled me. It was a scene from the movies. We boarded and were seated comfortably next to thirty-inch portholes. As we descended, to eighty feet in some places, the clear and lovely world of the underwater Caribbean was revealed. I could have spent several hours watching the fish and the divers snaking in and out of the coral reefs. This was a good experience and worth the price.

* Our third day out, we arrived in Martinique at about 2:00 p.m. This is the largest of the Windward Islands (about 600 square miles) and the only one which is French. Although discovered by Columbus in 1493, Martinique was colonized by France and definitely maintains its Gallic influence. The women are renowned for their beauty, style and their lovely complexions. In 1902, Mt. Pelee, the highest peak, erupted and wiped out the

entire city of St. Pierre, which up to then had been called the little Paris of the West Indies. The city was destroyed and according to legend, all but one inhabitant were killed. The ruins of old St. Pierre, which can still be seen in places, are extremely interesting, and the St. Pierre tour is worth the trip. It also takes you through Fort-de-France, the capital city of Martinique.

The Balata Botanical Gardens, a part of the rain forest outside Fort-de-France, is another tour interesting to flower lovers and walkers. You have an opportunity to roam through the gardens at your own pace. This tour ends with time for shopping in the capital city.

The "Kon Tiki Cruise" is a combination of relaxation and riot - no doubt due to the endless rum punches served aboard while you cruise the bay of Fort-de-France, stop at a beach for a swim and return to the tunes of the islands - the limbo, the conga, Merengue and the steel-band version of the rousing "When the Saints Come Marching In."

* Barbados was settled by the English in 1627 and unlike the rest of the Caribbean islands, has never been under any other rule. Today Barbados is an independent country within the British Commonwealth - and the entire island is like a little bit of England - with good weather.

This island was lush and gorgeous like all the others, but it was also elegant, with the British colonial perfectionism in evidence.

The "Harrison's Cave Tour" offers a running dialogue through Bridgetown, the capital (spots that sound so familiar - Trafalgar Square with the Admiral Nelson statue and an area called Bloomsbury), and past a sugar factory and panoramic views of the ocean and the island. You are transported through the cave on a comfortable electric tram - the easy way to view the stalagmites and stalactites of the ancient underground palace.

MV THE VICTORIA

The "Gun Hill Signal Station/St. John's and Flower Forest Tour" is a leisurely three-hour bus ride through the flowered countryside of Barbados with stops at historic sites.

The "Carlisle Bay Centre Tour" is really a delight. This is a shopping center, resort and beach area done in classic Barbadian-Caribbean architecture. This is a lovely place that offers not only shopping, but good eating, windsurfing, swimming, diving, glass-bottomed boats. Rather than pay the land tour rate, however, you can get there on your own in a taxi for under $10, rent any kind of water equipment you fancy at lower prices than the tour provides -- and shop and eat as you please.

* We pulled into St. George's, Grenada, early on Friday morning -- again, that intoxicating smell of this island, the original Spice Island of legend. This is an island whose culture is a blend of the original Caribs, the French, the British and its now mainly African-descent population. It has a very Mediterranean look to it.

Tours include the "St. Paul's Westerhall Point Tour," a ride through the capital of St. George's, which continues through the island itself, a mountainous, and of course, lush landscape full of nutmeg smells and awesome vistas.

The "Ridge Beach Drive and Swimming Excursion" highlights a few of the historic sites - Government House, the Governor General's residence, the small fishing village of Woburn, the sugar cane fields - and winds up at famous Anse Beach for a couple of hours of relaxation.

The "Rhum Runner," true to its name, supplies you with endless rum punches while you view the waters around Grenada through a glass-bottomed boat. You'll stop for an hour and a half at BBC Beach to snorkel, swim or sunbathe.

All three of the Grenada shore tours include time at beaches, so bring your swimgear and towels. Changing rooms are provided.

* La Guaira, Venezuela, is the debarkation point for a bus ride to Caracas, capital of Venezuela. This is a half-day tour of a major metropolitan city (population four million), so be prepared to wear comfortable shoes and clothing suitable for touring churches and historic buildings; in other words, no short skirts or shorts. Caracas is a beautiful city, birthplace of Simon Bolivar, liberator of the country.

* After a day at sea we returned to San Juan. If you did not tour San Juan before the cruise and if you have time before you leave, take the "Old and New San Juan City Tour" - or at least take a taxi to see the sights. Old San Juan is a cobblestoned beauty of a town.

You can also tour to El Yunque Rain Forest. This is where you can see coffee growing wild and ferns reaching to thirty feet.

The El San Juan Hotel, one of the hot spots of the world as far as class accommodations, is worth the tour. The well-kept grounds, the old-world charm, the light and delicious buffet at the El San Juan will impress you, no matter how jaded or sophisticated you might be.

CONDADO PLAZA HOTEL AND CASINO

Spend a few days in San Juan if possible, as I did, and try to stay at San Juan's Condado Plaza - an experience in itself. It's worth a few day's stay before or after your cruise. It was designed for the business traveler, equipped with conference rooms, private offices, equipment such as computers and Fax machines. You can hold down the fort even though you may be a thousand miles away from your corporate office.

And when the work is over, the fitness center will ease the tension of the most over-worked executive - or the over-shopped sightseer. Universal weight machines, free weights, aerobicycle, computerow, cross country ski simulator, versa-climber treadmill, electronic bicycles - you need it, Condado has it. They also have a steam room, Finnish sauna, whirlpool, tanning beds and licensed massage service. Men's and women's locker rooms with personal services such as facials and skin treatments offer luxurious privacy.

And there are five swimming pools, an outdoor Jacuzzi, the beach within walking distance and a multitude of water sports. Six restaurants cater to nearly every food whim.

The $4 million casino is shiny and spangly - true casino glitz with all the games - blackjack, roulette, craps, baccarat and mini-baccarat. They installed 300 of the latest in slot machines. And they're opened from noon to 4:00 a.m. daily. Nearby is Isadora's dance hall - fancy; wear your glittery clothes and your dancin' shoes. The Copa Room puts on the shows with top name entertainment and international dance troupes. Several bars allow for quiet sipping to leisurely sunsets or piano music - the Casino Lounge, La Cantina Bar, La Fiesta Lobby Lounge. On Sunday evenings, native dancers whoop it up poolside. A native-fare buffet offers fine local foodstuffs. It's called the LeLoLai Festival. Make reservations.

The Condado Plaza works with the El San Juan Hotel and Casino to entertain its guests. The El San Juan is luxurious and venerable, a historic spot on the island. You can sign your expenses at the El San Juan to your Condado Plaza room account.

Condado Plaza is one of those places to stay that will suit you to your heart's content. It's a splurge, but what fun. And even more important, the employees make you feel at home, comfortable and catered to.

MV THE VICTORIA

SHIPBOARD

Just lying on the deck is a pleasure aboard a cruise ship, and on the Victoria you never have to wait for a waiter - they're Johnny-on-the-spot. There are dozens of private corners on the ship, also, if you need a little solitude, or a lot for that matter. Traveling alone as I did, you will find that on a Greek-crew ship, you'll be making friends right and left. They seem to encourage that breakdown of reserve that keeps us from opening up to strangers and new people. After the first night's buffet and the getting-to-know-you session with the cruise director, a single (a person without traveling companions) will have made friends and feel right at home. A cruise ship is unlike anywhere else on earth for this kind of ready camaraderie, and the Victoria enjoys one of the easiest atmospheres among them all.

The Victoria has a gym - weight room, bicycle equipment, etc. - and sauna, a casino, two seawater swimming pools with temps of about eighty degrees, a golf putting facility, a gift shop, a beauty salon/barber shop and a masseuse. The movie theater shows current films.

ACTIVITIES

Although the ports of call are an enticement and may in fact be your reason for the cruise to begin with, activities on board are plentiful, varied and fun. Sometimes the hurly-burly of getting to and from shore excursions can simply wear you out, and a day spent on board, even in port, will return you to an even keel.

And even if you've spent the whole day ashore, evening activities abound - until dawn, if you're into dancing.

Speaking of dancing - the dance lessons entitled "Learn to Dance Like Zorba" are a riot. Greeks love dancing almost as they love their ouzo, and they're more than willing to teach you. You can also attend a Latin dance class and learn the Merengue, the limbo, the samba. The Miss Victoria contest, a kind of lottery-choice dance contest that had nothing to do with dancing ability or beauty, was one of the best events of the cruise. (Maybe because I came in second.)

Indoor games tournaments are scheduled daily - Scrabble, Trivial Pursuit, backgammon, bridge. Cash-prize bingo is a drop-in and participate marathon, and "Sport of Kings Horseracing" invites you to see six of the world's finest horses head to head at Grenada Downs, with an exciting-finish daily double on the final day of the cruise. Outdoor games tournaments include trap shooting, golf putting, Ping-Pong and shuffleboard.

Various lectures and arts and crafts hours are available, also. The travel talk and slide shows on Grenada, Barbados and Caracas are extremely good and can prepare you for shore excursions on your own if you're tired of guided tours. Bring your pen and paper and map out your own strategies for seeing the sights in port. We went to a vegetable-carving and napkin-folding demonstration - which is right up my cooking alley.

There are special activities for children and daily children's hour for special games. There are also gatherings for singles only and for grandparents only.

On our day at sea, between Venezuela and San Juan, we participated in an afternoon of crazy deck games and wacky pool games, including a beer-drinking contest. There was also an opportunity that day to assemble our costumes for the talent show that evening. We attended a morning rehearsal, which turned out to be as much fun as the main event. Garbage bags run a close second to sheets as attire for hokey talent. Even if you're shy, try to do this. It's so much fun and everyone, passenger and crew alike, is full of goodwill and laughter for this event. If nothing else, dress up so you can join the Carnival Parade. Many people bring their costumes along, but making things up the day of the parade/talent show is like being a kid again, dressing in outlandish get-ups to strut your stuff.

OTHER CRUISES

MV The Victoria offers the seven-night cruise above, from San Juan to Venezuela and back and a fourteen-night cruise from San Juan to St. Thomas, Santo Domingo, Aruba, La Guaira, Puerto Ordaz, Ciudad Guyana, Tobago, Barbados, Bequia, St. Maarten and back to San Juan. All of these cruises offer air/sea rates for travel to and from the home port. You can also opt for their "extend-a-cruise" package if you combine two consecutive cruises.

Chandris Fantasy Cruises' Amerikanis offers a six-night cruise from San Juan to Bermuda to New York City and an eight-night cruise from New York City to San Juan, Bermuda and the Caribbean islands of St. Maarten, Antigua and St. Thomas as well as a seven-night cruise from San Juan to St. Thomas, Guadeloupe, Barbados, St. Lucia, Antigua, St. Maarten and back to San Juan. There is a series of special cruises including a six-night cruise from San Juan to St. Thomas, Guadelupe, Barbados, St. Lucia and San Juan and an eight-night Christmas cruise from San Juan to St. Thomas, Guadeloupe, Barbados, Bequia, St. Lucia, Antigua and back to San Juan.

The MV Azur seven-night cruise leaves San Juan and travels to St. Thomas, Bequia, Barbados, Martinique, St. Kitts and back to San Juan.

The year-round Mexico and Key West cruises aboard the ss Britanis leave Miami, call on Key West, Playa del Carmen, Cozumel and return to Miami. These are five-night trips. The

MV THE VICTORIA

Nassau cruise aboard the Britanis is two-nighters from Miami to Nassau and back, year-round.

There are also five and six-night cruises to Bermuda from New York and weekend cruises from New York to nowhere and back - pure getaway entertainment with dancing, gambling, eating and relaxing on the ocean.

The Grand Cruise Around South American in 50 Days leaves Miami, stops at Cozumel on the Yucatan Peninsula, takes you through the Panama Canal, and stops at Callao, Valparaiso, Puerto Monte, Tierra del Fuego and then travels through the Straits of Magellan. On the eastern coast of South America you stop at Buenos Aires, Montevideo, Rio de Janeiro, Salvador, Recife, Belem, Devil's Island, Barbados, St. Thomas and debark in Miami.

All five Chandris ships in the Caribbean offer Christmas and New Year's cruises. They are seven-night stints from Miami or San Juan. "Sea and Stay" packages include pre-cruise stays in Miami, Orlando or San Juan.

Chandris in the Mediterranean offers an eleven-night cruise to the Black Sea, Greece, the Greek Isles and Turkey from Venice; a ten-night cruise to Greece, Egypt, Israel, Turkey and the Greek Isles from Venice; and a seven-night cruise to Yugoslavia, Greece, Turkey and the Greek Isles from Venice.

All Chandris cruises offer a Honeymoon package, which includes not only the cruise but a chilled bottle of Asti Spumanti, a honeymoon cake, a photo album with three photos, a honeymoon cocktail party and a basket of fruit in your cabin. Honeymooners save $100 per cabin by reserving ninety days in advance.

MV THE VICTORIA

CLOTHING AND WEATHER

Warm, sunny, humid. Bring light clothing, a light jacket, a raincoat or umbrella, comfortable walking shoes, swimwear, your own beach towel, touring clothes (no shorts or mini-skirts), evening clothes. It rains unexpectedly and often in the Caribbean. The sun is also intense. Be prepared with appropriate clothes and sun screen or suntan lotion and a hat.

BOOKING YOUR CRUISE

Chandris Fantasy Cruises
900 Third Avenue
New York, NY 10022
Telephone 212-223-3003
Cable Chandrik
Telex 175511
Fax 212-735-0577
Reservations 800-621-3446
or call your travel agent.

ENTERTAINMENT

The sounds of music aboard the Victoria were everywhere. Either calypso, Latin or Greek. It made for a party mood. The showband was excellent and the Martinique Folkloric Show was a stand-up success. Dance music by the Victoria Showband had me tapping my feet.

We were entertained one evening by a great review - dancing, juggling, jokes and singing. On another night the cast put on a Latin review, which was also excellent. These were top-flight professional entertainers and they were well-practiced and smooth.

In all the lounges, various kinds of music performances played into the evening. The disco club was the late-night spot.

CREW

The ship's crew was great, a friendly bunch. The captain, A.S. Varsamis, was particularly thoughtful, friendly and personable. At his cocktail party he explained his duties first as the captain guiding the ship, but as importantly, making his guests feel welcomed. He did a superb job. Captain Varsamis has been in the business all his life and loves it. He was charming, polished and interesting to talk with - not only about the sea, but about books, world affairs, travel and food. I will consider him also as my new friend.

FOOD

Chandris Cruises hire a food concession out of Miami that services fourteen cruise lines in the Caribbean. The presentation was always beautiful, the food good. The executive chef, who works in Miami, was trained in Austria and worked there in the hotels. He said it was difficult to please everyone on board a cruise ship, but I felt he did a superhuman job. When you realize the proportions of the average food consumption on board the Victoria for a week (450 passengers), you can be as amazed as I was that it all looks so sumptuous and tastes so good. Examples: red meats, veal, pork, liver - 4,350 pounds; fowl - 3,300 pounds; fish, shellfish - 2,175 pounds; bread flour - 2,200 pounds; cake flour - 600 pounds; sugar - 850 pounds; butter - 500 pounds; eggs - 45 cases; bananas - 500 pounds; and nearly 500 cases of grapefruit, kiwi, melons, pineapples, lettuce, potatoes and tomatoes.

RECIPES

Chilled Green Apple and Watercress Soup

1/2	bunch watercress
2	c. apple juice
2	large green apples
1	c. sour cream
1	c. heavy cream
1	oz. calvados brandy
	juice of 1/4 lemon
	salt to taste

Puree watercress in blender with 1 cup apple juice. Peel and grate apples. Mix together with remaining ingredients and chill. Serve in chilled cups.

Serves 8

Salad Nicoise

1	lb. small red potatoes
1	lb. whole green beans
1	lb. tomatoes, fresh
10	oz. vinaigrette dressing
10	large lettuce leaves
5	eggs, hard-boiled
10	anchovy fillets
1	oz. capers
20	small black olives

Boil potatoes until done. Cool, peel and slice. Boil green beans until al dente and cut in half. Dip tomatoes in boiling water, remove skin and cut in quarters. Blend with vinaigrette dressing. Arrange on lettuce leaves and decorate with eggs, anchovies, capers and olives. (Tuna fish can be used in this salad.)

Serves 10

Spinach Pie Victoria

1	lb. red onions, finely chopped
1/2	c. scallions, chopped
1/4	c. olive oil
3	lbs. spinach, chopped
	salt, pepper and nutmeg to taste
12	oz. feta cheese, crumbled
4	oz. ricotta cheese
2	eggs
8	oz. butter, melted
1	lb. filo dough
	eggwash

Saute onions and scallions in olive oil. Add spinach and seasonings and cool. Add cheeses and eggs and blend well. Butter baking pan and place 3 sheets of dough with butter brushed between them into pan. Add spinach mixture and top with 4 buttered dough sheets. Eggwash tops and bake at 350° F for 45 minutes.

Serves 10

Conch Fritters

1	lb. conch, frozen, cleaned
1	stalk celery
1	medium onion
2	eggs
1/2	c. milk
1/2	lb. flour
1/2	oz. baking powder
1	sm. chile pepper, finely chopped
	hot peanut oil

In a food processor grind conch, celery and onion through a coarse blade. Beat eggs and milk, mix flour and baking powder and add to conch mixture. Add chile peppers and drop small balls into hot peanut oil. Fry until golden brown. Serve with cocktail sauce or tartar sauce.

Serves 10

Brazilian Churrasco Steak

10	8-oz. New York strip steaks
1	large red onion, chopped
4	cloves garlic, minced
1	c. fresh lemon juice
	salt and pepper to taste
20	slices rye bread, spread with salsa mayonnaise (recipe follows)
3	avocados, peeled and sliced
10	romaine lettuce leaves, washed and dried

Brazilian Churrasco Steak (Cont.)

Marinate steaks in onion, garlic, lemon, salt and pepper for one hour, turning frequently. Grill steaks to desired doneness. Spread salsa mayonnaise on bread, top with sliced steak, avocado and romaine lettuce.

Serves 10

Salsa Mayonnaise

3	egg yolks
2	c. olive oil
1	clove garlic, pureed
1/2	lemon, juice and zest
1	small white onion, pureed
1	Tbsp. jalapenos, minced
	salt and pepper to taste

Whisk egg yolks and olive oil together to make a creamy mixture. Blend the rest of the ingredients gradually into mayonnaise mixture. Serve with Brazilian Churrasco Steak.

Serves 10

Shrimp Cilantro

2	lbs. large shrimp
8	oz. butter, melted
2	cloves garlic, crushed
3	shallots, chopped
1	c. white wine
	salt and pepper to taste
1	Tbsp. cilantro, chopped
1/4	c. heavy cream

Peel and clean shrimp, leaving the tails on. Saute shrimp in butter, garlic and shallots. Add half the wine and simmer 3 to 4 minutes. Remove shrimp, keeping hot. To the same saute pan add the remaining wine, cilantro, salt and pepper and reduce by half. Add heavy cream and shrimp. Serve shrimp over saffron rice and coat with sauce.

Serves 8

Kahlua Pie

2	oz. chocolate, semisweet
2	envelopes Sanka
2	oz. warm coffee
16	oz. whipping cream
3	oz. instant vanilla filling
3	oz. Kahlua
1	9" graham cracker pie shell
	toasted almonds
	coffee grounds

Melt chocolate, dilute Sanka in warm coffee and add to chocolate. Whip cream to soft peaks and gently blend in vanilla filling, coffee-chocolate mixture and Kahlua. Fill pie shell and chill until firm. Decorate with whipped topping, toasted almonds and coffee grounds.

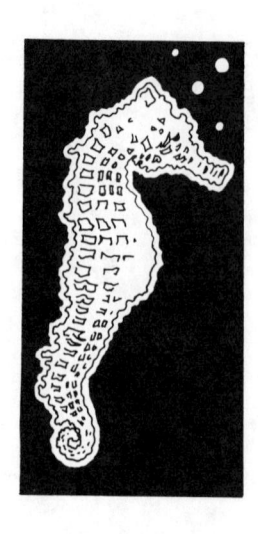

Serves 8

SS AMERIKANIS

CHANDRIS FANTASY CRUISES

SS AMERIKANIS

The Chandris Fantasy Cruises are indeed fantasy-like. Chandris knows their business and carries it out with good taste and great goodwill - these are the two definite marks of Chandris Cruises. The crews are sincerely upbeat and personable, and they'll do anything that needs to be done to make the ship run smoothly. It doesn't take a waiter to bring you a drink, for anyone is happy to oblige. The ambience is simply friendly. To carry this off amid elegance and charm makes this line special among the many I've traveled.

Having been in the Caribbean cruise market for twenty-eight years, Chandris knows its business well. Twenty-eight percent of the cruise market in Bermuda belongs to Chandris. Also, in the year 1987, Candris carried more passengers from the port of New York than any other cruise line.

In the spring of 1990, Chandris Celebrity Cruises will launch its newest ship, the MV Horizon. The Horizon will debut from New York on seven-night cruises to Bermuda with her sister Celebrity Cruise ship the ss Meridian. The Horizon will then sail on seven-night Caribbean cruises from San Juan to Martinique, Barbados, St. Lucas, Antigue and St. Thomas. Currently being built at the Meyer Werft shipyards in Papenburg, Germany, the Horizon will accommodate 1,400 passengers. It will be 682 feet long and hold 680 cabins, eighty percent of which are outside. Standard cabins are 171 square feet, which is a cut above most luxury cruise line vessels being built today.

There will be seven elevators, a showroom that will hold 1,000 patrons, two swimming pools, three Jacuzzis, a health club - sounds like my kind of ship for a vacation come 1990.

The interiors will be decorated by firms from Athens, London, Venice and Miami. As Chandris's executive director said, "There are many new things on the Horizon. . . ." I can't wait to see it. Chandris Celebrity Cruises will initially operate two ships, the

SS AMERIKANIS

MV Horizon and the SS Meridian. The Meridian will debut in the beginning of 1990 with seven-night cruises from POA Everglades, Florida to Antigua, St. Thomas and Nassau. At the conclusion of her preview series, the Meridian will join the Horizon for seven-night cruises to Bermuda. The Meridian will be the $40 million reconstructed Galileo.

EMBARKATION

This was one of the easiest boardings I've ever had, partly because I was transferring directly from the Chandris Cruises' MV The Victoria to the Chandris' SS Amerikanis tied up next door at the pier. A porter carried my bags and I simply followed him to my stateroom.

This is a spacious ship, seven decks with public rooms galore for relaxing. And relaxing was the main order of the day, for this was a trip from San Juan to Bermuda, taking two days at sea, with Thursday and Friday in Bermuda and then a day of sailing to New York City.

I really appreciated this easy-going, relaxing trip. This particular sailing was called a "positioning" cruise, which meant the ship was returning to New York to set up for its regular six-day sailings to Bermuda during the summer season. In the winter, between the first part of December through the end of April, the Amerikanis departs from San Juan every Monday evening for a seven-day trip through the Caribbean. The ship was not filled to capacity on this positioning cruise, which also lent a certain looseness and intimacy to the atmosphere, both from passengers and crew.

PORTS OF CALL

* Bermuda has been a British colony for 375 years. It is thoroughly British, clean and lovely. It contains a population of 350,000 and no one is allowed to move to Bermuda now. The harbor at

St. Georges, the original capital until Hamilton was declared official in 1815, is spotless and picturesque, even though it is a major industrial port of the island.

This is an elegant island, gorgeous and lush with its tapestry of flowering trees and shrubs. It is no doubt the prettiest and cleanest island I've seen in any of my travels. The native limestone buildings are pastel-hued, mostly pink, reflecting the pink sand beaches formed from the coral reefs.

The "Bermuda Super Deluxe Attraction Tour" is four hours of sightseeing which includes a ride around Harrington Sound, a visit to the Crystal Caves, the Aquarium, the Museum and the Zoo, shopping, a Dancing Dolphin Show and a visit to the Bermuda Perfumery where perfume is made from the island flowers. This is the comprehensive tour, interesting and informative. I found the perfume factory fascinating.

The "St. Georges' Highlights Tour" is two hours of guided monologue through the quaint and lovely old town. You can also do this on your own for the price of cab fare, consulting a map as you go. Bermuda's public transportation is excellent - the pink Bermuda bus is good and the minibus service between Dockyard and Somerset Bridge allows a request-stop system.

A glass-bottomed boat tour over the coral reefs of Bermuda's islands is pleasant also.

Since we had two days in Bermuda, I followed my own nose and the advice of a few of the crew members and did my own thing. I enjoyed this break from guided tours and saw what I wanted to see, at my own pace. Bermuda is an island of flowers, 700 miles out to sea from the U.S. coast. It is only twenty miles long and the public buses and taxis for hire are cheap and plentiful. Mopeds are for hire (no cars to rent) but it's almost too dangerous to ride a moped and you are warned against them by the cruise

SS AMERIKANIS

line, for the British road system prevails - driving on the left - and the roads are narrow and often steep. Beaches have public facilities for changing and renting equipment. Shopping is world-famous, with a plethora of British Wedgewood, Irish Waterford, woolens and linens. The currency is the Bermudian dollar, which is usually on a par with the American dollar. Both are accepted as are travelers checks and credit cards.

There are eight golf courses on Bermuda.

In the evening, two good reviews are available to you with reservations - the Hamilton Princess "Big, Bad and Beautiful Review" and the Southampton Princess "Anniversary Show." Dress for these with jacket and cocktail attire.

Points of interest include Fort St. Catherine, St. Georges Historical Society Museum, the Bermuda National Trust homes, Devil's Hole.

The "National Trust Homes Tour," which you can take on your own, is a good one. This is a very English-type holiday activity (touring of stately homes in England is practically a national pastime) with a very island-type flavor to it. The houses are chosen for their historic and architectural value. Each visit costs $2 or you can purchase a combination ticket for $3.

A few of the trust homes you might be interested in: Camden, the official residence of Bermuda's Premier; Verdmont, a seventeenth-century mansion full of antique furniture, china and portraits; Tucker House and the Confederate Museum, two prime examples of St. Geroge's best treasures. These stately homes are scattered throughout Bermuda, so call the Bermuda National Trust for maps and hours.

Along this line, during the season (winter), the Bermuda Garden Club sells tickets to their open homes tour. The newspaper called

Bermuda Weekly will be the place to look to see if you're in town at the right time. The tour lasts for six weeks and covers fifteen to twenty houses. They are picked for their architecture, or history, and always for their gardens. As in many communities, the money is used for student scholarship.

To feel like you're "in," in Bermuda, there are a few things to look for that you can then discuss with Bermudians or other people who have traveled to Bermuda. The first is a man named Johnny Barnes. Johnny stands each day in the traffic roundabout at the Foot of the Lane in Paget waving and smiling and calling out to passing motorists, "God bless you!" Or, "Mornin', love!" He'll make your day.

Another sign of your being a well-traveled insider in Bermuda is to know about "Weatherbird," a carved owl who is clothed each day according to the holiday, the weather or a major event in the UK. During Wimbledon, for example, "Weatherbird" is dressed in whites and given a racket. He sits at the Blue Hole Boatyard on Harbour Road in Paget - facing incoming traffic in the morning, and turned to face the homegoers in the afternoon. On really blistery hot days, he wears swimtrunks and sunglasses.

And lastly, if you are curious why there are so many oriental-style gates throughout the island, remember that the British Empire was big in the Orient for many a decade. The Moongate style of garden enhancement was introduced during the mid-1800s and has stuck around, for anyone who walks beneath its arch will be blessed with a happy life.

SHIPBOARD

All the expected amenities are here -- hairdressing salon, gym, sauna, massage, gift shop, casino, hospital, bars, cinema, television and a library in four languages (German, Spanish, French, English). The Amerikanis clientele is sophisticated and cosmopolitan - there aren't too many ships in the Caribbean that cater to so many nationalities.

ACTIVITIES

Along with the Ping-Pong, golf putting, trapshooting, quiz games, horseracing, bingo, Trivial Pursuit, shuffleboard, walk-a-thons, exercise classes, dance classes, bridge, backgammon, water polo and happy hours, there were lessons in ice carving, duty-free sales in the gift shop on specific hours, singles get-togethers, sing alongs, make-your-own costume parties and dart tournaments.

But just because it's there doesn't mean you must join in. This is an easy ship to lose yourself on - as in finding a place to get away from the crowd.

LOOK OF THINGS

A beautifully appointed ship, the Amerikanis, maybe because of the dearth of passengers, was really a luxury environment. I had a cabin of huge proportions with windows all around - I had nearly a panoramic view of Bermuda, of the ship itself, of the endless ocean once we were underway. This was luxury. I had a sitting room; my bathroom was large, with room to move around in, and the tub was done in a decorator teal blue; my closet space was enough for several trunk's worth of clothing; I had a television and a telephone.

I was taken through several other cabins, and all of them were commodious, tastefully decorated, with ample closet space and comfortable bathrooms. Many of the cabins were divided by a room sectioner, which allowed for the beds on one side and a sitting-room atmosphere on the other.

Connecting cabins would be ideal for families traveling together; some cabins connected via the sundecks. Nice arrangements and good looks; in fact, some of the most tastefully appointed and roomy rooms I've seen in my cruise ship travels.

OTHER CRUISES

See this section in the chapter on MV The Victoria.

CLOTHING AND WEATHER

It rained in Bermuda. As with all Caribbean trips, be prepared for wet and warm; be prepared for casual ashore and dressy for dinner on shipboard. Bermuda, in its very English properness, may inspire you to dress up a little more even when you're touring ashore. You'll feel in style and comfortable if you wear nice skirts and maybe a casual open shirt with cotton suit jacket.

BOOKING YOUR CRUISE

Chandris Fantasy Cruises
900 Third Ave.
New York, NY 10022
Telephone 212-223-3003
800-233-0848
Cable Chandrik
Telex 175511
Fax 212-735-0577
Reservations 800-621-3446
or call your travel agent

ENTERTAINMENT

Good variety shows, with magicians, dancers and comedians, were the order of the evening on the Amerikanis. Also, the mini-cabaret show was exciting, and the general level of musical entertainment in the lounges and bars was excellent. All the entertainers on this ship seemed to love their work and it showed. What a way to work - at something you love to do aboard a floating palace in the Caribbean. Some of the bars and lounges would have a piano bar, taking requests; others would be playing fifties music, or Latin, swing music from the '30s and '40s, or late-night melodies for lovers. Dancing in the ballroom attracted a flood of people. This phenomenon of customers-as-extraordinary-dancers is something that you see on cruise ships that you seldom see in land lubbers ballrooms. Wonderful ballroom dancers whirl one another through the steps as if they're Fred and Ginger.

FOOD

The food aboard the Amerikanis had the same look, the same attractive presentation, as the food aboard the Victoria, but for some reason, it tasted better. Maybe I was just hungrier? I don't know. I gained weight, but I could have watched my food intake. I could also have requested low-cal food, because all cruises will accommodate dietary differences if notified ahead of time - Kosher, low cholesterol, vegetarian. Just ask. I think I just wanted to eat and ignore the consequences for once.

At a lunch party for models who were aboard for photo sessions for new brochures for the cruise line, we were served the most delicious hors d'oeuvres - Taramosalata. It's made with mashed potatoes, garlic, olive oil and fish eggs - ah to die for. All this with ouzo and Greek music. What a way to travel.

porpoise

RECIPES

Italian Salad Dressing

1	oz. Dijon mustard
1	c. wine vinegar
1	c. olive oil
2	c. vegetable oil
	Worcestershire sauce
2	shallots, chopped
1	clove garlic, chopped
1	bunch parsley, chopped
1	bunch fresh oregano, chopped
	salt and pepper to taste

Mix mustard with vinegar. Slowly add oils and remaining ingredients.

Yields 1 quart

Fettucine and Smoked Salmon

1	lb. fettucine
1/2	lb. pancetta*
1	carrot, julienned
1	stalk celery, julienned
	salt and pepper to taste
12	slices smoked salmon
6	Tbsp. tomato sauce
6	Tbsp. Mornay sauce*

Fettucine and Smoked Salmon (Cont.)

Cook fettucine al dente. Cut pancetta in cubes and saute in its own fat. Remove fat. Add carrot, celery and salt and pepper. Mix with fettucine. Divide fettucine onto 6 plates and top with smoked salmon. Top one slice of salmon with tomato sauce, the other with Mornay sauce.

Serves 6

* see glossary

Grilled Chicken Dijonnaise

3	chickens, cut in half
1	c. olive oil
8	oz. Dijon mustard
1	bunch fresh basil, minced
2	shallots, minced
1	c. white wine
	breadcrumbs
	salt and pepper to taste

Marinate the chicken halves in olive oil, half the mustard and the basil for 6 hours. Remove from marinade and cook on a grill until almost done. Remove from grill and keep warm. In a saute pan, simmer shallots in wine. Add remaining mustard and mix well. Brush chickens with this mixture and sprinkle with breadcrumbs and salt and pepper. Place chickens under a broiler until breadcrumbs are golden and juices run clear.

Serves 6

Salmon in Foil

1/2 lb.	salmon fillets
1	carrot, julienned
1	leek, julienned
1	zucchini, julienned
	parsley, basil, chervil, salt and pepper to taste
2	oz. butter, cut in patties
1/2	c. white wine

Place salmon on a piece of aluminum foil. Top with carrot, leek, zucchini, seasonings, butter and wine. Seal the foil and bake for 13 minutes at 350° F.

Braised Halibut

1	carrot, julienned
1	leek, julienned
1	stalk celery, julienned
1	turnip, julienned
2	shallots, chopped
6	halibut steaks
1	c. white wine
2	c. fumet * (see glossary)
2	oz. butter
1	bunch each basil and dill, minced

Place carrot, leek, celery, turnip and shallots on a cookie sheet. Add halibut steaks, moistened with white wine and fumet. Add butter, basil and dill and bake at 350° F for 15 minutes.

Serves 6

Mushroom and Leek Pie

1	prepared pie crust
1/2	lb. mushrooms, sliced
1/2	lb. leeks, julienned
1/2	lb. tomatoes, sliced
1/2	lb. onions, shredded
4	eggs
1	pt. milk
	nutmeg to taste
	salt and pepper to taste
1	bunch fresh basil, minced
1	lb. Swiss cheese, shredded

On pie crust place sliced mushrooms, leeks, tomatoes and onions. Mix eggs with milk, nutmeg, salt and pepper and basil. Add egg mixture to the pie. Top with shredded cheese and bake 20 minutes at 350° F.

Serves 6

Red Berries in Champagne Saboyon

2	oz. strawberries
2	oz. blackberries
2	oz. raspberries
2	oz. butter
1/2	c. Grand Marnier
6	oz. sugar
1	c. champagne
2	egg yolks
6	scoops vanilla ice cream

Saute berries in butter. Flame with Grand Marnier. Prepare saboyon in a saucepan by mixing sugar and champagne. Whip in egg yolks. Continue to whip on low heat until smooth. Place ice cream in brandy snifters and top with berries and champagne saboyon.

Serves 6

Apples Flambe Chandris

2	apples, peeled, cored and sliced into rings 1" thick
2	oz. sugar
1/2	c. rum
1/2	tsp. cinnamon
1/2	tsp. grated lemon zest
1	c. apple juice
	freshly grated ginger to taste
2	oz. butter
1/2	c. calvados
1/2	tsp. balsamic vinegar
	vanilla ice cream

Marinate apple rings in 1 ounce of the sugar, the rum, cinnamon, lemon zest, apple juice and ginger for 1 hour. Saute the apples in 1 ounce of the butter, flame with calvados, then add remaining sugar to caramelize. Add marinade, let thicken a bit, then add the remaining butter in small pieces. Add balsamic vinegar. Serve with vanilla ice cream.

Serves 6

LAMBERT BRIDGE

Library Reserve

CABERNET SAUVIGNON
DRY CREEK VALLEY

Supple, elegant, and soft on the palate. Deep and inviting, beautifully structured fruit of black currants, wild berry, with long linger, clean finish.

The winemakers favorite food pairing is de-boned Greek Leg of Lamb, prepared with spinach, pine nuts, virgin olive oil, feta cheese and pressed garlic. Exterior is rubbed with olive oil and dressed with Dijon mustard and fresh parsley.

LADY A

BARGE FRANCE

The Lady A is a converted grain barge that slowly plies the Canal de Bourgogne in France's Burgundy area. A barge as a cruise? Oh yes. It is the height of luxury as far as accommodations, la haute cuisine as far as food and the nth degree of relaxation as far as vacation.

The owners of the Lady A, David and Lisa Bourne, work with Sea Air Holidays cruises out of Stamford, Connecticut. You can book through Sea Air. The Bournes' bought the commercial barge, had several feet taken off so they could fit her into the canal locks and inland waterways of France, cleaned her thoroughly, decorated her with care and class ... and went into business.

And what a business it is. David, the captain, is a lifelong sailor and boatman (the Mediterranean, the Atlantic, the Caribbean, he had been around the world by ship three times by the time he was eighteen). Lisa, first mate and chef, has a background in good food (her mother), good wines (her father) and a degree in art design. She also worked on yachts in the Caribbean with David, sailed the Med, and thus knows her business when on a boat. Together they made the Lady A a luxury, designing the window dressings, choosing the furniture and planting the flowers in the pots - but Lisa alone does the cooking

EMBARKATION

Coming from the United States, I flew New York City-Lyon, France, took a train to Dijon, in Burgundy, and met the captain, David, at La Cloche, a hotel in downtown Dijon. David picked me and the rest of the passengers up - all five of us. The boat holds six cruisers. In their Mini-Bus, he drove us to the canal and brought us aboard to enjoy a champagne cocktail and off we went. At a snail's pace, mind you, up (or down),the canal. Sea Air Holidays package provides the lodging in Dijon before the trip.

The canal system of France was instituted in the seventeenth century by King Henry IV. Much study was done, pathways decided on and watershed accounted for. Trees were planted along the tow paths to halt erosion. But the first barge from Paris to Dijon did not navigate until 1833. Five reservoirs feed the Canal de Bourgogne during the dry months of summer. The locks, designed by a man named Paul Riquet in the early 1600s, still work - they are masterpieces of engineering.

PORTS OF CALL

One of the luxuries of the barge cruise was that we could alter the itinerary as far as the shore excursions were concerned. David and Lisa told us our options and we could then opt. David said that if he had a group that wanted to see churches, he'd oblige; or only wineries? Fine. Or if they wanted to stay aboard all day and all night with no land forays, he and Lisa would have no problems with that either. As the captain said, "Our customers are in command of their own vacations."

We chose to take a few excursions, and because David was the tour guide, we felt we were getting an insight into things from a very personal point of view. An eighty-year-old English gentleman on our cruise said it best: "Ah, yes, the shore expeditions - we enjoyed them because David went out of his way to explain so that we knew enough about the country and its history to appreciate it. If I was wanting another holiday, I'd have no hesitation in coming on the Lady A again."

In this regard, David and Lisa plan to do all the waterways of France and Europe, not just in the Burgundy area.

The highlights of the shore excursions are as follows:

* Your first day and night you will probably spend in Dijon, acclimating yourself to jet lag and French customs. It is an old,

old town, the center point of European civilization in the fifteenth century and the medieval capital of the Duchy of Burgundy. The town is, obviously, historical, but it is also a center of the fine arts, with the Musée des Beaux-Arts, an art gallery second in France only to the Louvre. Dijon's cultural history dates back to the twelfth century when the dukes of the region began erecting buildings and sculptures, treasures which still validate the wealth and power they had then. Town houses in Dijon, protected by the government, date from the fifteenth century. The half-timbered houses reminded me of Elizabethan England.

Dijon is also a city of parks and trees, 600 hectares, or about 1,500 acres of lakes and wide open spaces. Dijon is the largest city in the Burgundy region and the center of some of France's most famed cuisine, specializing in Coq au Vin, hearty red wines and the tantalizing mustards known internationally as Dijon-made. Dijon is also the home of Kir, that lovely aperitif of cassis (black currant liqueur) and champagne.

* An excursion to the Chateau de Clos de Vougeot, a twelfth-century manor (castle to Americans) is one of the first options on the first day out. The Chateau was built by Cistercian monks.

* The Chateau de Commarin, a privately owned home, is sometimes open for Lady A cruisers. The Chateau was completed in 1346. It has been owned by the same family since. The chateau is a museum of seventeenth-century furniture and fifteenth-century tapestries, which have been exhibited in Paris, London and New York. Its claim to fame is that it is the home of tennis, which is historically disputed, but a nice story to hear from David's store of knowledge. They say the indoor tennis courts were there before the stables - which makes tennis very old indeed.

* We visited the Abbey of La Bussiere. The grounds here were so lovely - peonies, pools with floating black swans, waterfalls -a quiet, reflective place, surely suited to the black-robed nuns who,

like the swans on the water, floated through the grounds with serenity and grace, well worth a stop and a stroll. The gardens are not only beautiful and beautifully cared for, they are also 700 years old.

* Later in the week we stopped at the fifteenth century Hospice de Beaune. This imposing - and somewhat daunting - edifice was opened in 1443 as a charitable hospital for the poor. A shared bed was the norm.

* We then went for a little wine-tasting at the Marché aux Vins. With our small sommelier cups in hand we were invited to taste-test thirty (30!) burgundy wines. Some of these wines were out-of-sight expensive. And of course the ones we liked best.

* The Chateauneuf was a wealthy merchant's hilltop trading post. A small museum there is of interest. The view is lovely.

* And every day, you can bike along the tow path of the canal (the Lady A has bicycles for each passenger), meeting the Lady A at any point to hop aboard. I biked one day and then walked along the path the rest of the days, getting my exercise. It was lovely, tree-lined, quiet, bucolic. Walking at a good clip I could keep ahead of the barge. Also, maneuvering the fifty locks on our trip, we were invited (but not obliged) to help get the boat situated, the sluices opened or closed - exciting times. Either watching or participating.

SHIPBOARD

The best of it all was shipboard. The surroundings were so luxurious - the good, polished woods, the expensive draperies and curtains, the well-chosen furniture, the healthy and lovely marigolds, nasturtiums, impatiens and geraniums that flowered in every corner - it was a pleasure to be aboard.

The lounge was comfortable, spacious and beautiful, books available, board games and card games and even an electronic keyboard for anyone with a yen to play for the rest of us. But we were never bored enough to resort to even these placaters. The passing scenery was so lovely, the company so pleasant, the information from the captain and first mate so interesting, that we never picked up a deck of cards.

The galley is small and ultra-compact, but very modern and efficient.

The three cabins each have a toilet and shower and are decorated beautifully and comfortably.

Most cruise barges that ply the canals in France are owned by absentee companies and crewed by hired people. The Lady A is owned and operated by the Bournes, which made the service and life aboard very personalized, as if we were guests aboard a private barge being served dinner in our friend's dining room.

The Lady A was a comfort, it was peaceful, clean, well-equipped, friendly and fancy. The Bournes were constantly concerned about our well being and our bellies. Their enthusiasm and genuine friendliness made the trip even more pleasant than it would have been just lazing through the locks of central France. It is an ideal vacation for older people, although by no means should it be considered a retirement-only cruise. Six friends can rent the barge and have a high old time. Or you can take your chances and meet a cross-section of Europe or America once aboard. Because of the limited number of passengers aboard a barge trip, it's a good idea to have someone with you whom you like to travel with. Also, traveling in a country where English is not always spoken, it helps to have someone with you to share your experiences without having to struggle in a foreign language. The crew speaks English, of course, as well as several other languages.

MONEY ETIQUETTE

All shore excursions are part of the price of your cruise aboard the Lady A. This includes one or two meals ashore at famous inns or farmhouses along the way. All food aboard and all house wines are included in your ticket. Expensive regional wines and all champagnes are extra. Tipping is up to the passengers. Aside from the captain and his wife, the Lady A held one crew member who helped with serving, clean-up and room maintenance.

CLOTHING AND WEATHER

Dress was always casual aboard the Lady A - slacks or shorts or cotton skirts. But when going ashore, conservative outfits - slacks and a jacket for men, a casual suit or shirtwaist for women - would be the order of the day. Shorts and daring dress is frowned on in middle France, especially if you are touring cathedrals and monasteries. Sunning on the deck in my shorts I felt comfortable; riding a bike along the tow path in my shorts I felt okay; in town, shorts will make you feel out of place.

Bring an umbrella, a light jacket, a light raincoat, good walking shoes, rubber-soled shoes for shipboard, a sun hat. The weather will vary during the summer cruises from cool to hot, from humid to very dry, depending on the month of the year. The climate of France is considered mild, but it does have its extremes. Pack for comfort, not for fancy times.

BOOKING YOUR CRUISE

See Air Holidays, Ltd.
733 Summer Street
Stamford, CT 06901
Telephone 203-356-9033
1800-732-6247
Telex 6819262 SEAIR

or call your travel agent

PASSPORT

You will need a passport and check with your travel agent to see if you will also need a French visitor's visa, which you can obtain through a French consulate in the United States. Always apply early, for as you know, bureaucracy grinds slowly. Your travel agent can help you get a visa and passport.

OTHER CRUISES

* Alsace aboard the Stella Maris takes passengers from Strasbourg to Waltenheim to Saverne to Lutzelbourg to Xouaxange to Mittersheim and back to Strasbourg. You'll pass through steep, pine-clad hills via a boat "elevator" that raises the Stella 130 feet to the top of a mountain, giving you views of the Vosges River valley below. This is the French/German area of France, so you'll alter your eating habits from sauerkraut and sausages to French haute cuisine by candlelight aboard the Stella.

* The Midi aboard the Anjodi is another six-day holiday, this one along The Midi Canal of Southern France. You begin at Montpellier, cruise through territory once settled by Greeks and Romans, swim in the Mediterranean, travel through the world's oldest canal tunnel, visit vineyards and medieval castles.

* Sea Air Holidays also offers five- and seven-day trips along the coast of Portugal, with excursions into Spain and to the island of Madeira. Travelers fly into Lisbon, Portugal to commence these cruises.

* Canary Island and West Africa cruises are available also via Sea Air. You fly into Lisbon and then on to Madeira to begin your cruise of Agadir in West Africa, and the Canary Islands of Lanzarote, Las Palmas, Tenerife, Gomera.

* On Sea Air ships with capacities from thirty to ninety passengers, you can travel to Ecuador and the offshore Galapagos Islands in South America, or up the Amazon on a Mississippi paddleboat-type luxury cruiser called the Flotel Orellana.

FOOD

A run-down of our menu the first day aboard will give you an idea of how we ate for a week. Breakfast (petit déjeuner) was traditional continental - fresh brioches or croissants with coffee or tea and homemade jellies and jams. We were served lobster bisque with fresh salads, Charcuterié (cold cuts) and cheese for lunch (Déjeuner). For dinner (Diner or Souper) we had a leg of lamb, stuffed with garlic and cooked in herbes de Province, Ratotouille, flageolets and a cheese tray after dinner and then peaches in wine and peach liqueur. Plus the wines with the meal - in Burgundy, some of the best being Beaujolais, Beaune, Bourgogne (Burgundy), Chablis, Cote de Beaune, Cremant de Bourgogne. Elegant eating, well done with little fuss.

RECIPES

Vinaigrette

5	Tbsp. Dijon mustard
6	cloves garlic, crushed
1/2	tsp. salt
1/2	tsp. pepper
1/4	c. chives, chopped
4	Tbsp. red wine vinegar
2	c. sunflower oil

Whisk mustard, garlic, salt, pepper, chives and vinegar briskly in a bowl. Add oil while whisking and vinegar to taste. Keep refrigerated and shake before using.

Makes 2 1/2 cups

Soupe de Poissons (Fish Bisque)

1	can Soupe de Poissons*
9	baguette croutons
1	c. Gruyere, Jarlsburg or Emmenthale cheese, grated

Rouille

1/2	c. mayonnaise
1	tsp. paprika
1/2	tsp. cayenne
1/2	tsp. garlic, crushed
1	tsp. ketchup (optional)

Soupe de Poissons (Cont.)

Heat can of soup and 3/4 can of hot water. Do not boil. Make croutons, grate cheese, make Rouille by blending all remaining ingredients. Let Rouille sit for a bit to blend flavors. Serve soup in individual bowls with croutons, Rouille and cheese on top.

Serves 4

*Available in larger gourmet stores

Pomplemousse au Fruit de Mer (Seafood-Stuffed Grapefruit)

6	grapefruits
3/4	c. mayonnaise without lemon
	dash cayenne pepper
1	can baby shrimp
1	can crabmeat
1	Tbsp. parsley, chopped
	mint

Cut grapefruits in half and carefully remove the meat with a grapefruit knife. Place in separate bowl. Add to bowl the mayonnaise, cayenne, shrimp, crabmeat and parsley. Mix together well. Spoon into empty grapefruits and garnish with chunks of crab and a sprig of mint.

Serves 6

Artichoke Quiche

1	10" pie crust
8	eggs
3/4	c. crème fraîche*
1	tsp. salt
1	tsp. pepper
3/4	c. Gruyère cheese, grated
1	Tbsp. dried tarragon
1	can artichoke hearts
	sliced tomato

Preheat oven to 250° F. Make pie crust. Places eggs, crème fraîche (or sour cream) in large mixing bowl and mix well, adding salt and pepper, cheese and tarragon. Whisk briskly. Pour into pie crust. Drain artichokes and cut in half or thirds. Place around top of quiche. Place tomato slices around top. Bake 1 hour or until golden on top.

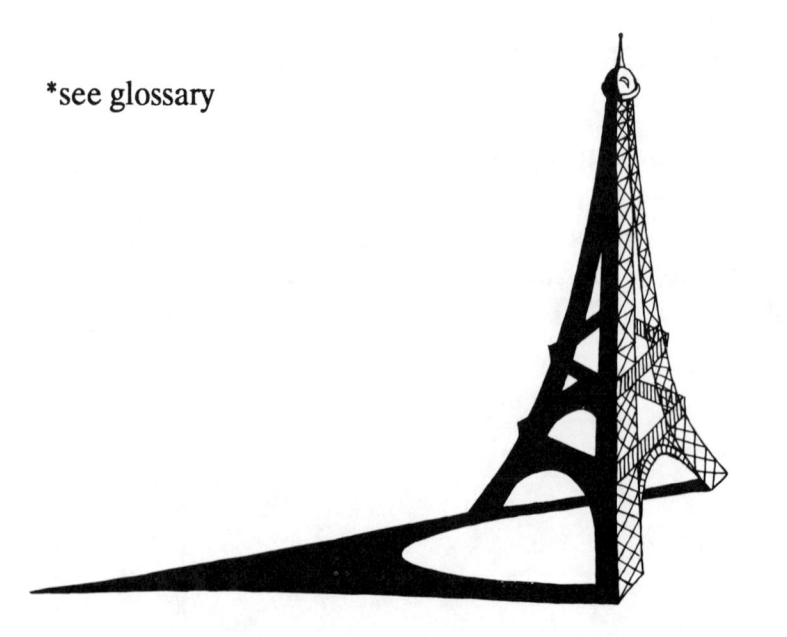

Serves 8

*see glossary

Lady A Loaf

2	c. flour
4	eggs
3/4	c. oil
1/3	c. dry white wine
1	c. green olives, pitted
1	c. smoked ham, cooked (or smoked chicken)
1/2	c. Gruyère cheese, grated
1	tsp. baking powder
1/4	tsp. salt

Place all ingredients in a bowl and mix well. Pour into cake tin placed in water bath* and bake at 350 degrees for 1 hour or until an inserted toothpick comes out clean.

Serves 8 to 10

*See glossary

Cuisses de Canard au Vin Rouge & Porto (Duck Legs)

6	duck legs
1	Tbsp. butter
	salt
1	c. red wine
6	shallots, finely chopped
1	tsp. thyme
1	c. mushrooms, chopped
1/2	c. crème fraîche*
1/2	c. port

Brown duck legs in butter, salt them and add wine, shallots and thyme. Let simmer covered for 1 hour. Remove legs and keep warm. Add mushrooms to sauce. Add crème fraîche and let reduce. Add port and reduce again. Adjust seasoning. Serve sauce over duck legs. Serve with thin green beans (French style) and sauteed potatoes.

Serves 6

*See glossary

LADY A

Pork and/or Chicken St. Lucia

1	large chicken, cubed, or 2 lbs. boned pork, cubed, or 1 small chicken and 1 lb. pork, cubed together
1	large onion, chopped
3	cloves garlic, crushed
1	Tbsp. powdered ginger
1	Tbsp. powdered mustard
1	tsp. salt
1	tsp. pepper
	dash Worcestershire sauce
	dash Louisiana hot sauce
	parsley
1	small can pineapple juice
	same amount (1 small can) dark rum
1	can pineapple chunks
	roasted almonds, slivered

Mix pork and/or chicken with all ingredients except pineapple chunks and almonds. Let stand for a couple of hours. Slowly bring to boil in a heavy saucepan with tight lid. Simmer about 1/2 hour. Just before serving, add pineapple chunks and sprinkle with almonds. (Stir in a little dark brown sugar to neutralize taste if hot sauce is too hot.)

Serves 6

Shrimp Endaxi

2	lbs. medium shrimp, shelled
4	cloves garlic, chopped
1	Tbsp. butter
2	Tbsp. flour
1	Tbsp. butter
1/2	c. milk
2	egg yolks
1/2	c. sour cream
1	tsp. parsley
2	tsp. tarragon
1	Tbsp. lemon juice
1	16-oz. can tomatoes, stewed
1	can mushrooms, chopped
	Parmesan cheese, grated

Saute shrimp with crushed garlic in butter, covered. Make a sauce bechamel* with flour, butter and milk. Add egg yolks, sour cream, parsley, tarragon and lemon juice. Transfer shrimp with juices into casserole. Add stewed tomatoes (without their juice), mushrooms and bechamel sauce. Add more tarragon and gently mix. Sprinkle with Parmesan cheese and heat in 350° F oven for 10 minutes.

Serves 6

*See glossary

Tarte au Citron (Lemon Tart)

1/2	c. flour
1	c. butter
1	tsp. vanilla
1	tsp. sugar
3	eggs
1	c. sugar
3/4	c. melted butter
	juice of 2 lemons
3	egg whites
1	lemon, sliced

Make pâte brisée* with flour, butter, vanilla and sugar. Line pie dish with this mixture. Mix eggs with sugar and melted butter. Add lemon juice. Pour over the dough and cook in 350° F oven for 20 to 25 minutes, or until lemon filling starts browning. Meanwhile, whip the egg whites very stiff. Spread over the cooked tart and garnish with lemon slices. Place back in oven for about 7 or 8 minutes, or until egg whites are golden. Cool before serving.

Serves 6

*See glossary

Sugarless Banana's Flambe

4   ripe bananas
2   Tbsp. butter
1/2   c. dark rum

Cut bananas lengthwise in half. In a skillet, melt butter (don't brown). Gently place bananas in butter and saute over low heat, slowly, turning only once with a spatula. Preheat serving dish by placing over skillet. Place bananas on serving dish and immediately pour rum over the top and ignite.

Serves 4

SONNIE'S FAVORITES

SONNIE'S FAVORITES

Ray's Italian Pink Lemonade

4   oz. sweet-and-sour bar mix
1 1/2 oz. club soda
2   tsp. sugar
1   oz. grenadine
1   lemon wedge

Blend sweet-and-sour bar mix with water and use 4 oz. of this mixture. Add club soda, sugar and grenadine. Pour over crushed ice. Squeeze lemon juice on top and serve with a straw. This recipe was given to me by Ray Salemi who is a bartender on the Mississippi Queen.

Brie Wheel in Puff Pastry

1   pkg (2 sheets) Peppridge Farms puff pastry
2   8 oz. wheel of Brie cheese
8   oz. Boursin or Alouette cheese

Place defrosted puff pastry sheet on a cookie tray. Remove rind from the Brie cheese and place in center of puff pastry. Spread 2 oz. of the Boursin cheese on the Brie cheese, turn over and spread 2 oz. of the Boursin cheese on other side. Wrap the brie in the pastry and trim the excess. Place seam side down on cookie tray and decorate the top with the trimmings. Repeat for the second wheel of Brie. Bake at 375° F for 25 minutes

Serves 10

Mushroom Barley Soup

4	lbs. brisket
4	qts. water
2	tsp. salt
2	onions, chopped
4	carrots, diced
1/3	c. parsley, chopped
1	c. barley
1	lb. mushrooms, sliced

In a stock pot, place brisket, water, salt, onions, carrots and parsley. Bring to a boil, lower heat, cover and simmer for 3 hours. Cool and refrigerate overnight. Skim off fat. Remove brisket from the broth. Add barley to broth. Bring to a boil, lower heat and simmer for 1 hour. Add mushrooms and continue to simmer for 30 minutes.

Serves 6 to 10

Red Bean Soup

1/2	lb. andouille* sausage, cubed
3	scallions, chopped
1	large can kidney beans, pureed with their liquid
1	c. canned chicken broth

In a saucepan, brown the andouille sausage, add the scallions and saute until golden. Add the pureed kidney beans and their liquid together with the chicken broth. Bring to a boil, cover and simmer for 30 minutes.

Serves 2

Chile Cheddar Soup

1	Tbsp. oil
1	Tbsp. butter
1	onion, diced
1	49 1/2 oz. can Swanson's chicken broth
4	oz. diced green chiles
8	oz. cheddar cheese, grated

In a stockpot, heat oil and butter, add onions and saute until transparent. Add green chiles and chicken broth. Bring to a boil and simmer for 45 minutes. Add cheddar cheese and stir until melted.

Serves 4

Almost Diet Roquefort Salad Dressing

4	oz. Roquefort cheese
3	Tbsp. parsley
3	Tbsp. tarragon vinegar
3	oz. cream cheese
1	c. diet mayonnaise
2	oz. buttermilk
1	oz. yogurt

Place all ingredients in a food processor and mix until well blended. Serve over a mixed green salad.

Yields 2 cups

Salsa Dip

1/2	bunch cilantro
2	bunches green onions, cut in 1" pieces
1	onion, cut in quarters
1	lb. can ortega chiles
4	1 lb. cans tomato sauce
4	tomatoes, cut in quarters
1	c. water
4	avocados
1	yellow chile pepper, seeded and chopped

Place all ingredients in a food processor and mix until well blended.

Yields: 1 gallon

Pepper Hash

3	lb. head of cabbage, chopped fine
1	medium green onion, chopped fine
1	small onion, chopped fine
1	large jar pimientos, drained and chopped
1	large green bell pepper, chopped fine
1	c. sugar
1	c. white vinegar
1	c. vegetable oil
1/2	Tbsp. salt
1/2	tsp. pepper
2	Tbsp. celery seed

Pepper Hash (Cont.)

Place first 5 ingredients in a large mixing bowl. Place the remaining ingredients in a saucepan and bring to a boil for 1 minute. Mix together with chopped vegetables and refrigerate for 24 hours before serving.

Serves 10

Carol's Potato Cheese Casserole

6	medium potatoes, cooked and cooled
3/4	c. butter
1	can cream of chicken soup, undiluted
1	pint sour cream
1	Tbsp. instant minced onions
12	oz. cheddar cheese, shredded
	corn flakes

Peel and grate potatoes, place in a 2 1/2 quart casserole. Heat butter and soup together, until boiling. Remove from heat and blend in sour cream, onions and most of the cheese. Stir the soup mixture into the potatoes, blending evenly. Sprinkle with the rest of the cheese. Add crumbled corn flakes on top. Bake at 350° F for 45 minutes.

Serves 8

Steamed Carrots in Orange Juice

1	lb. carrots, peeled and cut into 3" pieces
1	c. orange juice
1/2	c. brown sugar
1	Tbsp. butter, melted
1	Tbsp. cornstarch

Steam carrots until tender. Place the carrots in a serving bowl. In a saucepan blend together orange juice, sugar and butter. Heat until almost boiling. Dissolve cornstarch with water and stir into mixture in the saucepan. Stir until thickened. Pour over carrots and serve.

Serves 6

Linguine with Cheese and Clams

4	Tbsp. butter
4	Tbsp. oil
3	cloves garlic, minced
2	6 1/2 oz. cans minced clams, reserve clam juice
4	Tbsp. parsley, chopped
1	c. grated Jack cheese
8	oz. cooked linguine

Melt butter and oil. Add garlic and saute for 4 minutes. Add reserved clam juice and parsley. Simmer for 15 minutes. Add clams and cheese. Simmer for 4 minutes. Pour sauce over warm linguine and serve immediately.

Serves 2

Chris's Favorite Tuna Casserole

1	lb. package wide egg noodles
1	small onion, chopped
3	stalks celery, chopped
1/4	c. butter
1	can cream of mushroom soup
1	can cream of chicken soup
1	large can evaporated milk
1	jar pimientos
1	large can white tuna fish
1	package frozen petite peas
1	lb. cheddar cheese, grated
	potato chips, crushed

Cook the noodles being careful not to overcook. Saute onion and celery in butter until transparent. Mix together the mushroom soup and the chicken soup with the milk. Add this mixture to the sauteed vegetables. Add pimientos, tuna and peas. Place into large casserole, add drained noodles and 1/2 of the cheese. Mix together. Place remaining cheese on top of casserole and add crushed potato chips. Place casserole in a preheated 350° F oven and cook for 30 minutes or until cheese melts.

Serves 6 to 8

SONNIE'S FAVORITES

Gingered Sea Bass

2	lb. sea bass fillets
1/4	c. peanut oil
2	Tbsp. ginger, grated
4	scallions, chopped
1/4	c. soy sauce
2	Tbsp. cilantro, chopped

Steam sea bass for 10 minutes or until opaque. Place on a serving dish and keep warm. In a skillet heat oil, add ginger and scallions. Pour over fish and add soy sauce and cilantro.

Serves 4

Chicken and Cellophane Noodles

2	pkg. cellophane noodles*
1	Tbsp. peanut oil
1	lb. chicken thigh meat, cubed
2	scallions, thinly sliced
2	Tbsp. fish sauce*
1	Tbsp. soy sauce
1/2	c. chicken stock or water

Place cellophane noodles in a ceramic bowl, cover with water and place in microwave on high for 3 minutes. Let stand for 10 minutes. Drain and cut into bite-size pieces. Heat wok on high, add oil, chicken and scallions. Stir fry for 3 minutes. Add fish sauce, soy sauce and chicken stock or water. Simmer for 3 minutes. Add cellophane noodles, return to a boil and cook for another 3 minutes, stirring constantly. Serve immediately.

Serves 2

*Available in oriental markets

SONNIE'S FAVORITES

Pecan and Apple Crisp

1/2	c. brown sugar
1	tsp. cinnamon
5	Granny Smith apples, cored and sliced
1/2	c. raisins
2	Tbsp. lemon juice
1/2	c. brown sugar
1/2	c. white unbleached flour
4	Tbsp. butter, melted
1	c. pecans, chopped

Preheat oven to 350° F. Butter pie pan. Mix together sugar, cinnamon, apples, raisins and lemon juice. Pour into pie pan. Combine sugar, flour and butter. Blend well and add pecans. Sprinkle mixture on top of apples. Bake at 350° F for 50 minutes.

Serves 6

INDEPENDENCE HALL

Dry Creek Vineyard

SONOMA COUNTY
CHARDONNAY
ALCOHOL 13.6% BY VOLUME

The lively alluring aromas of apples, spice and vanilla complement ripe fruit flavors and warm oak tones.

Food Pairing: Salmon, crab, mussels, lobster, abalone as well as veal and fowl dishes.

FOOD GLOSSARY

AL DENTE - Pasta or vegetables cooked only until firm and crunchy, not soft or overdone.

ANDOUILLE SAUSAGE - A Cajun sausage made from pork chitterlings and tripe. Available in specialty stores or from mail-order houses.

BÉCHAMEL SAUCE - Basic white sauce, thickened and flavored with onion.

BLANCH - To briefly heat foods in a large quantity of boiling water; sometimes the foods are placed in ice water afterwards to stop the cooking process.

BRAISE - To sear meat over high flame in oil and then cook slowly in an oven in a covered dish with a small quantity of liquid.

BROWN SAUCE - Made from brown roux, brown stock, browned mirepoix, tomato puree and herbs cooked together slowly, skimmed and strained.

CLARIFIED BUTTER - Heat whole butter very slowly. Remove white deposit that forms on top. Strain the butter through a sieve into a small bowl, leaving the milky solids in the bottom of the pan. Store uncovered in refrigerator, as it will keep indefinitely. Butter so treated has a higher burning point.

CRÈME FRAÎCHE - Heat one cup whipping cream in a saucepan. Remove from heat and mix in 2 Tbsp. buttermilk (at room temperature). Cover and keep in a warm area, 24 to 48 hours or until slightly thickened. Refrigerate until ready to use.

CRESPELLE - A pancake, usually stuffed like a crepe.

DEGLAZE - Pour wine or other liquid into pan in which food has been roasted or prepared in butter or oil (food has been removed and just the pan juices remain).

DEMI GLACE - Reduced brown sauce.

EGG WASH - 1 egg, beaten with 1 Tbsp. water.

FILE POWDER - Sassafras leaves that have been dried; used to thicken gumbos.

FUMET - Reduced fish stock, sometimes containing wine.

FUSILLI - Thin, spiral-shaped pasta.

HOLLANDAISE SAUCE - Divide 1/2 c. butter into 3 pieces. Put 1 piece in top of double boiler with 2 egg yolks and 1 Tbsp. lemon juice. Stir constantly with a whisk until butter is melted. Add second piece of butter and then the third piece. Add 1/3 c. boiling water and 1/4 tsp. salt.

LIME, ORANGE OR LEMON ZEST - The grated outer covering of lime, orange or lemon, just the skin part, as the white part becomes bitter.

KAMANU - A deep sea fish called rainbow runner, also called Hawaiian Salmon.

MORNAY SAUCE - Bechamel sauce with butter, Parmesan cheese and Gruyere cheese blended in.

PANCETTA - Italian bacon.

PÂTE BRISÉE - Pie dough.

REDUCE OR REDUCTION - To boil down a liquid and to thicken its consistency and concentrate its flavors.

ROUX - A mixture of butter and flour. Melt butter in saucepan. Add flour slowly and whisk until thick. This is used to thicken sauces and soups.

SEAR - To brown the surface of meat quickly with high heat.

TASSO - Cajun ham.

WATER BATH - Place the receptacle in which you are cooking the ingredients into a larger receptacle, to which an amount of water has been added.

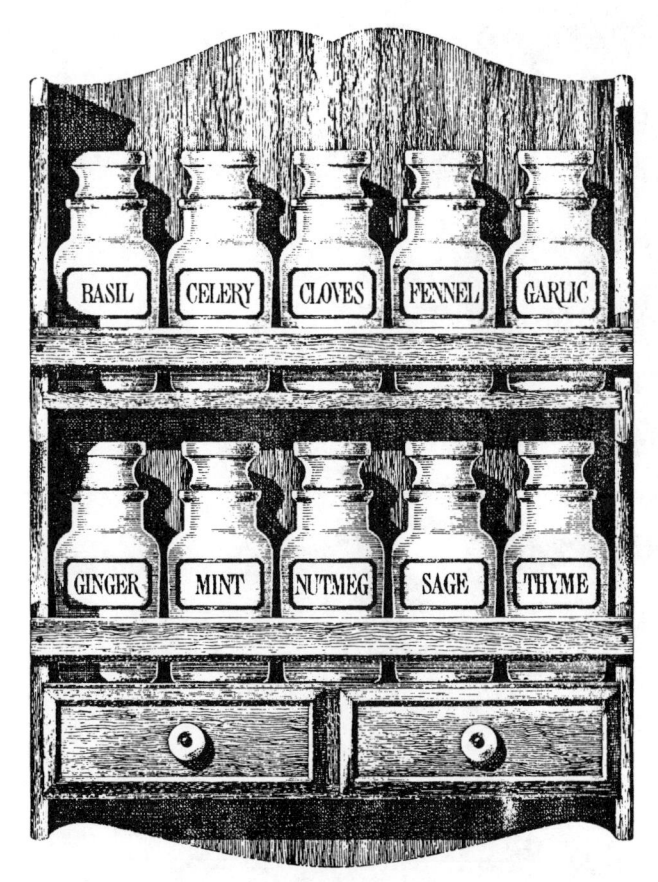

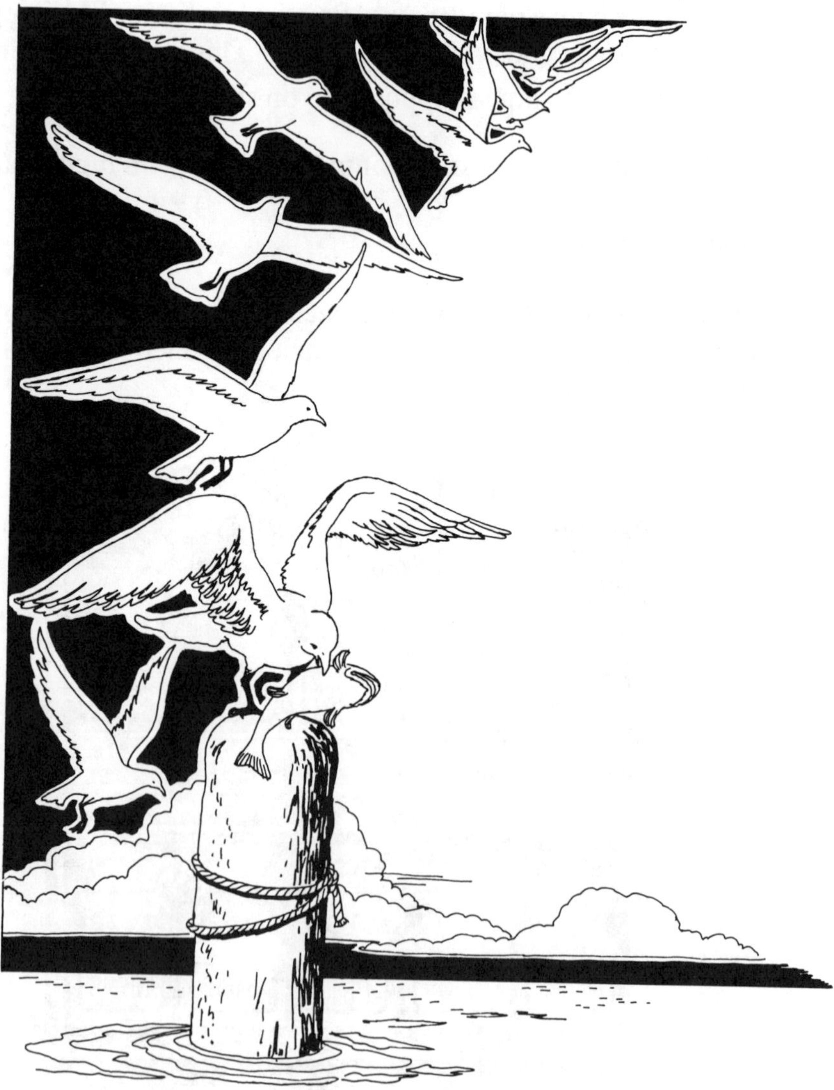

SHIP'S GLOSSARY

ABEAM - anything off to one side.

ABOARD - on a ship, as opposed to on shore.

AFT OR ABAFT - to the rear of the ship.

ALLEYWAY - a passageway or hall on a ship.

AMIDSHIPS - (midships) - middle section of a ship lengthwise.

ASHORE - on shore, as opposed to on a ship.

ASTERN - behind the rear of a ship.

BALLAST - weight put in the hold of a vessel to keep an even keel.

BEAM - the width of a ship at its widest point.

BELLS - 30-minute nautical time units.

BOW - (stem) - front end of a ship.

BRIDGE - the location of the ship's wheel, where the captain is found.

BULKHEAD - the wall in a ship.

CAPTAIN - the master of a ship.

COMPANIONWAY - interior stairway on a ship.

CROW'S NEST - lookout platform on top of a ship's mast, used in sailing days to keep a lookout for other ships and upcoming clouds.

DAVIT - device used for raising and lowering lifeboats.

DEBARK OR DEBARKATION - to get off a ship in port.

DECK - the floor on a ship.

DRAFT - the depth of the ship below water line.

DRAUGHT - depth of water needed for the ship to float without touching bottom.

EMBARK OR EMBARKATION - to board a ship.

FATHOM - 6 feet.

FORWARD - front of ship or direction of front of ship.

FREE PORT - port where no customs duty or regulations are imposed.

GALLEY - kitchen.

GANGWAY OR GANGPLANK - the ramp used to board a ship from a pier.

GROSS REGISTER TON - unit of 100 cubic feet used to measure the internal capacity of a ship.

HEAD - the bathroom.

HELL - the hollow, bottom part of the ship.

HELM - the steering.

HOLD - interior of a ship where cargo can be kept.

KEEL - a thick plate running the length of the bottom of the ship; the main frame of the ship is attached to this.

KNOT - the speed of one nautical mile per hour (1.5 m.p.h.); one nautical mile equals 6,080 feet.

LEAGUE - three nautical miles.

LEE - the side away from the wind.

LEEWARD - same as lee.

LOG - the daily record of the ship's speed and progress.

MS, SS - motor ship, steamship.

MANIFEST - passenger, crew and cargo list.

MOOR - to anchor or secure the ship at a port.

PORT - the city or dock where a ship is tied up; the left side of the ship when facing forward.

NAUTICAL MILE - 6,080 feet.

PITCH - the rise and fall of the ship in stormy weather.

PORT - the city or dock where a ship is tied up; the left side of the ship when facing forward.

PORTHOLE - any small opening on the side of a ship.

QUAY - (pronounced key) any landing place built along the edge of a body of water.

ROLL - sideways motion of a ship during stormy weather.

RUDDER - a vertical blade at the stern of a ship used to steer it.

RUNNING LIGHTS - small red and green lights on the side of ships to show other ships which way you're going.

SCUPPERS - drains along the ship's rail.

SOUNDING - the measurement of the depth of water.

STABILIZER - a retractable fin extending from both sides of the ship that make the ride smoother.

STACK - metal chimney or funnel.

STARBOARD - the right side of a ship when facing forward.

STERN - aft or rear end of the ship.

TENDER - small vessels used for transporting passengers from ship to port when the ship is at anchor.

TOPSIDE - upstairs.

UNDER WAY - either moving or ready to move, with anchor up.

WAKE - path of the boat.

WEIGH ANCHOR - raise the anchor.

WINDWARD - the side of the ship exposed to the wind.

ABBREVIATIONS

MS - motor ship

MV - motor vessel

SS - steamship

OFFICERS

CAPTAIN/MASTER - the boss; the captain has complete authority and control of the ship.

STAFF CAPTAIN - second in command.

CHIEF ENGINEER - oversees the function of the engine room and all technical aspects of the ship.

CHIEF RADIO OPERATOR - keeps the ship in contact with the rest of the world through the telex, radio and telegraph equipment.

CHIEF PURSER - controls all financial matters. The ship's banker, postmaster and problem-solver for on-board service.

CHIEF STEWARD/HOTEL MANAGER - maintains lodging facilities aboard.

CABIN STEWARD - takes care of your cabin and your personal needs.

MAITRE D' - takes charge of seating in the dining rooms and makes arrangements for food service.

CHIEF COOK - prepares all menus, orders all supplies and oversees the kitchens and food preparation.

CRUISE DIRECTOR - directs all entertainment and activities for a cruise.

EXCURSION MANAGER - handles shore tours.

INFORMATION OFFICER - handles inquiries from passengers, lost and found, etc.

BAR MANAGER - directs wine cellars and bars.

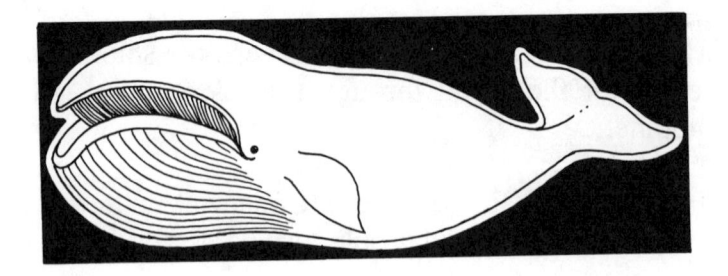

Index

A

A Bite to Remember	204
Agnolotti con Gamberi e Zucchini	244
Alaskan Gluhwein	132
Almost Diet Roquefort Salad Dressing	352
Appetizers	
Baked Stuffed Mushrooms	153
Brie Wheel in Puff Pastry	350
Butterfly Noodles with Salmon in Cream Sauce	184
Crabmeat au Gratin Appetizer	152
Creamed Herring Housewife Style	183
Fried Zucchini	76
Shrimp Cocktail, American Sauce	108
Apples Flambe Chandris	329
Artichoke Quiche	342

B

Baked Chicken Dijon	139
Baked Quail Perigourdine	293
Baked Stuffed Mushrooms	153
Banana Nut Bread	261
Banana's Foster	171
Basil Vinaigrette	262
Beef Macaroni Soup	262
Beef, Lamb & Venison	
Brazilian Churrasco Steak	311
Fillet of Beef in Dusseldorf Mustard Sauce	85
Korean Barbecued Beef	134
Lamb Roast with Pine Nut and Parmesan Crust	86
Lancashire Hot Pot	133
Odyssey Lamb	208
Petite Marmite	291
Prime Rib of Beef	140
Roast Rack of Lamb with Mint Pesto	228
Steak au Poivre	135
The Midwest	202

Beer and Cheese Soup	155
Blackened Chicken	163
Blush Fizz	72
Braised Halibut	326
Brazilian Churrasco Steak	311
Bread Pudding	165
Brie Wheel in Puff Pastry	350
Butterfish	187
Butterfly Noodles with Salmon in Cream Sauce	184

C

Caesar Salad	78
Cafe Latte Custard	229
Cajun Cucumber Stirfry	168
Cakes, Pies & Tortes	
Carrot Cake	57
Deep Dish Apple Pie	272
French Silk Pie	272
Kahlua Pie	314
Kugelhopf	111
Lemon Tart	347
New England Cheesecake	89
Pecan and Apple Crisp	359
Sacher Torte	92
Calaloo Mussel Soup	106
Calamari Salad	77
Carol's Potato Cheese Casserole	354
Carrot Cake	57
Chicken & Duck	
Baked Chicken Dijon	139
Baked Quail Perigourdine	293
Blackened Chicken	163
Chicken and Andouille Gumbo	160
Chicken and Cellophane Noodles	358
Coq au Vin	38
Cuisses de Canard au Vin Rouge & Porto	344
Duck a l'Orange	84
Duck and Orange Salad	107
Duck Legs	344
Grilled Chicken Dijonnaise	325
Grilled Chicken with Herbal Marinade	158

Pat's Caribbean Chicken	267
Pork and/or Chicken St. Lucia	345
Sauteed Chicken Breast in Sorrel Sauce	56
Southwest Special	203
Chicken and Andouille Gumbo	160
Chicken and Cellophane Noodles	358
Chile Cheddar Soup	352
Chile con Carne	266
Chilled Cantaloupe with Champagne	288
Chilled Cream of Papaya Soup	59
Chilled Green Apple and Watercress Soup	308
Chilled Zucchini Soup	80
Chocolate Mousse	228
Chocolate Souffle	91
Chris's Favorite Tuna Casserole	356
Cocktails	
Alaskan Gluhwein	132
Blush Fizz	72
Chilled Cantaloupe with Champagne	288
Electric Lemonade	73
Flaming Lampadina Cocktail	74
Jaeger Tea	131
Kir	73
Northern Lights	132
Ray's Italian Pink Lemonade	350
Vicksburg Mint Julep	166
Cold Lemon Souffle	110
Conch Fritters	311
Coq au Vin	38
Corn and Oyster Soup	167
Crabmeat au Gratin Appetizer	152
Crawfish Etouffee	156
Crawfish Hollandaise	159
Cream of Mushroom Soup	264
Cream of Nothing Soup	263
Cream of Shiitake Soup	222
Creamed Herring Housewife Style	183
Creamy Lemon Sauce	211
Creole Tartar Sauce	158
Crepe Dame Blanche	39
Cuisses de Canard au Vin Rouge & Porto	344

D

Deep Dish Apple Pie	272
Desserts	
Apples Flambe Chandris	329
Banana's Foster	171
Bread Pudding	165
Cafe Latte Custard	229
Chilled Cream of Papaya Soup	59
Chocolate Mousse	228
Chocolate Souffle	91
Cold Lemon Souffle	110
Crepe Dame Blanche	39
Deep Dish Apple Pie	272
French Silk Pie	272
Frozen Souffle au Grand Marnier	294
Grasshopper Pudding	271
Kahlua Pie	314
Kugelhopf	111
Lemon Tart	347
Macademia Nut Gelato	88
New England Cheesecake	89
Pecan and Apple Crisp	359
Red Berries in Champagne Saboyon	328
Sacher Torte	92
Salzburger Nockerin	137
Sugarless Banana's Flambe	348
Vienna Apple Strudel	58
White Chocolate Truffles	90
Zuppa Inglese	136
Discover America	200
Duck a l'Orange	84
Duck and Orange Salad	107
Duck Legs	344
Dungeness Crab Newburg in Vol-au-Vent	109

E

Eggplant and Red Pepper Soup	224
Electric Lemonade	73

F

Fettucine and Smokes Salmon	324
Fillet of Beef in Dusseldorf Mustard Sauce	85
Fish	
A Bite to Remember	204
Braised Halibut	326
Butterfish	187
Chris's Favorite Tuna Casserole	356
Gingered Sea Bass	357
Grilled Mahi Mahi w/ Black Bean Papaya Salsa	227
Grilled Snapper and Crawfish Hollandaise	159
Odyssey Treat	202
Orange Roughy	83
Red Snapper Premier	37
Roast Kamanu w/ Macadamia Nut Butter	226
Salmon in Foil	326
Salmon Mousse with Red Bell Pepper Sauce	289
Sauteed Dover Sole Fillets Genoise	55
Fish Bisque	340
Flaming Lampadina Cocktail	74
French Leek and Tomato Pie	269
French Silk Pie	272
Fresh Horseradish	140
Fresh Strawberry Sauce	89
Fried Zucchini	76
Frog Legs Aux Fines Herbes Caribe	290
Frozen Souffle au Grand Marnier	294

G

Gamberi alla Marinara	242
Gingered Sea Bass	357
Gnocchi de Patate alla Ligure	242
Grasshopper Pudding	271
Green Tagliatelle with Smoked Salmon	245
Grilled Chicken Dijonnaise	325
Grilled Chicken with Herbal Marinade	158
Grilled Mahi Mahi w/ Black Bean Papaya Salsa	227
Grilled Snapper and Crawfish Hollandaise	159

H

Havana Oxtail Soup	54
Herbal Tomato Soup	265
Honey Creamy Dressing	201

I

Italian Salad Dressing	324

J

Jaeger Tea	131
Jalapeno Sweet Potato Pancake	170

K

Kahlua Pie	314
Kir 73	
Korean Barbecued Beef	134
Kugelhopf	111

L

Lady A Loaf	343
Lamb Roast with Pine Nuts and Parmesan Crust	86
Lancashire Hot Pot	133
Lasagne 205	
Legumi Ripieni alla Italiana	246
Lemon Mustard Dressing	200
Lemon Tart	347
Linguine with Cheese and Clams	355
Little Italy	199
Lobster Bisque	79
Lobster Soup	186

M

Macademia Nut Gelato	88
Manicotti	82
Marinade	205
Marinara Sauce	199
Marinated Mussels	75
Mint Sauce for Lamb	209
Mushroom and Leek Pie	327
Mushroom Barley Soup	351

N

New England Cheesecake	89
Northern Lights	132

O

Odyssey Lamb	208
Odyssey Treat	202
Orange Roughy	83
Oyster and Artichoke Soup	154
Oyster Artichoke Soup	161

P

Paros Eggplant	207
Pasta	
Agnolotti con Gamberi e Zucchini	244
Fettucine and Smoked Salmon	324
Green Tagliatelle with Smoked Salmon	245
Lasagne	205
Linguine with Cheese and Clams	355
Little Italy	199
Manicotti	82
Spaghetti Alla Puttanesca	81
Tagliatelle Verdi al Salmone	245
Pat's Caribbean Chicken	267
Pecan and Apple Crisp	359
Pepper Dill Dressing	156
Pepper Dressing	187

Pepper Hash	353
Pesto Genovese	87
Petite Marmite	291
Petite Marmite Garnish	292
Pomplemousse au Fruit de Mer	341
Pork and/or Chicken St. Lucia	345
Potato Dumplings Ligurian Style	242
Potato Soup Schaffhausen Style	185
Pralines	164
Prime Rib of Beef	140

Q

Quiches	
Artichoke Quiche	342
French Leek and Tomato Pie	269
Mushroom and Leek Pie	327

R

Ravioli with Shrimp and Zucchini	244
Ray's Italian Pink Lemonade	350
Red Bean Soup	351
Red Berries in Champagne Saboyon	328
Red Snapper Premier	37
Risotto ai Funghi	241
Risotto with Mushrooms	241
Roast Kamanu w/ Macadamia Nut Butter	226
Roast Rack of Lamb with Mint Pesto	228
Romaine with Bleu Cheese Dressing	138
Romaine with Egg Mustard Dressing	137

S

Sacher Torte	92
Salad Dressings	
Almost Diet Roquefort Salad Dressing	352
Basil Vinaigrette	262
Honey Creamy Dressing	201
Italian Salad Dressing	324
Lemon Mustard Dressing	200

Pepper Dill Dressing	156
Pepper Dressing	187
Sesame Oriental Dressing	203
Vinaigrette	340
Salad Nicoise	309
Salads	
Caesar Salad	78
Calamari Salad	77
Discover America	200
Duck and Orange Salad	107
Pepper Hash	353
Romaine with Bleu Cheese Dressing	138
Romaine with Egg Mustard Dressing	137
Salad Nicoise	309
South Pacific	201
The Midwest	202
Salmon Chowder	225
Salmon in Foil	326
Salmon Mousse with Red Bell Pepper Sauce	289
Salsa Dip	353
Salsa Mayonnaise	312
Salzburger Nockerin	137
Sauces	
Crawfish Hollandaise	159
Creamy Lemon Sauce	211
Creole Tartar Sauce	158
Fresh Horseradish	140
Fresh Strawberry Sauce	89
Marinara Sauce	199
Mint Sauce for Lamb	209
Pesto Genovese	87
Salsa Mayonnaise	312
Sauteed Chicken Breast in Sorrel Sauce	56
Sauteed Dover Sole Fillets Genoise	55
Scallopine di Vitello al Limone	247
Seafood	
A Bite to Remember	204
Calamari Salad	77
Conch Fritters	311
Crawfish Etouffee	156
Dungeness Crab Newburg in Vol-au-Vent	109
Gamberi alla Marinara	242
Marinated Mussels	75

Seafood Newburg	268
Shrimp and Crawfish Diane	169
Shrimp Cilantro	313
Shrimp Cocktail, American Sauce	108
Shrimp Creole	162
Shrimp Endaxi	346
Soft-Shell Crab Belizaire	168
Soft-Shell Crabs	157
Stuffed Shrimp Imperial	210
Seafood Newburg	268
Seafood Stuffed Grapefruit	341
Sesame Oriental Dressing	203
Shrimp and Crawfish Diane	169
Shrimp Cilantro	313
Shrimp Cocktail, American Sauce	108
Shrimp Creole	162
Shrimp Endaxi	346
Shrimp Marinara Style	242
Soft-Shell Crab Belizaire	168
Soft-Shell Crabs	157
Soup	
Beef Macaroni Soup	262
Beer Cheese Soup	155
Calaloo Mussel Soup	106
Chile Cheddar Soup	352
Chilled Green Apple and Watercress Soup	308
Chilled Zucchini Soup	80
Corn and Oyster Soup	167
Cream of Mushroom Soup	264
Cream of Nothing Soup	263
Cream of Shiitake Soup	222
Eggplant and Red Pepper Soup	224
Fish Bisque	340
Havana Oxtail Soup	54
Herbal Tomato Soup	265
Lobster Bisque	79
Lobster Soup	186
Mushroom Barley Soup	351
Oyster and Artichoke Soup	154
Oyster Artichoke Soup	161
Petite Marmite	291
Potato Soup Schaffhausen Style	185
Red Bean Soup	351

Salmon Chowder	225
Soupe de Poissons	340
Tortilla Soup	223
Soupe de Poissons	340
South Pacific	201
Southwest Special	203
Spaghetti Alla Puttanesca	81
Spinach Pie Victoria	310
Steak au Poivre	135
Steamed Carrots in Orange Juice	355
Stuffed Shrimp Imperial	210
Sugarless Banana's Flambe	348

T

Taglitelle Verdi al Salmone	245
Tarte au Citron	347
The Midwest	202
Tortilla Soup	223

V

Veal	
Scallopine di Vitello al Limone	247
Veal Piccata	270
Veal Piccata	270
Veal Scollopine with Lemon	247
Vegetables	
Cajun Cucumber Stirfry	168
Carol's Potato Cheese Casserole	354
Fried Zucchini	76
Jalapeno Sweet Potato Pancake	170
Legumi Ripieni alla Italiana	246
Paros Eggplant	207
Pepper Hash	353
Spinach Pie Victoria	310
Steamed Carrots in Orange Juice	355
Stuffed Vegetables Italian Style	246
Vicksburg Mint Julep	166
Vienna Apple Strudel	58
Vinaigrette	340

W

White Chocolate Truffles — 90

Z

Zuppa Inglese — 136

EDITORS: Colleen O'Brien/Anne Witzleben
PUBLISHER: The Tastes of Tahoe®
PRINTER: Publishers Press, Inc.
CLIP ART: Dover Publishing Co.
FRONT COVER: Bonnie Kezer, ASID of Bonnie Kezer Interior Design
PROOFREADERS: Colleen O'Brien/Anne Witzleben
COMPUTER CONSULTANTS: John H. Welsch/Paul Clothier

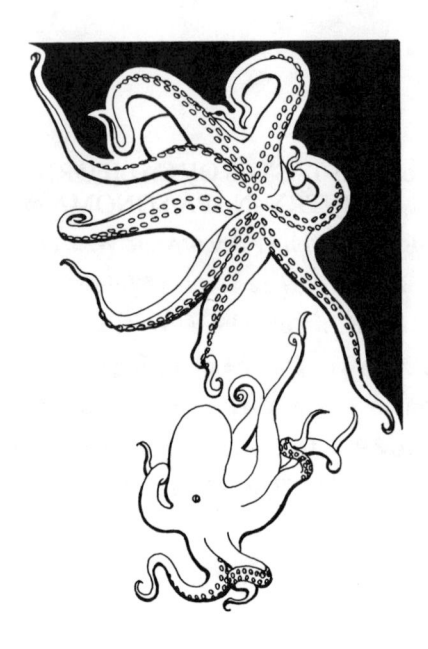

All Tastes of Tahoe books are available at special quantity discounts when purchased in bulk by corporations, organizations and special-interest groups. Custom imprinting can also be done to fit special needs. For comments, re-orders, the address of your nearest distributor, or information, please contact:

The Tastes of Tahoe®
P. O. Box 6114
Incline Village, NV 89450
702-831-5182

THE TASTES OF TAHOE®
P. O. BOX 6114
INCLINE VILLAGE, NV 89450
702-831-5182

Please send_____ copies of THE TASTES OF CALIFORNIA WINE COUNTRY -NAPA/SONOMA @ $11.95 each

Please send_____ copies of THE TASTES OF CALIFORNIA WINE COUNTRY -NORTH COAST @ $11.95 each

Please send_____ copies of COOKING IN STYLE @ $9.95 each

Please send_____ copies of THE BEST OF THE TASTES OF TAHOE @ $11.95 each

Please send_____ copies of THE TASTES OF CRUISING @ $11.95 each

Add $1.50 postage and handling for the first book ordered and $.50 for each additional book. Enclosed is my check for $_____

Name_____

Address_____

City_____ State_____ Zip_____

This is a gift. Send directly to:
Name_____

Address_____

City_____ State_____ Zip_____
Autographed by author. ☐
Autographed to:_____

CALLAWAY

VINEYARD & WINERY

"CALLA-LEES"
Chardonnay

TEMECULA, CALIFORNIA

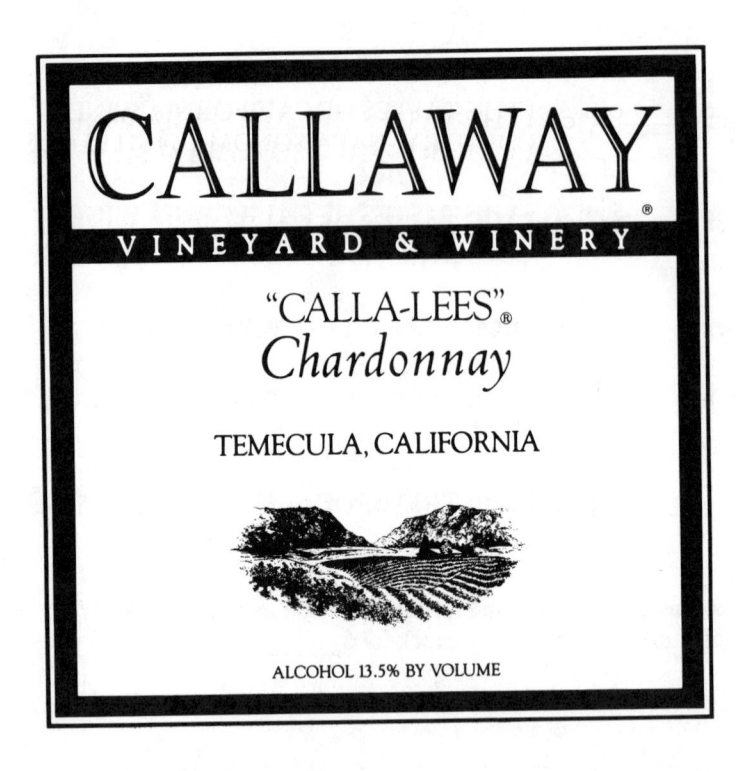

ALCOHOL 13.5% BY VOLUME

Green/gold color, mild aroma of green apples. Complexity enhanced due to non-oak aged/sur-lies style of winemaking.

Food Pairing: Lobster bisque, grilled seabass, roast duckling

THE TASTES OF TAHOE®
P. O. BOX 6114
INCLINE VILLAGE, NV 89450
702-831-5182

Please send_____copies of THE TASTES OF CALIFORNIA WINE COUNTRY -NAPA/SONOMA @ $11.95 each

Please send_____copies of THE TASTES OF CALIFORNIA WINE COUNTRY -NORTH COAST @ $11.95 each

Please send_____copies of COOKING IN STYLE @ $9.95 each

Please send_____copies of THE BEST OF THE TASTES OF TAHOE @ $11.95 each

Please send_____copies of THE TASTES OF CRUISING @ $11.95 each

Add $1.50 postage and handling for the first book ordered and $.50 for each additional book. Enclosed is my check for $_____

Name_____

Address_____

City_____ State____ Zip_____

This is a gift. Send directly to:
Name_____

Address_____

City_____ State____ Zip_____
Autographed by author. ☐
Autographed to:_____

ABOUT THE AUTHOR

Lake Tahoe's restaurant voyeur, Sonnie Imes, is an impresario of haute cuisine, low cuisine and everything in between - as long as the "tastes" are there.

Under her imprint of "The Tastes of Tahoe," Sonnie has published ten guidebooks/cookbooks to the best eateries at Lake Tahoe, Reno, California Wine Country and now, her latest "The Tastes of Cruising."

Sonnie knows whereof she speaks when she reviews a restaurant or cruise ship, for she is a chef herself, both gourmet and down home. She has taught the art of cooking at Sierra Nevada College, produced and directed her own television show on PBS, "A Taste of Tahoe," featuring chefs from area restaurants who prepared gourmet specialties on the air, and paid enough visits to restaurants and cruise ships worldwide, sampling their fare with critical palate, to have developed a discriminating knowledge of what tastes good.

Sonnie's next book will include cruise/food critiques of China, Australia, England, Scandinavia, the Mediterranean, Figi, South America and the Amazon......And at some point Sonnie plans to do an entire book solely on inland waterway cruising in Europe, the United States and wherever else cruise ships ply the rivers and canals of a country. Look for her books on every kind of restaurant and cruise ship - her only criterion being that the "Tastes" are there.

NOTES

NOTES

NOTES

NOTES

NOTES

NOTES

NOTES

NOTES

NOTES

NOTES

NOTES

NOTES

SIMI
SINCE 1876

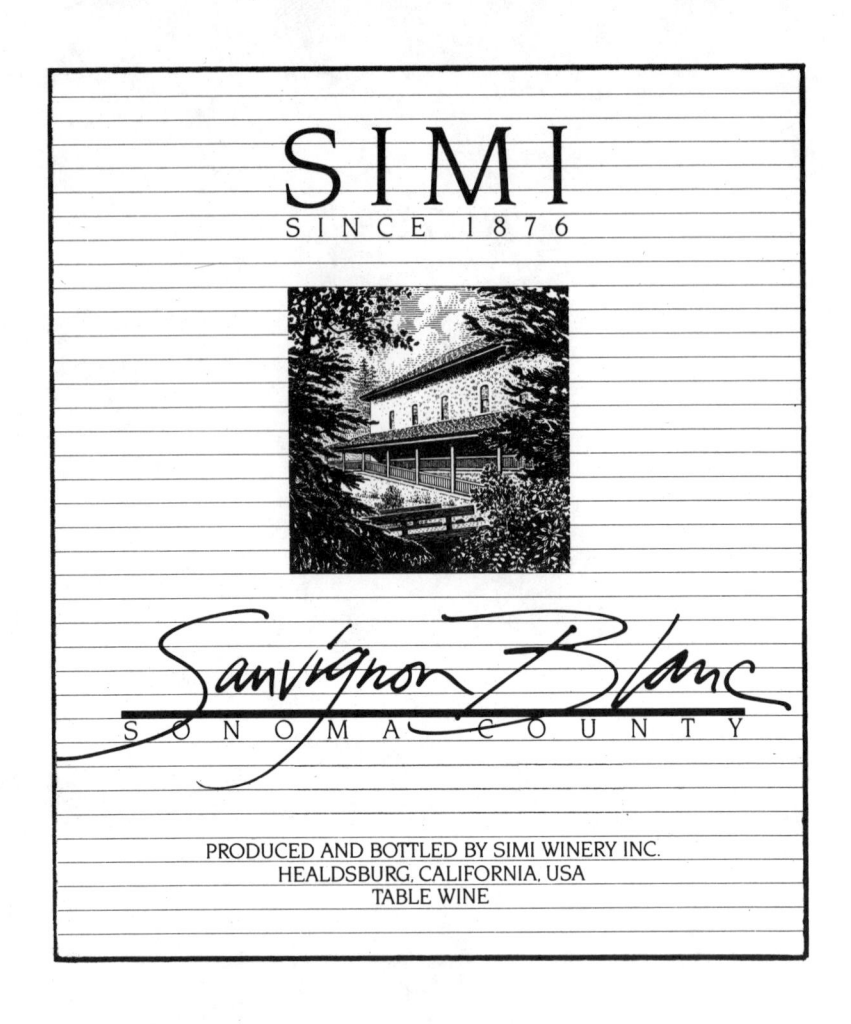

Sauvignon Blanc
SONOMA COUNTY

PRODUCED AND BOTTLED BY SIMI WINERY INC.
HEALDSBURG, CALIFORNIA, USA
TABLE WINE

A lively wine with floral notes, spice, some oak and the sweet smell of hay. Citrus and melon flavors, with a soft, mouth-filling texture.

Food affinities: Prawns and shrimp - fresh crab - oysters - goat cheeses - Pasta Primavera